Decolonizing Educational Assessment

Ardavan Eizadirad

Decolonizing Educational Assessment

Ontario Elementary Students and the EQAO

Ardavan Eizadirad
Toronto, ON, Canada

ISBN 978-3-030-27461-0   ISBN 978-3-030-27462-7   (eBook)
https://doi.org/10.1007/978-3-030-27462-7

This Palgrave Macmillan imprint is published by the registered company Springer Nature
Switzerland AG.
The registered company address is: Gewerbestrasse 11, 6330 Cham, Switzerland

To my loving grandparents Zinat (RIP) and Nosratollah,
my unconditionally supportive parents Kamal and Parvaneh,
my brother Arsalan,
and my best friends Pedro and Rohan.

To all the children, youth, parents, educators, and community activists who
every day in their different roles and capacities fight to make this world a
better place by standing up to inequitable unjust practices within
institutions.

"In the hood many hearts have turned into stones as a survival mechanism.
Through communities of love and resistance we can penetrate the stones, heal,
hope, and create new possibilities and alternatives for sustainable change."
Ardavan Eizadirad

FOREWORD

This book needs to be read by parents who have young children attending schools in Ontario.

Ardavan Eizadirad has written an important book about the impact of standardized testing on young students. There have been strong criticisms of standardized testing including Diane Ravitch's *The Death and Life of the Great American School System: How Testing and Choice are Undermining Education*. One of the problems with these tests is that they are not precise. Another is that they drive the curriculum and narrow its focus to language and math with little emphasis on other subjects such as social studies, arts, and sciences.

Decolonizing Educational Assessment: Ontario Elementary Students and the EQAO adds an important contribution to the literature on standardized testing because Ardavan interviewed students and their parents in Grade 3. We hear the *voices* of the students and the pressures that they experience in taking these tests. Students talk about feeling nervous during the tests and the pressure to complete the tests on time. Ardavan asked students to rate their level of anxiousness with the tests on a scale of 1–10 and the ratings were in the area of 8–10. Parents of the students saw how anxiety was also manifested at home affecting the students' sleep and behaviour.

Ardavan finds that the Grade 3 EQAO standardized test is more harmful than beneficial for healthy development of children. The tests lead to

---

John Miller is also the author of *The Holistic Curriculum*

invisible scars and trauma which include continuing sense of failure and lowering of self-confidence and self-worth with an increase in self-doubt. The book focuses specifically on effects of these tests on racialized students where the negative effects of the tests are magnified.

Ardavan does not just identify the problem with standardized tests but makes several recommendations of how the system can be improved. For example, he recommends that school boards and schools offer more mental health and mindfulness initiatives for racialized children and parents. In sum there are a total of 11 recommendations that the Ministry of Education and school boards should seriously consider.

Decolonizing Educational Assessment: Ontario Elementary Students and the EQAO challenges us to find a way of testing that does not harm students but supports their healthy growth and development.

Professor in Curriculum,   John Miller
Teaching and Learning,
University of Toronto,
Toronto, ON, Canada

Acknowledgements

The paradox of "the hood" is that you see good and evil in the same frame: loving community and institutional abandonment simultaneously. Looking at my life retrospectively, I continuously navigate many different spatial worlds, with each setting having its own set of written and unwritten rules and codes. Along the journey, I have found inspiration, love, and constructive knowledge in people and places society has given up on and abandoned, but their beautiful souls, energy, and spirits ignite every particle in my being to continue to care, to be a better person, and through my everyday decisions and actions try to make this world a better place. My interactions with people from all walks of life have made it clear to me that dismantling the "norms" in our society and questioning hierarchical inequitable power relations that currently exist are at the core of the struggle to revolutionize our minds, spirits, and imaginative souls.

Many people have opened my eyes, heart, mind, and soul to new perspectives and heightened my level of understanding and critical thinking over the years. I have to begin by thanking the almighty Allah for always being there for me no matter what. I am grateful to my parents, Kamal Eizadirad and Parvaneh Eisakhan, for being an exemplar of a beautiful marriage that demonstrates unconditional love and support every step of the way. Thanks to my grandmother Zinat (RIP) and grandfather Nosratollah for providing love, support, and insightful advice in critical times in my life. Thanks to my brother Arsalan for always being there to bounce ideas off one another and share a good laugh. I am grateful to Pedro Rabie for being my day 1 broski and always there no matter what time it is to listen and provide support and guidance. We've been through so much together in every stage of our lives. I cannot wait to see our children play together as we carry this friendship and brotherhood for years to come. I am also thankful and appreciative of Shemeka Coombs for all the memories and experiences over our decade-long relationship as it contributed to my growth and development.

I have to give a big shout out to the scholars who have contributed to my intellectual growth: Peter Trifonas, John Portelli, and Jack Miller. You are amazing human beings whose work and actions are inspiring! You have guided and pushed me to be the best I can be and live life to the fullest every day. Your feedback and support along my academic journey has been tremendous. I am glad to have crossed paths with you and hope to continue our friendships for many years to come as academic scholars but more importantly as friends.

I am grateful to Devon Jones for his guidance and mentorship, but more importantly for being a living embodiment of praxis in relation to community work, advocacy, sacrifice, and standing up to institutional forms of injustice. He exemplifies what it means to merge school and community into one socio-culturally relevant and responsive enterprise through Youth Association for Academics, Athletics, and Character Education (YAAACE), a non-profit organization he co-founded in 2007 and continues to operate and expand in the Jane and Finch community. I am honoured to be part of the YAAACE family since its inception.

Thanks to so many other wonderful people and organizations who have contributed to my development and growth over the years: my extended family in Canada including Uncle Parviz and Aunt Haideh; my family back home in Iran; Mike Falloon and the Toronto Association of Basketball Officials family; Wheelchair Basketball family; Michelle Fraser, Eric Tiessen, and the Toronto District School Board family; Rachel Berman and the Ryerson family; Parissa Safai and the York University family; Don Montgomery Community Centre crew; and my life-long friends Rohan Brown, Kenneth Toppin, Nathaniel Rollocks, Mina Awad, Paul Sargeant, Dwayne Brown, Augustine Obeng, Ajmer Darawal, Reza Rahimzadeh, Shaheer Jalalzai, and Mark Perera.

Thank you to the 416, also known as City of Toronto, the most beautiful city in the world and the place which I cherish and proudly represent! Finally, thanks to all the children, parents, and educators who took time out of their busy lives to be part of this book and allowed me to learn from their lived experiences.

CONTENTS

LIST OF FIGURES

CHAPTER 1

My Spiritual Journey as an Educator

I firmly believe understanding where an author is coming from in terms of their background, culture, history, and lived experiences contributes to better understanding his/her viewpoints and their stance on the topic or social issue being studied. Therefore, I start this book with my spiritual journey as an educator explaining how certain major events, both positive and negative, contributed to my growth and development, molding my approach to teaching and learning. My unique lived experiences across different socio-spatial locations which include both positive and negative events, some which I had control over and others which I did not, have impacted me in transformational ways shaping my values, ethics, and morals towards education both within the classroom and in the larger context of the communities which I belong to. My passion for being an educator and a community activist, ranging from working with elementary to post-secondary students, stems from the belief that educators play a pivotal role in cultivating student and young adult potential and empowering them to be agents of social change in their lives and in their communities.

CONNECTING WITH NATURE AND ANIMALS IN THE EARLY YEARS

My journey began in Iran where I was born in Rasht, the capital city of the Gilan Province. I was the second-born child, having a brother who is four years older than me. I was raised in a supportive and loving two-parent

A. Eizadirad, *Decolonizing Educational Assessment*,
https://doi.org/10.1007/978-3-030-27462-7_1

1

household. At the time of writing this book, my parents have been married for 37 years. In Iran, my dad worked for the government as an agricultural engineer and as a result we would relocate frequently depending on the project that he was assigned to work on. My mom stayed at home to raise my brother and me as we were from a higher socio-economic status and there was no need for her to work.

One of the most memorable places I lived in Iran was in the City of Damavand located near the Caspian Sea and in close proximity to Alborz Mountains. While living in Damavand I learned to appreciate interconnectedness with animals and nature. Due to the nature of my dad's job, which involved taking care of various animals, plants, and trees, from an early age I learned to respect animals and nature. One day when I was pulling a leaf from a tree, my dad stopped me and explained to me that when I pull the leaf from the tree it is as if I pinch the tree really hard and it creates a sharp pain for the tree. He explained to me that "trees and plants also have feelings" and that as part of his job he attends to the needs of the trees and plants such as watering and providing them with care through the various seasons in order for the trees and plants to yield a large produce. From that day on, I became fascinated by nature and its complexities and components that are unseen to the naked eye.

While in Damavand I also developed a special connection towards loving animals. As a family, we owned about a dozen chickens and hens which we cared for outside of our house and used their eggs. Although I would be playful towards the chickens, I did not develop a deep connection with animals until my family decided to get a dog. One of my dad's friends had to leave the country and he offered to give us his German Shepherd dog. In Iran, it is not custom to bring dogs inside the house and therefore the dog was kept outside in a closed spacious area.

I have two vividly profound memories with our German Shepherd which we named Gorgie. The previous owner recommended that as means of getting the dog to understand that he now has a new home and owner, we should keep him tied stationary outside for a week and feed him regularly. After a few nights we decided it was enough and untied him overnight. When we woke up in the morning and went to check up on Gorgie, we noticed that he was nowhere to be found. We called the owner to notify him and were puzzled by what we heard: Gorgie had somehow used his sense of smell and found his way back to his previous owner's home which was approximately 8 kilometres away from our house. This was shocking and fascinating to me as it was a reflection of Gorgie's loyalty to his previous owner. From that point on, I felt a special connection with animals where I learned to treat them with respect, recognizing that they also have souls which experience happiness, sadness, and various other emotions.

The other vivid memory with Gorgie was one that almost cost him his life. As a means of keeping wolves away from attacking sheep and chickens, my dad's company would sometimes plant poisoned meat in the mountain areas to scare away the wolves and to reduce their numbers. In the middle of the night, we heard Gorgie howling by our window. He seemed very weak and in a poor condition. We immediately took him to a nearby veterinarian my dad personally knew to figure out what was wrong with him. After doing some diagnostic testing, the veterinarian indicated that Gorgie had possibly licked a poisonous substance. He pointed out that luckily he had consumed only a small amount or else he would have died right away. Nonetheless, he stated that Gorgie could potentially die unless he receives an anti-toxin shot. The unfortunate thing was that we had to wait until 9 a.m. for the pharmacy to open as there were no 24-hour emergency pharmacies for animals where we lived. For the time being, we decided to take him back home to get him some rest until the pharmacy opened up. Upon arrival at home, my mom sat beside Gorgie and cried for hours while petting him. It is a scene that I will remember for the rest of my life. During this time, my dad notified some people at his work about the incident and what happened next is astonishing; one of the elders of the area who was a well-known farmer came by to see Gorgie's condition and she recommended that we feed him yogurt as it naturally cleans and refines the stomach through its natural bacteria and helps with digestion. We did just that and amazingly within an hour Gorgie's condition drastically improved to the extent that he returned to his old energetic, playful self. From that incident, I recognized that Gorgie was officially a member of our family and that my parents cared for him just as much as they would care for my brother and me.

IMMIGRATING TO CANADA FROM IRAN

Life seemed simple and everything was going well until my parents gave me the abrupt news in early 1998 that they were planning to relocate to Toronto, Canada. Being in Grade 3 at the time, immigrating to a new country permanently was a complex topic to holistically grasp and understand its magnitude. I became angry and frustrated that I had to say goodbye to many family members and friends not knowing when I might see them again. This meant I also had to say goodbye to Gorgie; we gave him to a close family friend to take care of.

In October 1998 we left Iran and travelled to Toronto to start a new life as a family with eight suitcases, sponsored by my uncle and aunt who lived in Canada. I was ten years old and started Grade 4 upon arrival to Canada. As a young child, I did not understand many things, such as why my parents decided to leave Iran to start a new life somewhere else when we were living a comfortable life back home. It was a difficult transition for my family and me due to changes in our lifestyle accompanied with cultural changes and language barriers. My dad was not able to find a career in his professional field as his educational background and professional work experiences were not accepted as relevant and hence he settled for doing alternative precarious jobs to support our family. My mom also began working in the fast-food industry to support our family financially. Although at the time as a young child I could see the symptoms of stress in my family, I did not holistically understand the extent of sacrifices and adjustments my parents were making in terms of their lifestyle.

With maturity comes wisdom and as I grew older through reflection and contemplation I began to understand, realize, and respect my parents so much for what they had sacrificed to start a new life in Canada. They sacrificed a comfortable lifestyle in order to be able to live in a country that aligns with their personal values, morals, and ethics such as democracy and freedom of self-expression. They also wanted their children to have better opportunities in life and to live in a more democratic country that offered them their human rights. My parents' actions demonstrated to me the importance of listening to your heart and soul and willing to take risks and sacrifice privileges to pursue one's aspirations and dreams. By wanting to provide a better future for my brother and I, as well as certain personal freedoms for themselves, they risked it all, including a lifestyle associated with middle to upper socio-economic status to start from scratch knowing it will not be easy and nothing is guaranteed. What amazes me up until this day is my parents' positive attitude towards the hardships they experienced as part of settling in Canada. We are now considered a middle-class family, but it took many sacrifices and hardships to get there. My parents are my role models as they have demonstrated to me the importance of always being grateful and to embrace the difficult times as part of the journey to achieving one's goals and attaining success. Hardships are not endpoints but rather middle points and processes as part of our larger life journey. These various life experiences as a collective, including my family's journey to Canada from Iran, have made me realize that happiness cannot be bought but rather co-exists in our interactions with the world and the meaningful relationships we build and maintain throughout our lifetime with others.

Growing Up in Toronto

The start of Grade 12, my final year of high school, was a dark period in my life where a series of major negative events occurred within a short span of time profoundly impacting my development, growth, and level of maturity. The first event was the passing away of my grandmother due to cancer which was the first time I had to deal with death on a personal level. This had a profound impact on me as it made me question the purpose of life and why people suffer. I would contemplate these questions daily and read many religious and spiritual books in order to make sense of death. I came to realize that death is part of the cycle of life and once we accept this, we can live more in tune within each moment by appreciating all experiences whether positive or negative for their essence and what they invoke in us. As a means of coping with my grandmother's death, I played lots of basketball and I got a tattoo in her memory, even though at the time I was under the age of consent to get a tattoo. I did it anyway knowing that my parents opposed having tattoos due to cultural and religious values.

Shortly after receiving the news of my grandmother's death, I found out my best friend was arrested and placed in jail awaiting trial for committing numerous illegal activities. I knew what he had done was wrong and that he had to face the consequences, but seeing him behind bars and how it impacted him and his family tore me apart. Not being able to talk to him on a daily basis and do the things we used to do made me angry and sad. I would compensate by writing him letters, visit him often in jail, and attend as many court dates as possible. We would get small joys out of our informal interactions such as simple eye contacts and hand gestures during trials at court. I learned through such experiences and his stories from jail that freedom is a privilege. I learned not to take things for granted, even small things such as being able to eat whenever you want. It was during this phase in my life that I began writing poetry as a means of channelling the tsunami of emotions I was experiencing from within. Listening to poetry and spoken word moved my soul and spirit by acknowledging the pains and emotions I was experiencing. I found inspiration in poetry and began writing to constructively express my thoughts, feelings, and emotions and to channel my energy into a positive outlet rather than allowing it to burst into arguments with others in my life such as teachers at school.

This process of healing, mourning, learning, and coping with loss and death was not smooth and linear. What was happening in my life outside of school largely impacted my behaviour and mannerism in school with my teachers and those in positions of authority. I was being more resistant and disruptive than usual. In retrospect, this could be attributed to the range of feelings and emotions I was trying to make sense of as a young teenager as well as the physical changes my body was experiencing going through puberty. These factors collectively influenced my decision-making, especially when I found myself in an intense situation where I had to make a quick judgement under peer pressure. Not being able to think straight, I was involved with an opportunistic theft where a couple of the members of our varsity high school basketball team stole some items from another school we were visiting as part of attending a basketball tournament. The police were involved and they were able to piece together what happened. This incident brought negative attention to a school which had an established identity of being a great academic school. As a consequence for my actions, I was offered a choice by the administrators at my high school: to serve a lengthy suspension of 30 plus days or transfer schools and start fresh at a new school without any note going under my student transcript regarding the theft incident. I chose the latter.

It was not easy breaking the news to my parents of what took place and why I needed to transfer schools midway through my high school senior year. They had sacrificed so much for me to receive a quality education and I was disappointing them. In retrospect, although difficult, those events built resiliency in me and gave me an opportunity to mature and gain insight and knowledge about life, who I am, and what I wanted to accomplish. Above all, these events contributed to making me a more spiritual person where I began living in the moment, feeling and appreciating interconnectedness to all life forms known and unknown, and gaining faith in understanding "everything happens for a reason." When one door closes, another one opens. I responded to the situation by focusing extra hard on my academic aspirations. This translated to having to take a full courseload my last semester at my new high school in addition to taking a class at night school to get all the necessary credits to graduate in time that year and be able to apply for various university programmes. Hard work paid off as I graduated on time and got accepted into York University for the following year where I began pursuing a career in teaching, wanting to make a difference in others' lives.

SHAPING MY PHILOSOPHY AND APPROACH TO TEACHING AND LEARNING

Reflecting my spiritual journey as an educator, from birth to my current way of being, it is clear to me that my lived experiences have had a profound impact on my spiritual identity as a person and my practices as an educator. My unique experiences, which include positive and negative events, have impacted me in transformational ways, in the process igniting my soul and spirit and molding my values, philosophy about education, pedagogical hands-on approach towards learning and teaching, and personal practices both within the classroom and in the community in alternative settings. As a life-long learner, I have learned so much from people from all walks of life ranging from children and youth to adults and seniors. I am grateful that my path intersected with theirs. Some of the most valuable lessons I have learned did not take place within the walls of a classroom but in the larger context of the community via meaningful bonds, connections, and conversations with people who shared their perspective and life experiences with me. By maintaining an open mind and heart and by allowing others' characters and colourful souls to speak to me through our interactions and conversations, I continue to experience growth and gain insight by gaining new perspectives, knowledges, and experiences.

My lived experiences profoundly shape my praxis as an educator. Freire (1970) defines praxis as "reflection and action upon the world in order to transform it" (p. 51). Freire (1970) argues that it is through "conscientization" (p. 67), a process of developing critical awareness about one's social reality through reflection and action, that objects come to see themselves as subjects beholding agency and having capacity to make a liberatory change at the micro and macro level. Conscious of my autobiographical history and life experiences such as being an immigrant and English as a Second Language (ESL) learner, I make extra efforts as a teacher to reach out to immigrant and ESL students to understand their life stories and how they enter the learning space physically, socially, spiritually, and emotionally. Providing various mediums for students to share and express their stories and simultaneously sharing my own journey and vulnerabilities allow me as an educator to build a connection and rapport with the students. This process allows the teacher-student duo to acknowledge they are not alone in experiencing difficulties. As well, it empowers the students by acknowledging their lived experiences as a form of valid and worthy knowledge that demonstrates strength and resilience. In a curriculum that often exclusively values content that can be quantified and assessed "objectively," it is important educators seek to understand students holistically including their socio-emotional well-being relative to their life experiences (Miller, 2016; Portelli & Vilbert, 2002). As Miller (2000) states, "soulful learning seeks to restore a balance between our outer and inner lives" (p. 5).

As an educator I often volunteer to coach basketball and other sports in schools and communities that I am involved in, such as in the Jane and Finch community located in the northwest of Toronto. My philosophy is that all educators at some point in their career should coach a team or lead a student club because they would get to see children and youth in a completely different light, particularly kids who are labelled by the system as "trouble-makers" or "low achievers." Through the game of basketball I have connected with many students on a whole new level, where not only do we acknowledge each other's passion for the sport, but more importantly we recognize the importance of working together to accomplish a collective goal that puts the team ahead of our own self-interests. This journey involves allowing one another to make mistakes both as players and as a coach, acknowledge our vulnerabilities, take risks, learn from making mistakes, and move towards being better prepared and more knowledgeable human beings as a means to better ourselves on the basketball court and beyond in the context of our lives within the meaningful relationships we create and maintain with others. These skills are transferrable to the classroom. It is important to note, the process of co-learning and collaborating is not always linear and smooth. It is unique each time depending on the personalities of the individuals, the needs of the student-athletes, their unique autobiographical life histories and experiences, the current developmental stage and maturity of the children/students, the socio-spatial context of the school and the surrounding community, and the power dynamics embedded within the space we utilize and interact within. Meaningful learning can take multiple pathways and it will bear fruit at different times for each individual.

I find teachers often penalize students harshly for making mistakes, whether by deducting marks on tests or assignments or attempting to correct their behaviours to the extent that it disengages students from their school experiences and creates doubt in students' minds about their competencies and potential. In many cases, frustrated students express themselves through behaviours that challenge the teacher and other authorities in positions of power. Consequentially, for not conforming to established routines and standards, students are labelled as "incompetent" or "at-risk" (Masood, 2008; Noguera, 2003) when the problem lies within hierarchical power relations embedded within schools that judge students exclusively based on narrow definitions of success, such as their intellectual capabilities measured by how they perform on tests and assignments. We need a shift towards understanding students from a holistic interdisciplinary perspective that "integrates body, mind, emotions, and spirit" (Miller, 2000, p. 110). My philosophy as an educator is that we need to explore how we can constructively share more power and control with students, to let them act on their ideas and to lead, while simultaneously being available and approachable for help and assistance in the background in a learning environment that is safe, supportive, and empowering.

After graduating from high school, I attended York University for my Bachelor of Arts in Kinesiology and Bachelor of Education. This was ideal for me as it reflected my two passions: sports and education. After completing my undergraduate studies, I subsequently attended the Ontario Institute for Studies in Education at University of Toronto for my Masters of Education in Social Justice and PhD in Curriculum, Teaching, and Learning. Pursuing graduate studies provided me with the language and the theoretical framework to analyse social issues from a critical lens. The Academy, referring to post-secondary education, particularly graduate studies, became a site of critique that contributed to my growth and development intellectually and subsequently my praxis as an educator and community activist. Engaging in dialogues and discussions with professors and other students shifted my paradigm to look at experiences and issues impacting various identities and communities from multiple perspectives other than my own point of reference. Delving into course readings from authors such as Paulo Freire, Frantz Fanon, Michel Foucault, Sherene Razack, and many others took me into different worlds and solidified my passion for non-fiction. It provided me with the expressive language to engage in the Academy with other scholars about issues and concerns that I was experiencing both in my life and in the communities that I was involved with. Reading and writing became an expressive outlet and a therapeutic medium for me to channel my ideas and emotions in a constructive manner.

It is important to emphasize that I am not implying that the entire experience pursuing graduate studies was positive. I also learned how rigid the Academy is, plagued with its own politics and hegemonic normalizing practices, and often any deviation from its current practices and expectations was met with resistance and consequences. Hence, just like my life, I learned to navigate the Academy as a system, paying particular attention to the power dynamics that govern classrooms and institutional policies and practices. This is a life skill that is essential for many racialized bodies to master, as in many cases their socio-economic survival depends on it. I learned that although institutions are resistant to change, it is possible through communities of learners with a similar passion and appetite for constructive change to cope with the struggles and challenges at the Academy, to heal from our traumatic experiences inside and outside of school campuses, and with hope work collectively and in solidarity towards challenging oppressive learning conditions at various levels.

It is significant that we all do our best in our various roles and capacities on a daily basis to create inclusive, safe, empowering, loving, and supportive learning environments where children, youth, and adults do not lose interest in education due to systematic barriers but rather become encouraged to make a difference in their own lives and in their communities by keeping an open mind and heart and pursuing their passions. As educators we have to deviate from obsession with control and excessive assessment and testing to seeing individuals holistically, in the process allowing learners to lead, make mistakes and learn from it, express their thoughts, feelings, and emotions, invite them to think, and challenge them to solve problems both within the classroom and in the larger context of their neighbourhoods and/or the world. At the core of my praxis as an educator and a community activist is the importance of using education as a tool to inspire, motivate, empower, and bring social consciousness to individuals and collective groups to resist and challenge injustice and inequity in its various forms and processes at the micro and macro levels. This is best accomplished when we make education socio-culturally relevant and responsive to the needs and lives of learners. As Ladson-Billings (1995) points out, culturally relevant pedagogy is an education "model that not only addresses student achievement but also helps students to accept and affirm their cultural identity while developing critical perspectives that challenge inequities that schools (and other institutions) perpetuate" (p. 469). As I continue to work in numerous racialized neighbourhoods in the City of Toronto as an educator, I strive to blur the hierarchical and dichotomous binary of teacher/student and work towards forming a community of learners within my classroom where collectively as life-long learners we horizontally share the power and work collaboratively to achieve co-constructed goals for the betterment of our well-beings, and the larger needs of the community and the planet which we co-exist within.

Gravitating Towards Studying the Impact of EQAO Standardized Testing

As an educator and as a community activist for the past ten years, I have worked in numerous Toronto racialized communities labelled "at-risk" by media representations, particularly in Jane and Finch and Scarborough involving various initiatives with a focus on advocacy and social justice advancement for minoritized and racialized identities through education, leadership, and coaching. In terms of terminology, it is important to distinguish that whereas the term "minority" refers to "a group of less than half of the total, a group that is sufficiently smaller in number," the terms minoritized and racialized have a focus on describing power relations referring to "groups that are different in race, religious creed, nation of origin, sexuality, and gender and as a result of social constructs have less power or representation compared to other members or groups in society" (Smith, 2016, para. 11). I have had the privilege of teaching and learning with kids, youth, and young adults ranging from elementary-aged children to post-secondary students from all walks of life. Being a racialized person, I found many children, youth, parents, and community members felt more comfortable turning to me to express some of their needs and concerns about various issues impacting them in the classroom, in the school, and/or in the community outside of school. Over time, based on the conversations and the feedback I received, I began to see a trend that one of the silenced issues in educational inequity is the impact of standardized testing on racialized students and parents (Au, 2010; Dei, 2008; James, 2012; Kearns, 2016; Pinto, 2016). This is a process that begins with the use of EQAO (Education Quality and Accountability Office) standardized testing in elementary schools in Grade 3 and is continued as children grow and mature and attend high school and post-secondary institutions. In particular, I became concerned about the organization and impact of provincial standardized testing introduced in Ontario in 1996 by EQAO, which is an arm's-length agency of the Ministry of Education (EQAO, 2012). Each year EQAO assesses students in all Ontario publicly funded schools in Grades 3, 6, 9, and 10 focusing on numeracy and literacy using criterion-referenced census-style standardized tests as a means of providing "an independent gauge of children's learning and achievement" (EQAO, 2012, p. 1). For all assessments, questions are linked to the Ontario Curriculum expectations and include a range of multiple choice, true and false, and open-ended response questions. The following school year, each student receives a personalized report that "describes his or her achievement on the test" in relation to Ontario's provincial curriculum expectations ranging from Level 1 being "below grade expectations" to Level 4 being "above grade expectations" (EQAO, 2012, p. 8). As well, each school and school board receive a detailed report about overall achievement of their student population and how they are doing collectively as a school board. The annual cost of administrating EQAO standardized tests is $32 million dollars (EQAO, 2012).

When I inquired about the short- and long-term impact of EQAO standardized tests through everyday conversations with many racialized children, youth, young adults, and parents, many expressed that writing EQAO standardized tests was nerve-wrecking for them and in some cases traumatizing by the amount of pressure they felt coupled with their fear of failure. I was astonished by the high number of people who in retrospect vividly remembered their experience writing the EQAO test in Grades 3 and 6 and described it as negative and detrimental to their development and growth. Many racialized identities explained how taking EQAO tests had a long-term lasting negative impact of making them feel "stupid" or "incompetent" and created fear in them associated with test-taking anxiety lasting a lifetime. As a result, it became important to me to conduct an exploratory qualitative research study to further more holistically capture the impact of Grade 3 EQAO standardized test preparation and administration on racialized children, parents, and educators as told through their voices. I interviewed eight families as case studies, predominantly racialized children who were in Grade 3 and had recently completed writing the EQAO test and their respective parent(s), to capture how the enactment of the test in their respective schools impacted them. Their responses are analysed and the findings presented throughout this book, but prior to that in the following upcoming chapters I will explore the history of standardized testing in Ontario, Canada, and what led to EQAO standardized testing becoming a dominant and normalized accountability tool in schools today.

REFERENCES

Au, W. (2010). *Unequal by design: High-stakes testing and the standardization of inequality*. London: Routledge.

Dei, G. J. S. (2008). Schooling as community: Race, schooling, and the education of African youth. *Journal of Black Studies, 38*(3), 346–366.

Education Quality and Accountability Office. (2012). *The power of Ontario's provincial testing program*. Toronto: Queen's Printer for Ontario. Retrieved from http://www.eqao.com/en/assessments/communication-docs/power-provincial-testing-program.PDF

Freire, P. (1970). *Pedagogy of the oppressed*. New York: The Continuum International Publishing Group Inc.

James, C. E. (2012). *Life at the intersection: Community, class and schooling*. Halifax, NS: Fernwood Publishing.

Kearns, L. (2016). The construction of 'illiterate' and 'literate' youth: The effects of high-stakes standardized literacy testing. *Race Ethnicity and Education, 19*(1), 121–140.

Ladson-Billings, G. (1995). Toward a theory of culturally relevant pedagogy. *American Educational Research Journal, 32*(3), 465–491.

Masood, O. (2008). *At risk: The racialized student marked for educational failure*. (Unpublished doctoral dissertation). University of Toronto, Toronto, ON.

Miller, J. P. (2000). *Education and the soul: Toward a spiritual curriculum*. New York: SUNY Press.

Miller, J. P. (2016). Equinox: Portrait of a holistic school. *International Journal of Children's Spirituality, 21*(3–4), 283–301. https://doi.org/10.1080/1364436X.2016.1232243

Noguera, P. A. (2003). Schools, prisons, and social implications of punishment: Rethinking disciplinary practices. *Theory into Practice, 42*(4), 341–350.

Pinto, L. E. (2016). Tensions and fissures: The politics of standardised testing and accountability in Ontario, 1995–2015. *The Curriculum Journal, 27*(1), 95–112.

Portelli, J., & Vilbert, A. (2002). Standards, equity, and the curriculum of life. *Analytic Teaching, 22*(1), 4–19.

Smith, I. (2016). Minority vs. Minoritized: Why the noun just doesn't cut it. Retrieved from https://www.theodysseyonline.com/minority-vs-minoritize

CHAPTER 2

Elementary Standardized Testing on the Bubble: To Eliminate or Maintain?

In September 2017, an independent review of student assessment and reporting practices in publicly funded schools in Ontario was announced by the provincial government and the Premier at the time Kathleen Wynne (Ontario Ministry of Education, 2018b). The review was titled *Ontario: A Learning Province* led by six expert researchers who were identified as Ontario's education advisers to the provincial government. The six members were:

- Dr. Carol Campbell, Associate Professor, Leadership and Educational Change, Ontario Institute for Studies in Education at the University of Toronto
- Dr. Jean Clinton, Clinical Professor, Department of Psychiatry and Behavioural Neurosciences at McMaster University
- Dr. Michael Fullan, OC, Professor Emeritus and former Dean of the Ontario Institute for Studies in Education at the University of Toronto
- Dr. Andy Hargreaves, Thomas More Brennan Chair in the Lynch School of Education at Boston College
- Dr. Carl James, Jean Augustine Chair in Education, Community and Diaspora, Faculty of Education, York University
- Kahontakwas Diane Longboat, Senior Project Manager, Guiding Directions Implementation, Centre for Addiction and Mental Health; ceremonial leader, educator, teacher of Indigenous spiritual ways and healer. (Ontario Ministry of Education, 2017)

© The Author(s) 2019
A. Eizadirad, *Decolonizing Educational Assessment*,
https://doi.org/10.1007/978-3-030-27462-7_2

The objective of the review was "to ensure that Ontario's assessment and reporting practices are culturally relevant, measure a wide range of learning and better reflect student well being and equity" (Ontario Ministry of Education, 2018a, para. 2). Consultation with various community members including parents/guardians, educators, students, and community members was conducted using various formats to "modernize student assessment and reporting tools" (Ontario Ministry of Education, 2018a, para. 3). Community consultation mediums used included in-person engagement sessions in various geographical locations in Ontario attended overall by more than 800 people, an online survey which 4100 people completed, 44 written submissions, and many other shared comments and viewpoints submitted through Twitter and webcasts.

The data was compiled and led to the production of a 106-page report released in March 2018 titled *Ontario: A Learning Province: Finding and Recommendations from the Independent Review of Assessment and Reporting*. The report makes 18 recommendations about various ways current assessment and reporting practices in education can be modernized to be more relevant and equitable. Under a subsection titled "Large-Scale Assessments," the report describes various concerns about Education Quality and Accountability Office (EQAO) testing in schools arising from the community consultations:

Clarifying and renewing the role of the EQAO agency

While EQAO has a national and international reputation for world-class assessment expertise, within Ontario, it has a very mixed perception publicly and among students, parents/guardians and educators. Views ranged from calls to abolish EQAO through to support for maintaining, but transforming it.

Reforming the design and administration of EQAO assessments

There was a strong consensus about the need for changes in EQAO assessments. There is a high level of concern about the current nature and impact of EQAO assessments given commitments to student equity, recognizing the culture and experiences of students, and minimizing undesirable indirect effects of assessments on students' learning and well-being. In particular, there were concerns about whether Grade 3 was an appropriate age for large-scale assessments in light of concerns about children's development, well-being and anxiety, whether Grade 9 was an inappropriate time as students were transitioning into the first year of secondary school and whether the OSSLT was outdated and should continue to be a one day assessment linked to a graduation requirement. (Campbell et al., 2018, pp. 7–8)

Recommendations 7 to 17 directly and indirectly are specific to EQAO activities, policies, and/or practices. Of particular interest is Recommendation 8 which states,

> Recommendation 8: Undertake a redesign of provincial large-scale assessments, aligned with the curriculum refresh and taking into account developments in student learning and assessment design, including equitable, inclusive and culturally relevant practices, student choice and voice in assessments, and integration of technology. Develop a parallel implementation process to:
>
> 1. Reform provincial large-scale assessments to:
>   a. Continue but substantially modernize Grade 6 census assessments of literacy and numeracy, plus consideration of transferable skills needed to equip elementary students as they proceed in their education;
>   b. Discontinue the OSSLT and design and implement a new Grade 10 census assessment of key knowledge, skills and competences, including consideration of literacy, numeracy and competences needed to equip students for success in post-secondary school destinations (e.g. apprenticeship, college, university, community living, or work). This would replace the OSSLT, but would not be linked to graduation requirements.
> 2. Phase out and end over a multi-year period:
>   a. the current Grade 3 EQAO assessments and make better use of the EDI to support early intervention; and
>   b. the current Grade 9 EQAO assessments and the OSSLT. (Campbell et al., 2018, p. 67)

Shortly after the release of these recommendations in late March 2018, which recommended phasing out "over a multi-year period" the Grade 3 EQAO assessments, EQAO responded with their own press release expressing, "agency concerned by recommendation to eliminate important source of data on early student learning" (EQAO, 2018, para. 2). The press release indicated that EQAO agrees that "further discussion is required regarding the recommendations of the Premier's education advisors" (EQAO, 2018, para. 1) to examine the implications of these potential changes. EQAO defended the need to maintain the Grade 3 EQAO standardized tests arguing, "The removal of this assessment would result in the loss of an important source of data on early student learning—data that is used not only to improve programs in elementary schools but also to monitor the effectiveness of public expenditures on education and the results of Ontario's Poverty Reduction Strategy" (EQAO, 2018, para. 7).

This brings us to a critical juncture in education socio-politically today in relation to EQAO standardized testing in Ontario. There is tension between the provincial government and EQAO with respect to whether or not to phase out the Grade 3 EQAO standardized testing as advised by Premier's education advisors or maintain it as argued by EQAO. To make matters more complex, in the June 7, 2018, provincial election a new Premier was elected from a different political party. Doug Ford of the Progressive Conservatives was elected defeating Kathleen Wynne of the Liberal Party who was the Premier since 2013. It is yet to be seen what direction and approach the new Premier takes to tackle issues related to EQAO standardized testing, but as of writing this book, his political party has introduced massive budget cuts within the public sector both in education and in healthcare. The Toronto District School Board has projected a $67.8 million-dollar budget shortfall for the 2019–2020 school year due to reduction in funding from the provincial government which will translate to a decrease in number of teaching positions and an increase in class sizes.

Effects of Standardized Testing: Pros and Cons

According to *Public Attitudes Toward Education in Ontario 2015: The 19th OISE Survey of Educational Issues*, under the subsection "Province-Wide Testing and Elementary Students," Hart and Kempf (2015) point out:

> Every-student testing in grades 3 and 6 has continued to attract opposition. In particular, the Elementary Teachers' Federation of Ontario (ETFO) has long opposed the policy. Only a small minority, of the public and parents, 14% in 2015, has opposed any form of province-wide testing. Supporters of provincial assessment generally favour every-student testing over testing only a sample of students. In 2015, however, there seems to have been some shift in opinion, with support for every-student testing falling slightly below 50% for the first time, with almost one in five favouring the sampling approach. (p. 3)

As the survey findings indicate, as of 2015, there has been a shift in the general public from a parents' perspective with respect to the appropriateness and effectiveness of millions of dollars spent every year testing every student in Grades 3 and 6 in domains of Reading, Writing, and Mathematics.

More research is required in this area to explore why there is a public shift in opinion and what it can be attributed to. Yet, EQAO continues to advocate for census-style assessments. In a December 2018 document titled *Supporting Student Learning Through Assessment and Accountability*, EQAO justifies census-based provincial assessments over sample-based assessments by listing multiple benefits:

- providing independent data to parents, guardians, and teachers to support the education of each child;
- providing independent data on all groups of students across the province;
- evaluating progress over time at the student, school, school board, and provincial levels;
- fostering accountability at the school, school board, and provincial levels;
- enabling discussions about improvements to learning programmes in schools and boards across the province; and
- allowing policymakers to better understand system-wide trends, and make student-focused and evidence-informed decisions accordingly.

The key question to consider as you read this book is whether there are more effective and alternative ways that can yield such aforementioned benefits. In other words, how can we obtain similar benefits without investing in standardized testing of every child?

As a follow-up study released in 2018, Hart and Kempf (2018), in the *Public Attitudes Toward Education in Ontario 2018: The 20th OISE Survey of Educational Issues*, express that when it comes to standardized testing,

> [t]here has been a sharp decline in the proportion of the public who are undecided on the issue. Both the percentage supporting and percentage opposed to every-student testing at the elementary level have gained as a result, but the opposition has drawn somewhat more support. (p. 30)

Hamilton, Stecher, and Klein (2002) outline a comprehensive list of various positive and negative effects associated with the use of standardized testing in schools, particularly as it impacts students, teachers, administrators, and policymakers (pp. 86–87). Although the mentioned effects on various educational stakeholders, as listed below in chart format, are not exhaustive in nature, it serves as a baseline reference guide to further contextualize how standardized tests can have multiple positive and negative effects depending on how they are enacted, implemented, and the results used. The goal is to present both sides of the argument, pros and cons of standardized testing, in seeking to explore, "What are the experiences, opinions, and concerns of racialized children, parents, and educators regarding how the EQAO standardized test impacts their identity, family, school and the larger surrounding community in which they live?" which is the main research question for this exploratory qualitative study.

Effects on students

Positive effects	Negative effects
Provide students with better information about their own knowledge and skills	Frustrate students and discourage them from trying
Motivate students to work harder in school	Make students more competitive
Send clearer signals to students about what to study	Cause students to devalue grade and school assessments
Help students associate personal effort with rewards	

Effects on teachers

Positive effects	Negative effects
Support better diagnosis of individual student needs	Encourage teachers to focus more on specific test content than on curriculum standards
Help teachers identify areas of strength and weakness in their curriculum	Lead teachers to engage in inappropriate test preparation
Help teachers identify content not mastered by students and redirect instruction	Devalue teachers' sense of professional worth
Motivate teachers to work harder and smarter	Entice teachers to cheat when preparing or administrating tests
Motivate teachers to align instruction with standards	
Encourage teachers to participate in professional development to improve instruction	

Effects on administrators

Positive effects	Negative effects
Cause administrators to examine school policies related to curriculum and instruction	Lead administrators to enact policies to increase test scores but not necessarily increase learning
Help administrators judge the quality of their programmes	Cause administrators to reallocate resources to tested subjects at the expense of other subjects
Lead administrators to change school policies to improve curriculum and instruction	Lead administrators to waste resources on test preparation
Help administrators make better resource allocation decisions, for example, provide professional development	Distract administrators from other school needs and problems

Effects on policymakers

Positive effects	Negative effects
Help policymakers to judge the effectiveness of educational policies	Provide misleading information that leads policymakers to suboptimum decisions
Improve policymakers' ability to monitor school system performance	Foster a "blame the victims" spirit among policymakers
Foster better allocation of educational resources	Encourage a simplistic view of education and its goals

GRADE 3 EQAO STANDARDIZED TESTING: A DEVELOPMENTAL PERSPECTIVE

While the pros and cons of standardized testing can be debated at length, another angle to examine EQAO standardized testing is from a developmental perspective examining the needs of children in the early years. In other words, is Grade 3 as a developmental stage where children are still growing, maturing, and developing physically, socially, psychologically, emotionally, morally, and spiritually an appropriate age to administer standardized tests? And if so, will the results be accurate and useful? As Russo (2012) points out, "By placing unrealistic demands upon children who are not developmentally ready, we are asking teachers to spend most of their time attempting to push children in ways that may set them up to fail" (p. 144).

Although EQAO standardized tests are administered in Grades 3, 6, 9, and 10, and there has been vast amounts of research on standardized testing in Ontario, majority of it has been conducted at the secondary high school level (Hori, 2013; Kearns, 2016; Kempf, 2016; Klinger, Rogers, Anderson, Poth, & Calman, 2006; Langlois, 2017; Lock, 2001; Masood, 2008; Spencer, 2006). There is a gap in the research focusing on testing in the elementary years. This could partially be attributed to the greater risk and complexity of gaining ethical clearance to work with young children. Nonetheless, it is an important area that needs further examination as currently all Grade 3 students attending public schools in Ontario write EQAO standardized tests.

As part of this exploratory qualitative study, I try to capture the subjective embodied lived experiences of Grade 3 students, parents, and educators about how they are impacted by preparing and writing the EQAO standardized test. The goal is to take a step towards better understanding the impact of EQAO standardized testing at the elementary level, particularly on racialized children and communities. Ontario Ministry of Education (2014) document *How Does Learning Happen? Ontario's Pedagogy for the Early Years* states, "children's early experience last a lifetime" because "During our first years of life, the brain develops at an astounding rate. Scientists now know this process is not just genetic but is dramatically influenced by our early experiences with people and our surroundings" (p. 4). Further emphasizing the importance of the early years as a time frame where children are constantly growing and changing, Fiore (2012) argues that, "One particular test or score does not paint a full, clear picture of a complex, developing child" and this is "supported by research that states that standardized testing of children under the age of 8 is scientifically invalid and contributes to detrimental labeling that can permanently damage a child's educational future" (p. 5).

Fiore (2012) emphasizes, beyond examining the pros and cons of standardized testing for its effectiveness, that it is just as important to consider the developmental stage of each child when evaluating and assessing their capabilities, because "recognizing the developmental appropriateness of assessment and research is fundamental to practices that protect children from less than ideal classroom activity and, in the worst cases, harm" (p. 187). One of the commonly cited harms of exposing young children to standardized testing is complications arising from stress rooted in fear of failure and anxiety about the impact of the test on their educational outcomes such as marks or advancement to the next grade (Au, 2010;

FairTest, 2017; Kearns, 2016; Kempf, 2013). This refers to the subjective perceived and embodied stress experienced by the children from their perspective. For example, even though the Grade 3 EQAO standardized test does not count towards student report card marks or their advancement to the next grade, the emphasis placed on the importance of the test by the vast amount of time and effort dedicated to preparing for the test by teachers and administrators can give students the impression that if they don't do well they are disappointing themselves, their parents, teacher(s), and potentially the perceived image of the school, hence creating a highly pressurized and stressful learning environment.

Weale (2017) reports that a survey was conducted in the United Kingdom to explore the impact of Standardized Assessment Tests (SATs) on primary school children. SATs are United Kingdom's version of EQAO standardized tests which focus on English and Mathematics testing for accountability purposes. These standardized tests are administered to children 7 and 11 years old. What stands out is that "8 out of the 10 primary school leaders reported an increase in mental health issues among primary school children around the time of the exams" (Weale, 2017, para. 2). This included symptoms such as increased signs of stress and anxiety with "some suffering sleeplessness and panic attacks" (Para. 1). Specific examples of stress experienced by students, as observed and reported by teachers and administrators who participated in the survey, included one child losing all their eyelashes due to stress and some children sobbing while doing the tests and given a time-out to recollect themselves before returning to their seats to complete the test (Weale, 2017). Overall, responses from 1200 teachers who participated in the survey indicate that many teachers feel that there has been an increase over the years "in general cases of stress, anxiety, and panic attacks," and "an increase in fear of academic failure and depression" (Weale, 2017, para. 7) amongst children since 2014 with the implementation of more standardized testing in schools.

FairTest (https://www.fairtest.org/), The National Center for Fair and Open Testing, is a national organization in the United States which "advances quality education and equal opportunity by promoting fair, open, valid and educationally beneficial evaluations of students, teachers and schools" (FairTest, 2018, para. 1). FairTest, through its weekly online newsletters, compiles and expresses relevant news about standardized testing locally, nationally, and internationally and "works to end the misuses and flaws of testing practices that impede those goals" (FairTest, 2018, para. 1). Examining the use of standardized testing on young children from a developmental perspective, FairTest (2017) has produced an information sheet titled "Fact Sheet for Families on Testing and Young Children." This factsheet is educational and intended for parents and activists outlining the harmful effects of using standardized testing on young children. It explains that "emphasis on testing has negative impact on children's healthy development and learning" (FairTest, 2017, p. 1). Other reasons listed to justify FairTest's stance on misuse of standardized testing on young children includes:

- Deprived of these engaging activities, children may lose interest in school and learning.
- Parents, teachers, and mental health professionals report many more symptoms of test stress among young children, including nausea, crying, panic attacks, tantrums, headaches, sleeplessness, depression, and refusal to go to school.
- Test stress is especially harmful to more vulnerable children, such as those with special needs or children whose first language is not English.
- Testing may make children feel "dumb," especially when tested on materials that are developmentally inappropriate. (FairTest, 2017, p. 1)

Overall, the objective of this study is to explore whether the same impacts are replicated in the context of Ontario as expressed by the voices of racialized children, parents, and educators. The goal is to present both sides of the argument, pros and cons of standardized testing, in seeking to explore "What are the experiences, opinions, and concerns of racialized children, parents, and educators regarding how the EQAO standardized test impacts their identity, family, school and the larger surrounding community in which they live?" A key feature of the data generated for this study is that the conversations and discussions are led by voices of children, parents, and educators who self-identify as racialized. The racialized perspectives of the children, parents, and educators expressed throughout the book provide an avenue to gain a better and more in-depth understanding about the subjective embodied experiences of preparing and writing the Grade 3 EQAO test and the extent that it is positive or negative and to further document specifically in what ways. This can then be compared to the dominant narrative disseminated by and through EQAO about the benefits and effectiveness of EQAO standardized tests for accountability outcomes.

I hope the content of this book serves as a platform to continue to engage in dialogues and conversations about the usefulness and effectiveness of standardized testing, particularly in the context of administrating them to young racialized and minoritized children in elementary schools. At the end of reading this book, I hope readers walk away further questioning where does the use of EQAO standardized testing fit in the equation for serving the needs of all students in the education system, particularly racialized students who come from marginalized communities? More importantly, I hope readers reflect to what extent EQAO standardized testing as an accountability tool helps or hinders closing the achievement amongst different social groups and what can be utilized as alternative decolonizing assessment models?

References

Au, W. (2010). *Unequal by design: High-stakes testing and the standardization of inequality*. London: Routledge.

Campbell, C., Clinton, J., Fullan, M., Hargreaves, A., James, C., & Longboat, K. (2018). *Ontario: A learning province. Findings and recommendations from the independent review of assessment and reporting. Ontario Ministry of Education.* Toronto: Queen's Printer for Ontario. Retrieved from http://www.edu.gov.on.ca/CurriculumRefresh/learning-province-en.pdf

Education Quality and Accountability Office. (2018). *About the agency.* Toronto: Queen's Printer for Ontario. Retrieved from http://www.eqao.com/en/about-eqao/about-the-agency

FairTest. (2017). Fact sheet for families on testing and young children. The National Center for Fair and Open Testing. Retrieved from http://www.fairtest.org/sites/default/files/YoungChildTestingFactSheet2017.pdf

FairTest. (2018). About FairTest: The National Center for Fair and Open Testing. Retrieved from https://www.fairtest.org/about

Fiore, L. (2012). *Assessment of young children: A collaborative approach.* New York: Routledge.

Hamilton, L., Stecher, B., & Klein, S. (2002). *Making sense of test-based accountability in education.* Santa Monica, CA: RAND.

Hart, D., & Kempf, A. (2015). *Public attitudes toward education in Ontario 2015: The 19th OISE survey of educational issues.* OISE, University of Toronto. Retrieved from https://tspace.library.utoronto.ca/bitstream/1807/76898/2/Final_Report_-_19th_OISE_Survey_on_Educational_Issues_2015.pdf

Hart, D., & Kempf, A. (2018). *Public attitudes toward education in Ontario 2018: The 20th OISE survey of educational issues.* OISE, University of Toronto. Retrieved from https://www.oise.utoronto.ca/oise/UserFiles/Media/Media_Relations/OISE-Public-Attitudes-Report-2018_final.pdf

Hori, M. M. (2013). *The Toronto District School Board & Structural Violence.* Mahad. M. Hori.

Kearns, L. (2016). The construction of 'illiterate' and 'literate' youth: The effects of high-stakes standardized literacy testing. *Race Ethnicity and Education, 19(1)*, 121–140.

Kempf, A. (2013, June 21). Standardized school tests stress students and system. *Toronto Star*. Retrieved from https://www.thestar.com/opinion/commentary/2013/06/21/standardized_school_tests_stress_students_and_system.html

Kempf, A. (2016). *The pedagogy of standardized testing: The radical impacts of educational standardization in the US and Canada.* New York: Springer.

Klinger, D., Rogers, W., Anderson, J., Poth, C., & Calman, R. (2006). Contextual and school factors associated with achievement on a high-stakes examination. *Canadian Journal of Education, 29(3)*, 771–797.

Langlois, H. (2017). *Behind the snapshot: Teachers' experiences of preparing students in lower socioeconomic status schools for the Ontario Secondary School Literacy Test.* Master of Teaching research paper, Department Curriculum, Teaching and Learning, University of Toronto, Toronto, ON.

Lock, C. (2001). *The influence of a large scale assessment program on classroom practices.* (Unpublished doctoral dissertation). Queen's University, Kingston, ON.

Masood, O. (2008). *At risk: The racialized student marked for educational failure.* (Unpublished doctoral dissertation). University of Toronto, Toronto, ON.

Ontario Ministry of Education. (2014). *How does learning happen? Ontario's pedagogy for the early years: A resource about learning through relationships for those who work with young children and their families.* Toronto: Queen's Printer for Ontario. Retrieved from http://www.edu.gov.on.ca/childcare/HowLearningHappens.pdf

Ontario Ministry of Education. (2017). *Ontario appoints new advisors to guide transformation in education system.* Toronto: Queen's Printer for Ontario. Retrieved from https://news.ontario.ca/edu/en/2017/08/ontario-appoints-new-advisors-to-guide-transformation-in-education-system.html?_ga=2.71555795.1779644130.1528468099-1009438681.1520260943

Ontario Ministry of Education. (2018a). *Independent review of assessment and reporting.* Toronto: Queen's Printer for Ontario. Retrieved from http://www.edu.gov.on.ca/CurriculumRefresh/student-assessment.html

Ontario Ministry of Education. (2018b). *Ontario's graduation rate.* Toronto: Queen's Printer for Ontario. Retrieved from http://www.edu.gov.on.ca/eng/

Russo, L. (2012). "Standardized" play and creativity for young children? The climate of increased standardization and accountability in early childhood classrooms. *Counterpoints, 425*, 140–156.

Spencer, B. (2006). *The will to accountability: Reforming education through standardized literacy testing.* (Unpublished doctoral dissertation). University of Toronto, Toronto, ON.

Weale, S. (2017, May 1). More primary school children suffering stress from SATs, survey finds. *The Guardian*. Retrieved from https://www.theguardian.com/education/2017/may/01/sats-primary-school-children-suffering-stress-exam-time#img-3

Royal Commission on Learning and the Birth of EQAO and the Accountability Movement in Ontario

Leading up to the 1990s, the province of Ontario had "no history of large-scale assessment and none with high-stakes for students, schools, and districts" (Volante, 2007, p. 2). The education system came under scrutiny by taxpayers, media outlets, policymakers, and parents in the early 1990s, being blamed as ineffective due to the compounding provincial government debt and the rising unemployment rate (Gidney, 1999). As Kempf (2016) points out, this mounting government pressure was "part of a larger push for accountability with taxpayer dollars on the one hand, and the call to for schools to get back to basics on the other" (p. 36). Schools were blamed for not preparing students adequately for the emergence of a knowledge-based economy. Public polls indicated majority of taxpayers and parents felt the education system was failing students by not being responsive to economical needs of a changing Canadian society in a manner that would keep Canada competitive internationally, particularly when globalization and unemployment were on the rise (Royal Commission on Learning, 1994; Ungerleider, 2003). This placed pressure on government officials and politicians to seek new changes and educational reforms as a means of restoring public confidence in the education system. The pressure for educational reform reached its climax when media outlets began emphasizing how Ontario students were doing poorly on international standardized tests in comparison to students from other provinces (Gidney, 1999; Morgan, 2006; Pinto, 2016).

© The Author(s) 2019
A. Eizadirad, *Decolonizing Educational Assessment*,
https://doi.org/10.1007/978-3-030-27462-7_3

In Ontario, three dominant political parties have been in power at various intervals. These include the New Democratic Party (NDP), the Liberals, and the Progressive Conservatives. The NDP is typically the most left-leaning party, the Liberals the centrist, and the Progressive Conservatives the most right-leaning party. This is important to keep in mind as we examine the drastic educational reforms introduced and implemented by the various political parties in Ontario beginning in the mid-1990s which led to the normalization of the accountability paradigm and the legitimization of province-wide standardized testing supported by the establishment of the Education Quality and Accountability Office (EQAO) in 1996. According to Morgan (2006), "In 1986, after 30 years of Conservative rule, a Liberal government came into power in Ontario led by David Peterson. It was defeated shortly afterwards by the New Democratic Party (NDP) in 1990" (p. 129) led by Bob Rae. After a 30-year Conservative dominance, there was an opening for other political parties to lead government and propose changes. Under the NDP government, on February 3, 1993, Dave Cooke was appointed Minister of Education and shortly after began implementing new changes to restructure the education system as a means of restoring public confidence in Ontario's education system. Changes introduced included "appointment of consultants to review potential amalgamations" (Sattler, 2012, p. 8) of various school boards to reduce education expenditures and implementation of "province-wide achievement tests for Grade 9 students in reading and writing and public reporting of the results" (Gidney, 1999, p. 223). As well, as a response to the public outcry and pressure to improve the education system, in May 1993, the NDP launched the *Royal Commission on Learning* (RCOL) which "initiated an opening of public opportunity structures that allowed for public input into educational governance" (Morgan, 2006, p. 129). It was a one-of-a kind comprehensive examination of education in Ontario since the 1968 Hall-Dennis report titled *Living and Learning* which reported on the overall aims and objectives of education in Ontario schools and how it can be improved. The putting together of the RCOL report involved consultation with "more than 4700 groups and individuals" through various mediums (Sattler, 2012, p. 9). The RCOL was to prepare recommendations about changes in "laws, policies, and procedures necessary and desirable to improve the efficiency, effectiveness, relevance, and accountability of education in Ontario" as a means to ensure that "Ontario youth are well-prepared for the challenges of the twenty-first century" (Royal Commission on Learning, 1994, pp. vi–vii).

The RCOL utilized a series of guiding questions to examine four key areas in education: a shared vision, programme, accountability, and education governance. The Commission released its findings in January 1995 in a 550-page report titled *For the Love of Learning* which made 167 recommendations in numerous areas related to curriculum, report cards, funding, and addressing the needs of specific student populations including Aboriginals, students with special needs, and minority groups. One of the primary focus areas of the recommendations was accountability. Under the subsection titled "Large-Scale Assessment of Student Achievement and the Effectiveness of School Programs," the Commission recommended establishment of the Office of Learning Assessment and Accountability as an independent arm's length testing agency to operate as a "watchdog for system performance" responsible for annual "construction, administration, scoring, and reporting" of standardized tests (Royal Commission on Learning, 1994, p. 256). At the elementary level, Recommendation 50 from the RCOL suggested "all students be given two uniform assessments at the end of grade 3, one in literacy and one in numeracy, based on specific learner outcomes and standards that are well known to teachers, parents, and to students themselves" (Royal Commission on Learning, 1994, p. 256). At the secondary level, the Commission recommended that in Grade 11 "a literacy test be given to students, which they must pass before receiving their secondary school diploma" (Royal Commission on Learning, 1994, p. 256). The secondary school literacy test would be a high-stakes test as successful passing of it would be a requirement for graduation and obtaining the Ontario Secondary School Diploma (OSSD) (Volante, 2007).

In 1995, the Progressive Conservative Party led by Mike Harris campaigned to fix the inadequacies in government and to introduce necessary reforms to make government policies and practices more "efficient" and relevant to the needs of the increasingly competitive and globalized knowledge-based Canadian economy. His political campaign slogan was called the Common Sense Revolution "coined as an election strategy to woo voters disenchanted by rising taxes, spiralling deficits and debt, and the intrusion of big government in their lives" (Basu, 2004, p. 623). Harris's Progressive Conservative Party defeated the NDP and achieved a majority government. Harris's approach to reform was authoritarian and aggressive compared to the NDP. It was guided by a philosophy of reducing the cost of education through "cut spending and downsize of school board budgets" which in 1996 resulted in an "expenditure reduction of $400 million from school board budgets" translating to a "dramatic $1 billion cut from the system" on a yearly basis (Sattler, 2012, p. 11). Harris's aggressive cost reduction and downsizing in education led to increased tensions between the government, teachers, and teacher unions as it caused elimination of various social programmes and laying off of teachers and support staff. The Harris years became known as the dark ages in education in Ontario where education at all levels was drastically altered and changed due to major funding reduction for "efficiency" purposes.

Two major changes occurred under the Mike Harris government which continue to have long-lasting effects even today. The first change is the introduction of Bill 104 titled the *Fewer School Boards Act* which "reduced the number of school boards from 129 to 72 with a corresponding decrease in the number of [school] trustees from 1900 to 700" (Sattler, 2012, pp. 11–12). The second major change, which was more controversial, is the introduction of Bill 160 titled the *Education Quality Improvement Act* which "centralized financial control at the provincial level by removing education funding from the residential property tax-base and eliminating school boards' local taxing power" (Sattler, 2012, p. 11). As Basu (2004) points out, as a result of the new changes, "the six cities and boroughs that made up the Municipality of Metropolitan Toronto were amalgamated into a single city of Toronto and the six boards of education were similarly merged into the new Toronto District School Board (TDSB) as part of a fundamental realignment of taxation and spending between the province of Ontario and its municipal government" (p. 626). These drastic changes provided the niche for the introduction and implementation of an accountability system centred on outcome-based results supplemented with the use of fear tactics by the government. The government informed school boards that it was illegal to operate on a deficit budget and obligated school boards to publish annual reports on their finances disclosing their spending. This placed school boards and schools under centralized surveillance by the government. Pinto (2016) summarizes and outlines the overall major changes implemented by Mike Harris's Progressive Conservative Party in education during his eight years in power; the sweeping education reforms "resulted in standardized and prescriptive curriculum, a reduction in number of years in secondary school with different graduation requirements, a new tracking system for students starting in grade nine, and standardized report cards" (Pinto, 2016, pp. 97–98).

In 2003, the Progressive Conservatives were defeated by the Liberals led by Dalton McGuinty and succeeded by Kathleen Wynne in 2013. The Liberals maintained the changes established and implemented by Mike Harris in education. In further demonstrating accountability to the public and restoring public confidence in the education system, the Liberals invested money into various specific programmes to "improve literacy and numeracy outcomes" on EQAO standardized tests and increase the over-all "high school graduation rates" (Pinto, 2016, p. 97). Liberals constantly make reference to the increase in high school graduation rates under their time in power as a proud thermometer statistic that symbolizes "the strength of the education system" (Ministry of Education, 2017, para. 6). According to an article published on May 8, 2017, on the Ontario Ministry of Education website (2017) titled *High School Graduation Rate Climbs to All-time High*, "Ontario's unprecedented investments in education have pushed the high school graduation rate to a historic new high, as more students than ever before are obtaining a high school diploma and gaining the skills and experience required for the jobs of tomorrow" (para. 1). The article further states, "In 2016, the five year graduation rate increased to 86.5 percent—up more than 18 percentage points compared to the 2004 rate of 68 percent" (para. 2). The Liberals are very proud of this statistic that at one point on the Ministry of Education's home webpage (Ministry of Education, 2018), located at the centre, was a line graph titled "*Ontario's Graduation Rate*" which displayed how the provincial four-year and five-year graduation rates has steadily increased from 2004 to 2016 while the Liberals were in power.

Although at the surface level the gradual increase in high school gradu-ation rates during an extensive time period when the Liberals have been in power appears to be a great statistic to be emphasized to the general public, however, this generic statistic does not tell a complete story to assist us in "understanding curriculum as racial text" (Pinar, Reynolds, Slattery, & Taubman, 1995, p. 23) and whether or not the unique needs of all students from various social groups are being met equitably by the education system and its policies and practices. In order to understand "curriculum as racial text," it is important to critically question and ask for graduation rates for specific social groups such as Indigenous, black/African, Latino, and Middle-Eastern students and how each group is doing compared to the overall provincial graduation rate given Ontario's multicultural classrooms where immigrants from various parts of the world are learning together.

According to the Colour of Poverty and Colour of Change (2019) Fact Sheet on "Racialized Poverty in Education and Learning":

- In 2015, there was a 69% high school graduation rate for Black students and 50% for Indigenous students, versus 84% for White students.
- Black and Indigenous students are more likely to be streamed into non-academic programs than White or some of the other racialized students. In 2015 the Toronto District School Board reported that 53% of Black students and 48% of Indigenous students, compared to 81% of White students, were enrolled in Academic programs of study; while 39% of Black students and 41% of Indigenous students, compared to 16% of White students, were in Applied programs.
- Black, Indigenous, and Eastern Mediterranean/Southwest Asian students were disproportionately expelled from TDSB primary/secondary schools. Black students were 12% of TDSB student population but represented 48% of all expulsions; Indigenous students were 0.3% of the population but faced 1% of all expulsions; Eastern Mediterranean/Southwest Asian students were 4% of the population but faced 8% expulsions. (p. 1)

These inequitable trends in education emphasize that we cannot exclusively focus on graduation rates. We have to focus on the experiences of various social groups so we can make educational policies and practices more inclusive and equitable relative to identified needs and systemic shortcomings.

Another critical perspective to consider is how each school is doing relative to its student demographics such as total number of racialized students, English as Second Language (ESL) learners, and students identified with exceptionalities. This holistic approach to understanding and contextualizing the overall graduation rate of a school tells a much more specific story that contains details about how students are doing, where inequities exist, and what can be done to better address the needs of specific student populations. By centring race as the main lens to examine curriculum and graduation rates, we can begin to understand graduation rates as racial texts and whether or not and to what extent specific institutional policies and practices such as EQAO standardized testing contributes to perpetuating subtle racism. As educators and researchers, we have to constantly ask who does the current enactment of curriculum and EQAO standardized testing benefit and who does it oppress, and more specifically in what ways and at what costs?

Examining the timeline of educational reforms implemented from the mid-1990s up until now in Ontario, introduced and implemented under three different political parties, there is a common thread that all political parties view education through an economic market-driven lens. All political parties and their affiliated policymakers invested in demonstrating accountability to the general public by introducing and maintaining policies and programmes that increased outcome-based results ranging from improvements in EQAO standardized test scores to increases in high school graduation rates (Sattler, 2012). The premise of the economic market-driven model of education is maximizing human capital of students to prepare them for the needs of the labour market (Apple, 2004; Portelli & Vilbert, 2002). Therefore, EQAO standardized tests and improvement in scores become a symbolic political tool for the government and politicians to demonstrate accountability by "monitoring and reporting to the public on the performance of the education system by the use of test results" (Basu, 2004, p. 625). What is important to engage with and question is the philosophical principles undergirding the push and focus on the knowledge-based economy; specifically, what are the limitations of the economic market-driven model of education and its dominant ideology that economical needs should drive schools and education rather than the needs of students and local communities? More importantly, under the market-driven model of education, which social groups are privileged and who is oppressed? These are questions that we grapple with throughout the remaining chapters of this book from multiple perspectives.

EQAO Establishment and Evolution: Normalization of Standardized Testing Culture

Based on the recommendations of the *Royal Commission On Learning* report, EQAO was established in 1996 as an arm's length agency of the government of Ontario responsible for creating and implementing annual criterion-referenced standardized tests as a means of providing "an independent gauge of children's learning and achievement" (EQAO, 2012, p. 1) across the province of Ontario. Comparing standardized testing in Ontario to other provinces and territories in Canada, Pinto (2016) points out Ontario is "the only Canadian province in which such assessment is not executed directly by the government" (p. 98). Typically standardized tests fall under two categories; norm referenced or criterion referenced. Kohn (2000) distinguishes between the two by explaining, "In contrast to a test that's 'criterion-referenced,' which means it compares each individual to a set of standards, one that's norm-referenced compares each individual to everyone else, and the result is usually (but not always) reported as a percentile" (p. 14). EQAO standardized testing is criterion referenced and uses the prescriptive Ontario curriculum expectations as the benchmark to assess students.

The establishment of EQAO occurred with the implementation of Bill 30 in 1996, known as the *Education Quality and Accountability Office Act* (Education Quality and Accountability Office Act, 1996). Under section 3 of the *Education Quality and Accountability Office Act*, the specific objectives of the EQAO agency are outlined and listed:

1. To evaluate the quality and effectiveness of elementary and secondary school education.
2. To develop tests and require or undertake the administering and marking of tests of pupils in elementary and secondary schools.
3. To develop systems for evaluating the quality and effectiveness of elementary and secondary school education.
4. To research and collect information on assessing academic achievement.
5. To evaluate the public accountability of boards and to collect information on strategies for improving that accountability.
6. To report to the public and to the Minister of Education and Training on the results of tests and generally on the quality and effectiveness of elementary and secondary school education and on the public accountability of boards.
7. To make recommendations, in its reports to the public and to the Minister of Education and Training, on any matter related to the quality or effectiveness of elementary and secondary school education or to the public accountability of boards. (Education Quality and Accountability Office Act, 1996, c. 11, s. 3)

The words "evaluate/evaluating," "quality," "effectiveness," and "accountability" are constantly repeated throughout aforementioned objectives of the EQAO agency. This aligns with the market-driven technocratic view of education where "effectiveness" and "quality" of the education system is measured, quantified, and "evaluated" based on performance of students on outcome-based criterion-referenced standardized tests to demonstrate "accountability" to the general public (Eizadirad, Martinez, & Ruminot, 2016).

IMPLEMENTATION OF LARGE-SCALE EQAO STANDARDIZED TESTING IN ONTARIO

According to the EQAO document (2013), *EQAO: Ontario's Provincial Assessment Program: Its History and Influence*, the main objective of the agency is "to monitor students' achievement at key points in their learning as a way of assuring the public that all students were being assessed in the same way and according to an established set of standards" (p. 5). Grades 3, 6, 9, and 10 are chosen as key points for students to be assessed in various subjects. The launch of annual yearly large-scale EQAO census-style criterion-referenced assessments began in 1996–1997 school year where all Grade 3 children in Ontario wrote the EQAO test in domains of Reading, Writing, and Mathematics "which required approximately 12 hours of testing over two weeks" by completion of three test booklets: two for language and one for math (EQAO, 2013, p. 7). The administration of Grade 6 EQAO tests began in 1998–1999 school year taking the same amount of time as the Grade 3 testing. End of Grade 3 was chosen for administration of the first set of EQAO standardized tests as it represented end of schooling in the primary division referring to Grades 1–3, and Grade 6 was chosen for administration of second set of EQAO standardized tests because it represented end of schooling in the junior division referring to Grades 4–6. In 2004, after a systemic review of its practices, EQAO reduced the amount of testing time by half from 12 to 6 hours, which gave students 2 hours to complete each testing booklet. The Grade 9 Assessment of Mathematics began in 2000–2001 with administration of different set of tests for applied and academic streams consisting of two test booklets. Lastly, the high-stakes Grade 10 Ontario Secondary School Literacy Test (OSSLT), which is evaluated on a pass or fail criteria and a successful pass is a requirement for obtaining one's Ontario Secondary School Diploma, was introduced and implemented starting in 2002 consisting of two booklets.

EQAO standardized tests continue to be implemented today in Grades 3, 6, 9, and 10 in Ontario. Recently, EQAO has invested in a platform called EQAO Online which is a multi-year project to move EQAO's provincial student assessments from paper-and-pencil to computer-based as a means of modernizing (EQAO, 2017a). In October 2016, students in Grade 10 were given the opportunity to complete the Grade 10 OSSLT online. Students were informed that if they pass the test online, they would not have to write it again in paper-and-pencil format at a later time in the school year. Being in a high school that day to assist in administering the test, it did not take long before many students began encountering various computer problems. These problems included individualized passwords not working to give students access to start the test, pages taking long to upload or refresh, or pages freezing while students were typing their responses. These issues caused students to be logged out of the test and to wait long periods for a test administrator to manually log them back in so they could continue finishing the test. Within hours, EQAO issued a statement cancelling the online test due to "technical issues" (Shum & Miller, 2016, para. 1).

DIFFERENCES BETWEEN HIGH-STAKES AND LOW-STAKES STANDARDIZED TESTS

Standardized tests can be categorized into high-stakes or low-stakes tests based on consequences associated with the test. According to Langlois (2017), "Low-stakes testing is any test that is used for diagnostic and accountability purposes and does not have any direct effect on the students, teachers or schools, whereas high-stakes testing may affect to influence decisions for the student, teacher, school or school board such as grade promotion, graduation, hiring, bonuses and increase or loss of funding" (p. 8). In Ontario, Grades 3 and 6 Assessments of Reading, Writing and Mathematics and the Grade 9 Assessment of Mathematics are considered low-stakes tests. The Grades 3 and 6 tests do not count as part of a student's mark or report card and does not influence advancement to the next grade (EQAO, 2011). The Grade 9 EQAO Mathematics test can count up to 30 per cent of the student's final mark depending on the discretion of the teacher (EQAO, 2011). On the other hand, the Grade 10 OSSLT is a high-stakes test "where a passing grade is needed in order for students to receive their Ontario Secondary School Diploma" (Langlois, 2017, p. 9). Upon failing the OSSLT multiple times, students can take a Ministry of Education designed Literacy course which lasts a semester offered at their respective schools as an alternative means to gain a pass designation for the OSSLT.

GOVERNING STRUCTURE OF EQAO

EQAO in 1997 created a 20-page document outlining its by-laws categorized into 11 specific articles which "relate generally to the transaction of the business and affairs of the EQAO" (EQAO, 1997, p. 1). In terms of its governing structure, EQAO is managed by "a nine member

Board of Directors appointed by the Ontario cabinet" (Pinto, 2016, p. 98) and a seven-member Executive Team led by a Chief Executive Officer (EQAO, 2018). The Board of Directors has a Chair who was Dave Cooke, who in mid-1990s was the Minister of Education and fundamental in establishing the RCOL; one of its recommendations led to the creation and establishment of the EQAO agency. Dave Cooke spent ten years on EQAO's Board of Directors with the last three years as the Chair. In October 2018, Dave Cooke vacated the Chair position and as of February 2019 Dr Cameron Montgomery was appointed as the agency's first full-time Chair. Cameron Montgomery has a PhD in Educational Psychology and has been a professor of education at University of Ottawa for 14 years. The Board of Directors also has a Vice Chair, David Agnew, who is the president of Seneca College. The Chief Executive Officer is currently Norah Marsh and she "reports directly to the Board and to the Minister of Education" (Pinto, 2016, p. 98). The Chief Executive Officer "is responsible for the operation of the Office, the implementation of policies established by the board of directors and the performance of such other functions as assigned by the board of directors" (Education Quality and Accountability Office Act, 1996, c. 11, s. 16).

GRADE 3 EQAO PROVINCIAL RESULTS AND FIVE-YEAR PATTERNS

The Grades 3 and 6 EQAO test results are not available for the 2014–2015 school year due to the work to rule campaign by elementary school teachers which resulted not administrating the EQAO standardized tests because of lack of progress in labour negotiations with the Liberal government. According to the EQAO (2017a), in the 2016–2017 school year 132 992 Grade 3 students across the province wrote the EQAO test in Reading, Writing, and Mathematics (p. 1). In 2017–2018, the overall number of students who wrote the test got reduced to 132 656 (EQAO, 2019, p. 1). For 2016–2017, the percentage of Grade 3 students at or above the expected provincial Level 3 achievement level was 74 per cent in Reading, 73 per cent in Writing, and 62 per cent in Mathematics. For 2017–2018, the percentage of Grade 3 students at or above the expected provincial Level 3 achievement level was 75 per cent in Reading, 72 per cent in Writing, and 61 per cent in Mathematics.

EQAO also aggregated data over a five-year period to report five-year patterns of student achievement going back to the 2012–2013 school year. Listed are some of the five-year patterns for the Grade 3 primary division:

- Percentage of students performing at or above the provincial standard in reading has steadily increased, from 68% to 74%.
- Percentage of students performing at or above the provincial standard in writing has decreased from 77% to 73%.
- Percentage of students performing at or above the provincial standard in mathematics has decreased, from 67% to 62%.
- Percentage of Grade 3 English language learners performing at or above the provincial standard has increased by eight percentage points in reading and decreased by four percentage points in writing, while it has decreased by five percentage points in mathematics. This pattern is similar to that for the overall Grade 3 student population.
- Percentage of Grade 3 students with special education needs performing at or above the provincial standard has increased by seven percentage points in reading and one percentage point in writing; in mathematics, it has decreased by five percentage points, from 34% to 29%. (EQAO, 2017b, pp. 26–31)

Although these statistics can be useful indicators "to provide students, parents, teachers and administrators with a clear and comprehensive picture of student achievement and a basis for targeted improvement planning at the individual, school, school board and provincial levels," (EQAO, 2017a, p. 4) it is significant to question, similar to earlier with overall graduation rates in Ontario, whether absolute numbers in terms of overall percentage of students in the province achieving at the provincial level tells a complete story that captures the complexities that goes into understanding student achievement and curriculum as racial text. For example, schools in which neighbourhoods are doing consistently well on EQAO scores? Which areas are consistently not doing well? What are the demographics and the student make-up of such schools? How are specific social groups such as racialized and Indigenous students doing when it comes to EQAO results? These specific questions will move provide a more thorough and in-depth understanding of how EQAO standardized tests impact various students and their identities.

REFERENCES

Apple, M. W. (2004). *Ideology and curriculum*. New York: Routledge.

Basu, R. (2004). The rationalization of neoliberalism in Ontario's public education system, 1995–2000. *Geoforum, 35*(5), 621–634.

Colour of Poverty and Colour of Change. (2019). Fact sheets. Retrieved from https://colourofpoverty.ca/fact-sheets/

Education Quality and Accountability Office. (1997). *Education quality and accountability office/Office de la qualite et de la responsibilite en education by-law no. 1*. Toronto: Queen's Printer for Ontario. Retrieved from http://www.eqao.com/en/about_eqao/about_the_agency/communication-docs/EQAO-By-Law-No1.pdf#search=eqao%20by%20law%20

Education Quality and Accountability Office. (2011). *EQAO tests in elementary school: A guide for parents*. Toronto: Queen's Printer for Ontario. Retrieved from https://www.rainbowschools.ca/wp-content/uploads/2016/04/EQAO_ParentGuide_PrimaryJunior2011.pdf

Education Quality and Accountability Office. (2012). *The power of Ontario's provincial testing program*. Toronto: Queen's Printer for Ontario. Retrieved from http://www.eqao.com/en/assessments/communication-docs/power-provincial-testing-program.PDF

Education Quality and Accountability Office. (2013). *EQAO: Ontario's provincial assessment program- Its history and influence 1996–2012*. Toronto: Queen's Printer for Ontario. Retrieved from http://www.eqao.com/en/about_eqao/about_the_agency/communication-docs/EQAO-history-influence.pdf

Education Quality and Accountability Office. (2017a). *Highlights of the provincial results*. Toronto: Queen's Printer for Ontario. Retrieved from http://www.eqao.com/en/assessments/results/communication-docs/provincial-report-highlights-elementary-2017.pdf

Education Quality and Accountability Office. (2017b). *Achievement results; Primary division*. Toronto: Queen's Printer for Ontario. Retrieved from http://www.eqao.com/en/assessments/results/assessment-docs-elementary/provincial-report-primary-achievement-results-2017.pdf

Education Quality and Accountability Office. (2018). *Board of Directors*. Toronto: Queen's Printer for Ontario. Retrieved from http://www.eqao.com/en/about-eqao/about-the-agency/board-of-directors

Education Quality and Accountability Office. (2019). *Highlights of the provincial results. Literacy*. Toronto: Queen's Printer for Ontario. Retrieved from http://www.eqao.com/en/assessments/results/communication-docs/provincial-report-highlights-literacy-2018.pdf

Education Quality and Accountability Office Act. (1996). *Education Quality and Accountability Office Act. SO 1996, c, 11*.

Eizadirad, A., Martinez, X., & Ruminot, C. (2016). Comparative analysis of educational systems of accountability and quality of education in Ontario, Canada and Chile: Standardized testing and its role in perpetuation of educational inequity. *Interfaces Brasil/Canadá, 16*(2), 54–88.

Gidney, R. (1999). *From hope to Harris: The reshaping of Ontario's schools.* Toronto: University of Toronto Press.

Kempf, A. (2016). *The pedagogy of standardized testing: The radical impacts of educational standardization in the US and Canada.* New York: Springer.

Kohn, A. (2000). *The case against standardized testing: Raising scores, ruining the schools.* Portsmouth, NH: Heinemann.

Langlois, H. (2017). *Behind the snapshot: Teachers' experiences of preparing students in lower socioeconomic status schools for the Ontario Secondary School Literacy Test.* Master of Teaching research paper, Department Curriculum, Teaching and Learning, University of Toronto, Toronto, ON.

Morgan, C. (2006). A retrospective look at educational reforms in Ontario. *Our Schools, Our Selves, 15*(2), 127–141.

Ontario Ministry of Education. (2017). *Ontario appoints new advisors to guide transformation in education system.* Toronto: Queen's Printer for Ontario. Retrieved from https://news.ontario.ca/edu/en/2017/08/ontario-appoints-new-advisors-to-guide-transformation-in-education-system.html?_ga= 2.71555795.1779644130.1528468099-1009438681.1520260943

Ontario Ministry of Education. (2018). *Ontario's graduation rate.* Toronto: Queen's Printer for Ontario. Retrieved from http://www.edu.gov.on.ca/eng/

Pinar, W., Reynolds, W., Slattery, P., & Taubman, P. (1995). *Understanding curriculum: An introduction to the study of historical and contemporary curriculum discourses.* New York: Peter Lang Publishing, Incorporated.

Pinto, L. E. (2016). Tensions and fissures: The politics of standardised testing and accountability in Ontario, 1995–2015. *The Curriculum Journal, 27*(1), 95–112.

Portelli, J., & Vilbert, A. (2002). Standards, equity, and the curriculum of life. *Analytic Teaching, 22*(1), 4–19.

Royal Commission on Learning. (1994). *For the love of learning: Report of the royal commission on learning [Short Version].* Toronto: Queen's Printer for Ontario.

Sattler, P. (2012). Education governance reform in Ontario: Neoliberalism in context. *Canadian Journal of Educational Administration and Policy, 128,* 1–28.

Shum, D., & Miller, A. (2016, October 20). EQAO cancels high school online literacy tests due to 'technical issues'. *Global News.* Retrieved from https://globalnews.ca/news/3015060/ontario-high-school-online-literacy-tests-run-into-technical-issues/

Ungerleider, C. (2003). *Failing our kids: How we are ruining our public schools.* Toronto: National Library of Canada Cataloguing in Publication.

Volante, L. (2007). Educational quality and accountability in Ontario: Past, present, and future. *Canadian Journal of Educational Administration and Policy, 58,* 1–21.

CHAPTER 4

Inequality of Opportunity: Experiences of Racialized and Minoritized Students

Anyon (1980) and Bourdieu and Passeron's (1977) work can serve as the platform to critically examine the reproduction of social class through standardized testing; specifically how formal and informal practices in schools and their associated power relations contribute to maintenance of a dominant, hegemonic culture which benefits and privileges white affluent students at the expense of marginalization to racialized students and those from lower socio-economic backgrounds. Anyon (1980) conducted a classical ethnography where she observed "work tasks and interaction in five elementary schools in contrasting social class communities" and noticed major differences in "classroom experience and curriculum knowledge among the schools" (p. 67). She concluded that that there is a "hidden curriculum in school work" that reproduces social class through development of specific symbolic capital that "yields social and cultural power" (p. 69), whereas in the working-class schools the school work was guided by "preparation for future wage labour that is mechanical and routine," in contrast, in affluent schools the children were given opportunities "to develop skills of linguistic, artistic, and scientific expression and creative collaboration of ideas into concrete form" (p. 88). Similarly, Bourdieu and Passeron (1977) in *Reproduction in Education, Society, and Culture* emphasize schooling reproduces certain knowledges that benefit dominant classes while marginalizing the working class. Bourdieu and Passeron (1977) argue that often those with greater socio-economic status (SES) are rewarded with the voice of

© The Author(s) 2019
A. Eizadirad, *Decolonizing Educational Assessment*,
https://doi.org/10.1007/978-3-030-27462-7_4

authority and legitimization of their knowledge and identities as learning content in schools reflect their social and cultural experiences.

McNeil (2000) makes the argument that standardized testing "in the name of 'equity' imposes a sameness and in the name of 'objectivity' relies on a narrow set of numerical indicators" to judge success (p. 4). Standardized tests homogenize the needs of all students within a school, expecting all students to do well regardless of their socio-economic status and access to opportunities and social support systems. As Nezavdal (2003) points out,

> [S]tandardized tests seek to assess individuals, young people who bring a different range of experiences to the classroom, through a most peculiar claim; that all students can learn differently and come from inequitable backgrounds but be evaluated in the same way, at the same time, by the same test—designed of course, by those who are the social power-holders. (p. 69)

Standardized tests fail to take into consideration systemic discrimination in education such as reproduction of Eurocentric knowledge and lack of representation within the curriculum content for racialized and minoritized students (McIntosh, 1988) leading to higher dropout rates for non-European student populations (Colour of Justice Network, 2007; Dei, Holmes, Mazzuca, McIsaac, & Campbell, 1995; James, 2012). According to the Colour of Poverty and Colour of Change (2019) Fact Sheet on "Racialized Poverty in Education and Learning," in 2015, there was a 69 per cent high school graduation rate for black students and 50 per cent for Indigenous students, versus 84 per cent for white students in Toronto public schools.

"Closing the achievement gap" in the context of both United States and Canada has become a popular buzz word often used by educational policy-makers and politicians, yet what is often not talked about are the disparities in the opportunity gap which as a process leads to the achievement gap as an outcome. Reporting on Ontario schools, Curtis, Livingstone, and Smaller (1992) point out that, "Working-class kids always have, on average, lower reading sores, higher grade failures, higher drop-out rates and much poorer employment opportunities" (p. 7). Race is a significant factor that impacts one's access to opportunities (Block & Galabuzi, 2011) including educational success, particularly when systemic discrimination is embedded within the fabric of institutional policies and practices.

Race(ing) to the Top: Educational Achievements of Racialized Students and Inequitable Accessibility to Opportunities

Racial tensions were high in Toronto, Ontario, and it reached a tipping point in May 1992 following two incidents: the shooting and killing of a 22-year old black man named Raymond Lawrence by a white police officer who was wearing plain clothes in the streets of Toronto and the acquittal of four white police officers caught on video brutally beating black driver Rodney King in the streets of Los Angeles (Paradkar, 2017). On May 4, 1992, as an expression of racial concerns and collective resistance to injustice, many people took to the streets to protest and resist the systemic discrimination racialized bodies were experiencing living in Ontario and to show solidarity with those in Los Angeles who were experiencing similar issues where systemic discrimination was more explicit and magnified. The protests in Toronto occurred along Yonge Street and escalated and became violent involving "looting, fires, smashing of windows, and pelting of police" leading to "30 people arrested and 37 police officers injured" (Paradkar, 2017, para. 4). Immediately after the incident, the Premier at the time, Bob Rae, assigned Stephen Lewis as his Advisor on Race Relations and delegated him to consult local communities and produce a report with recommendations to work towards racial solutions. The following month on June 9, 1992, Stephen Lewis produced his report titled *Report of the Advisor on Race Relations to the Premier of Ontario, Bob Rae*. Lewis (1992) outlines that in the span of one month he held "seventy meetings with individuals and groups in Metro Toronto, Ottawa, Windsor and beyond, supplemented by innumerable phone conversations" (p. 1). As one of his key observations, Lewis (1992) expresses,

> First, what we are dealing with, at root, and fundamentally, is anti-Black racism. While it is obviously true that every visible minority community experiences the indignities and wounds of systemic discrimination throughout Southern Ontario, it is the Black community which is the focus. It is Blacks who are being shot, it is Black youth that is unemployed in excessive numbers, it is Black students who are being inappropriately streamed in schools, it is Black kids who are disproportionately dropping-out, it is housing communities with large concentrations of Black residents where the sense of vulnerability and disadvantage is most acute, it is Black employees, professional and non-professional, on whom the doors of upward equity slam shut. Just as the soothing balm of "multiculturalism" cannot mask racism, so racism cannot mask its primary target. (p. 2)

Lewis describes through the examples he lists how systemic discrimination, specifically anti-black racism, within institutions trickles down to impact the daily lives of racialized bodies and communities leading to inequality of outcome in various settings including the education system. The various examples mentioned in the report demonstrate that race plays a key role in accessing opportunities. It is important to note that similar conclusions had previously been expressed and continue to be expressed by many community organizations and black, African, racialized, and minoritized scholars such as George Dei, Carl James, Patrick Solomon, and John Portelli in the context of Ontario. We need to take time to listen to the outlined concerns and work towards initiating and creating sustainable change to meet the needs of racialized students and communities.

Fast forward to 2008 and similar findings were expressed by McMurtry and Curling (2008) in their report titled *Review of the Roots of Youth Violence*. Youth and gun violence were a hot topic in Toronto following the death of 15-year-old grade nine student Jordan Manners on May 23, 2007, at C. W. Jefferys Collegiate Institute, a public high school located within the boundaries of the Jane and Finch neighbourhood (Eizadirad, 2016; James, 2012). Manners died in the school hallway as a result of a gunshot wound to the chest. This incident was the first of its kind in the City of Toronto where a student had died within a school.

In the aftermath of Jordan Manner's death, the Premier at the time Dalton McGuinty, approached Honourable Roy McMurtry and Dr Alvin Curling to "spend a year seeking to find out where it (youth violence) is coming from—its roots—and what might be done to address them to make Ontario safer in the long term" (p. 1). This led to the 2008 publication of *Review of the Roots of Youth Violence*. The report identifies numerous immediate risk factors that "create that state of desperation and put a youth in the immediate path of violence" (p. 5). The immediate risk factors identified are:

- having a deep sense of alienation and low self-esteem
- having little empathy for others and suffer from impulsivity
- believing that they are oppressed, held down, unfairly treated and neither belong nor
- have a stake in the broader society
- believing that they have no way to be heard through other channels
- having no sense of hope. (pp. 5–6)

The report goes on to outline "the roots" of youth violence, referring to "the major conditions in which the immediate risk factors grow and flourish" (p. 6). These include poverty, racism, poor community planning and design, issues in the education system, family issues, health issues, lack of youth voice, lack of economic opportunity for youth, and issues in the justice system. As Eizadirad (2016) states, *"Review of the Roots of Youth Violence* report dares to speak the truth by naming race and racism and putting a face to it in terms of institutional practices" (p. 178). The report identifies racism and poverty as major systemic barriers contributing to youth gravitating towards violence; "Alienation, lack of hope or empathy, and other immediate risk factors are powerfully, but far from exclusively, driven by the intersection of racism and poverty" (p. 19).

Dei (2000) deconstructs what racism is and how it works by emphasizing, "Racism is more than an ideology and structure. It is a process" (p. 36). *Review of the Roots of Youth Violence* reiterates this definition of racism and guides the discussion towards examining the consequences arising from consistent exposure to racism:

> But while race is not something that can create the immediate risk factors for violence involving youth, racism is. Racism strikes at the core of self-identity, eats away the heart and casts a shadow on the soul. It is cruel and hurtful and alienating. It makes real all doubts about getting a fair chance in this society. It is a serious obstacle imposed for a reason the victim has no control over and can do nothing about. (p. 9)

The report also emphasizes that the most harmful impacts are experienced within neighbourhoods plagued with poverty, making the connection that "when poverty is racialized, and then ghettoized and associated with violence, the potential for the stigmatization of specific groups is high" (p. 4). From this vantage point, we can begin to understand how unequal power relations and practices are perpetuated through racialization of specific social groups and neighbourhoods leading to inequality of opportunity.

It is important to recognize schools do not operate in bubbles, therefore, what occurs socio-politically in communities surrounding schools impacts what happens in schools and vice versa. Ricci (2004) argues that "standardized testing can have a negative impact on the quality of education students are receiving and the effects can be particularly detrimental to children whose race, culture, or first language is not that of the majority" (p. 346). This is the reality within the Toronto District School Board

(TDSB) as "schools with high dropout rates are those with the highest number of racialized students" (Colour of Justice Network, 2007). According to Brown (2009), in the TDSB, which is the largest and one of the most diverse school boards in Canada with 583 schools and serving more than 246,000 students, "students of African ascendance experience a 38% dropout rate and students from Central and South America had a 37% dropout rate" (p. 4). This is an alarming statistic that has persisted over the years. It is important to engage in dialogue and action to figure out why the needs of certain specific social groups are not being met, systemically leading to such high dropout rates across various socio-spatial locations in TDSB schools.

Kearns (2011) found similar findings at the secondary level with high school students who failed the Grade 10 Ontario Secondary School Literacy Test (OSSLT) administered by Education Quality and Accountability Office (EQAO). She interviewed 16 youth who failed the OSSLT and found,

> Youth who pass the OSSLT are privileged, rewarded, deemed to be good future citizens and active contributors to society, whereas those who fail are named as different, deemed not up to the standard, are considered to be not thriving, and, therefore, must work harder to become good future citizens. (p. 123)

More importantly, "the literacy test was alienating for some youth because it undermined some of their positive identity-confirming experiences, and forced them to negotiate a negative label" such as being "illiterate" (p. 124). Kearn's (2011) study depicts how standardized tests inscribe a negative label on to students which is powerful enough to create self-doubt in them and their motivation to succeed in school. The language of "at-risk" (Masood, 2008) and other negative labels such as "illiterate," often used as educational jargon to describe students, blames the individual "as the holder of the 'at-riskness' as opposed to multiple and complex, social, political, and economic factors" (Kearns, 2016, p. 127).

Similar concerns can be raised for newly arrived immigrants and ESL (English as a Second Language) learners who are struggling to master the dominant language used as part of administration of EQAO standardized tests. Toplak and Wiener (2000) examined "whether the demands placed on the children are consistent with what we know about the cognitive development of 8–9 year old children" and concluded, "although the Grade 3

Assessment is based on the Ontario Curriculum, many items exceed what should be expected from a typical Grade 3 student when children's cognition is considered" (p. 65). Toplak and Wiener (2000) argue,

> A fair test of reading in the third grade should, therefore, rely heavily on skills in sounding out words (decoding) and reading simple passages, and less heavily on making inferences and extending ideas from the text. The Grade 3 Assessment clearly falls short from the perspective of this developmental model. There is a heavy emphasis on text comprehension and inferences in the Grade 3 Assessment, and very little on reading and identifying words. (p. 71)

Toplak and Wiener (2000) further point to shortcomings with the math component of EQAO testing which requires mastery of English language to comprehend the word problems. They state, "The over-reliance on reading in both the Mathematics and Mathematics Investigations booklets makes the Grade 3 a test of mathematics achievement and a test of reading, in which one skill cannot be demonstrated adequately without mastery of the other" (p. 74). Therefore, some children might have the necessary mathematical skills to achieve at the provincially expected Level 3 or higher but due to not comprehending the question clearly they could get the answer wrong. This contributes to lowering their self-esteem and self-confidence. As Bower and Thomas (2013) state, "Assessment can disempower students by making them feel inadequate and generating feelings of avoidance" (p. 128).

Although theoretically standardized tests are supposed to help identify inequities in the education system and areas for improvement at the individual level as well as broader areas in school and school board district levels, and this is the dominant narrative disseminated by EQAO for justification of its practices (Nagy, 2000; Volante, 2006), in practice it has not led to closing the achievement gap along the lines of race and socioeconomic status over the years since its inception (Dei, 2008; Hori, 2013; James, 2012). Similar arguments have been made in United States and Europe to justify investment in more standardized testing for accountability purposes, such as the "Back to Basics" movement and slogans, yet ironically the achievement gaps amongst different social groups, particularly racialized and Indigenous students compared to white students and those from higher socio-economic backgrounds, have persisted and in some cases further intensified (Au, 2010). Examining the historical impact of standardized testing in the United States over time, Au (2010) explains,

> The historical roots of high-stakes, standardised testing in racism, nativism, and eugenics raises a critical question: why is it that, now over 100 years after the first standardised tests were administered in the United States, we have virtually the same test-based achievement gaps along the lines of race and economic class? (p. 12)

Although the context is different to varying degrees between how standardized tests are used and implemented in Canada compared to the United States and Europe, the outcome of racialized students doing more poorly relative to their white counterparts within the education system remains a persistent pattern in all countries. Canada is a country with a population of approximately 37 million people (United Nations Statistics Division, 2018) consisting of ten provinces and three territories. Ontario is Canada's largest province and it "represents approximately one-third of the nation's population" (Pinto, 2016, p. 96). In Canada, there is "no Federal Department of Education or a National System of Education" (Gardener, 2017, p. 7). Instead, each province and territory has its own exclusive legal jurisdiction over educational policies and practices (Volante, 2007). Educational policies for governance are established at the provincial level and communicated to local school boards. Local school boards and individual schools have the authority and flexibility to implement Ministry of Education approved policies and practices using various approaches to achieve the intended outcome-based results. Sattler (2012) explains that "the multi-level structuring of education governance addresses such issues such as geographic boundaries of school districts, administration and management of schools, locus of decision-making, role of parents and the community in school planning, type of school management, and the degree of state involvement and intervention in education decisions" (p. 3). This multifaceted approach to governance of education in Canada provides provinces, territories, and school districts with the power to be flexible in using different approaches and strategies to address local needs of students within their unique spatial geographies relative to the needs of the larger surrounding community.

Nezavdal (2003) critiques standardized testing as ineffective, arguing that standardized assessments are "a social construct" (p. 69). He goes on to explain, "these norms are not incidentally held but deliberately upheld to stream students to propel some forward while systematically impeding others" (p. 67). According to the Colour of Poverty and Colour of Change (2019) Fact Sheet on "Racialized Poverty in Education and Learning":

Black and Indigenous students are more likely to be streamed into non-academic programs than White or some of the other racialized students. In 2015 the Toronto District School Board reported that 53% of Black students and 48% of Indigenous students, compared to 81% of White students, were enrolled in Academic programs of study; while 39% of Black students and 41% of Indigenous students, compared to 16% of White students, were in Applied programs.

The use of standardized test policies as a normalized accountability tool in schools at all levels has "not improved reading and math achievement across states and have not significantly narrowed national and state level achievement gaps between white students and non-whites students or gaps between rich and poor students" (Au, 2010, p. 11; Curtis et al., 1992; Dei, 2008; Hori, 2013; James, 2012; Lewis, 1992; Ladson-Billings, 1994; Masood, 2008; McNeil, 2000; Pinto, 2016; Ricci, 2004).

Hori (2013) argues standardized tests have not assisted in closing the achievement gap in Toronto and instead has contributed to intensifying and widening the achievement gap by systemically closing accessibility to certain opportunities for racialized students and those from lower socio-economic status. In his report, controversially titled *vi-o-lence = The Toronto District School Board*, Hori (2013) argues "the Toronto District School Board commits structural violence against its most marginalized students" (p. 1). Hori (2013) defines structural violence as "unequal distribution of power" which leads to uneven distribution of resources and consequentially in the long term to "unequal life chances" (p. 6) in terms of upward social mobility. Using the Fraser Institute ranking of schools which is a score out of ten, Hori maps on a graph TDSB's 73 secondary schools' ranking averages calculated over a five-year period from 2007 to 2011. The overall rating of schools takes into account the following factors: average level achieved by students on the Grade 9 academic and applied mathematics tests administered by EQAO; the percentage of eligible Ontario Secondary School Literacy Test (OSSLT) writers who successfully completed the test on their first attempt or on a subsequent attempt administered by EQAO; and the percentage of tests below provincial standards which refers to overall percentage of students who wrote EQAO administered tests, whether the math test in Grade 9 or the Grade 10 OSSLT test, who were below the Level 3 provincial standard of performance. Hori (2013) concludes,

Toronto has a very visible socio-economic divide between its residents. As a matter of fact, most of the schools which had ratings above 6 were located in affluent neighbourhoods. On the other hand, the worst schools were located in the low-income areas. Toronto is generally presented as one city; however, the truth of the matter is that there are 3 different cities within Toronto. David Hulchanski's 3 cities report captures the divisions and segregations which define the city of Toronto. (p. 18)

Hori is referring to a study conducted by David Hulchanski (2007) titled *The Three Cities within Toronto* which provides the means to contextualize development of different neighbourhoods across the city spatially relative to important factors such as level of income, race, and socio-economic status. The study provides a comprehensive examination of income polarization among Toronto's neighbourhoods from 1970 to 2005, taking into consideration neighbourhood demographics. Findings indicate the emergence of three distinct cities within Toronto based on income change. "City #1" makes up 20 per cent of the city and is generally found in the downtown core of the city in close proximity to the city's subway lines. The neighbourhoods under "City #1" are identified as predominantly high-income areas where the average individual income has increased by 20 per cent or more relative to the Toronto Census Metropolitan Area average in 1970. "City #2" makes up 40 per cent of the city and is characterized my middle-income neighbourhoods. Individual incomes in "City #2" have fairly remained the same having undergone an increase or decrease of less than 20 per cent. "City #3" makes up 40 per cent of the city and the individual incomes in these areas have undergone a decrease of 20 per cent or more. Other than income, there are other major differences between "City #1" and "City #3" particularly in terms of number of immigrants and visible minorities living in the areas. Eight-two per cent of "City #1" is white compared to 34 per cent of residents in "City #3." As well, percentage of foreign-born people in "City #1" declined from 35 per cent to 28 per cent between 1971 and 2006, whereas in "City #3" the number of immigrants increased dramatically from 31 per cent in 1971 to 61 per cent in 2006 (p. 11).

Hulchanski's (2007) data demonstrates drastic differences in long-term neighbourhood trends in Toronto, and more importantly deconstructs the fallacy that neighbourhoods simply evolve "naturally." Long-term trends from the study, supported with data, demonstrate investments and resources are distributed inequitably throughout neighbourhoods in City of Toronto. Neighbourhoods composed of majority white residents are privileged at the expense of neglecting neighbourhoods composed of majority working-class racialized immigrants. Hulchanski's (2007) findings assist in contextualizing why it is significant to further examine experiences of racialized children and parents with EQAO standardized tests, as their socio-spatial location and access to opportunities and social services can impact the quality of education they receive in the schools located in their respective communities. Racialized children and parents' experiences with standardized tests will be unique and by listening to their voices describing their experiences it can provide us with new insights and understandings to assist in establishing more equitable institutional policies and practices to close the achievement gap between racialized students and their white counterparts.

Hori (2013) uses Hulchanski's (2007) report as a foundational framework to explore whether the same argument about inequitable spatial developments across neighbourhoods can be applied to quality of education received by students attending different schools in various neighbourhoods in City of Toronto. Hori (2013) conducts a comparative spatial analysis where he maps the overall rating of secondary schools as ranked by the Fraser Institute—which is based exclusively on EQAO standardized test scores—and looks for spatial patterns relative to whether the schools are labelled as low or high achieving. In order to provide some context, it is important to note that in 2005 the City of Toronto identified 13 "Priority Neighbourhoods" to receive extra attention for the purpose of neighbourhood improvements. In March 2014, the city expanded the programme to 31 neighbourhoods and renamed them from "Priority Neighbourhoods" to "Neighbourhood Improvement Areas" (City of Toronto, 2018). Given that Hori's study was conducted in 2013, he makes reference to "Priority Neighbourhoods" as part of his findings.

After mapping the overall ranking of schools across various neighbourhoods and searching for spatial patterns, Hori (2013) concludes, "the most vulnerable individuals in Toronto (the socioeconomically and ethnically marginalized youth who live in the 13 priority neighbourhoods) attend the worst high schools in Toronto" (p. 1). It is important to contextualize what Hori (2013) means by using the phrase "worst"; referring to schools based on how they are ranked by the Fraser Institute which exclusively labels schools and judges the quality of education they offer via performance of students on EQAO administered standardized tests. The ranking of schools by the Fraser Institute has high currency value in the public's eye as often schools are judged based on their overall EQAO test scores, to the extent that there is a correlation between property values and EQAO schools rankings. Schools with higher rankings are often located in affluent neighbourhoods and see a rise in property values, whereas schools at the bottom of the Fraser ranking list are located in "Priority Neighbourhoods" saturated with government housing and properties worth much less in financial value.

Hori supports his claims by pointing out that underperforming schools with the lowest rankings are predominantly located in "Priority Neighbourhoods" which spatially are located in Hulchanski's City #3 where the demographics of the neighbourhood is predominantly made up of immigrants and racialized and visible minorities whose individual incomes have undergone a decrease of 20 per cent or more since 1970. On the other hand, schools that had an overall school ranking of six or higher by the Fraser Institute were located in affluent high-income neighbourhoods which spatially are located in Hulchanski's City #1 where demographics of the neighbourhoods is 82 per cent white, and whose average individual incomes increased by 20 per cent or more relative to the Toronto Census Metropolitan Area average in 1970. Hori (2013) concludes, "TDSB provides a low quality of education to its most disadvantaged students, while providing a higher quality of education to its most privileged students" (p. 28), further reproducing social class disparities. Hori (2013) identifies this disparity in quality of education received by students from different socio-economic classes as a form of systemic structural violence as "education serves as a tool to oppress the most vulnerable individuals, and it serves as a tool to maintain, reproduce, and engender socioeconomic disparities" (p. 29). This process is labelled as "structurally violent" at a systemic level because "it denies students upward social mobility and therefore socioeconomically marginalized and racially excluded students get streamed towards less desired labour jobs" (p. 37). Hori (2013) and Hulchanski's (2007) findings collectively provide a holistic picture of the disparities and inequities that exist across neighbourhoods in the City of Toronto, and how racialized identities and communities are marginalized with respect to access to quality education, opportunities, and social services, while neighbourhoods occupied by predominantly white bodies and those from higher socio-economic status are privileged.

Williams, Jones, and Bailey (2013) similarly conducted a spatial analysis collecting and compiling data from multiple sources including the Department of Justice Canada, Toronto Census Tract, TDSB Learning

Opportunities Index, and the Fraser Institute to examine various disparities across different neighbourhoods in Toronto. The authors aggregated all data collected by postal code and found major disparities between neighbourhoods located in City #1 and City #3 (Hulchanski, 2007). For example, a comparison of the Jane and Finch neighbourhood, with postal code starting with M3N located spatially in City #3 and being one of the identified "Priority Neighbourhoods," to the Rosedale neighbourhood, with postal code starting with M4T located spatially in City #1 and being an affluent neighbourhood, showed major disparities in neighbourhood incarceration costs, police expenditures, percentage of families with one parent, total population 15 years and over with no certificate, diploma or degree, unemployment rate, median income, TDSB Learning Opportunities Index school rankings, and Fraser Institute school rankings (see Figs. 4.1 and 4.2 for specific numerical and statistical differences).

Findings by Hulchanski (2007), Hori (2013), and Williams et al. (2013) using comparative spatial analysis indicate that all neighbourhoods are not treated equally at a systemic level; white identities and elite spaces are privileged at the expense of marginalization and oppression to racialized identities and communities (Eizadirad, 2017).

Priority Neighbourhood: Jane-Finch	
Incarceration Costs (2008)	$36,856,603 (Postal Code M3N)
Police Expenditures (2011)	$30,576,947 (31 Division)
Data for Census Tract 0312.04 (2005)	Percentage of families with one parent: 39% (+22%)
	Total population 15 years and over with no certificate, diploma or degree: 47% (+27%)
	Unemployment: 12.1% (+5.4%)
	Median income (All private households): $37,056 (-$27,072)
TDSB Learning Opportunities Index School Rankings (2011)	Westview Centennial Secondary School (1/109) Brookview Middle School (15/479) Shoreham Public School (3/479) Driftwood Public School (9/479)
Fraser Report Rankings (Secondary Schools 2011-12)	Westview Centennial Secondary School (696/725)

Fig. 4.1 Jane and Finch neighbourhood (Williams et al., 2013)

Affluent Neighbourhood: Rosedale	
Incarceration Costs (2008)	$0 (Postal Code M4T)
Police Expenditures (2011)	$20,965,401 (53 Division)
Data for Census Tract 0344.02 (2005)	Percentage of families with one parent: 11% (-6%)
	Total population 15 years and over with no certificate, diploma or degree: 7% (-13%)
	Unemployment: 5.5% (-1.2%)
	Median income (All private households): $179,935 (+115,807)
TDSB Learning Opportunities Index School Rankings (2011)	Northern Secondary School (104/109) North Toronto Collegiate Institute (105/109) Whitney Junior Public School (479/479)
Fraser Report Rankings (Secondary Schools 2011-12)	North Toronto Collegiate Institute (14/725)

Fig. 4.2 Rosedale neighbourhood (Williams et al., 2013)

SCHOOL-COMMUNITY INTERFACE

We have to keep in mind that there is a dynamic nature to what occurs in communities surrounding schools and the learning quality and conditions within schools. We cannot treat them as separate entities but work to improve the learning and living conditions in both spaces as a collective. Placing blame on individuals and communities for underachieving does not constructively work towards finding constructive and sustainable solutions.

Polanyi, Wilson, Mustachi, Ekra, and Kerr (2017) provide more recent statistics about how the aforementioned disparities across race, class, and socio-economic status continue to persist in different sectors, in this case relative to child poverty rates across different neighbourhoods in Toronto. They point out:

> Between 2010 and 2015, low-income rates among children have decreased significantly in many downtown and southern Etobicoke neighbourhoods, while low-income rates have remained the same or increased in a number of Scarborough and other inner-suburb neighbourhoods. (p. 19)

Polanyi et al.'s (2017) study outlines how racialized neighbourhoods continue to be marginalized and oppressed through institutional systemic discrimination and abandonment which consequentially impacts children's learning and achievement levels in schools, particularly in the early years. Similar statistics emphasizing disparities between racialized and non-racialized neighbourhoods were outlined more than a decade ago by The Colour of Justice Network in 2007 stating, "racialized communities experience ongoing, disproportionate levels of poverty" supported by the fact that "between 1980 and 2000, while the poverty rate for the non-racialized European heritage population in Toronto decreased by 28 percent, the poverty among racialized families rose by 361 percent" (The Colour of Justice Network, 2007, p. 1). This indicates resources are distributed inequitably privileging white bodies and spaces at the expense of social exclusion and marginalization of racialized identities and communities. This is troubling given that "more than half of Toronto's population identify as racialized (51.5%)" (Polanyi et al., 2017, p. 1) and as Block and Galabuzi (2011) in their report titled *Canada's Colour Coded Labour Market: The Gap for Racialized Workers* point out, "Racialized Canadians earn only 81.4 cents for every dollar paid to non-racialized Canadians" (p. 11). These disparities at the systemic level along the lines of race, class, and socio-economic status have real-life implications and consequences. As the Racial Justice Report Card for Ontario (2014) states, "Statistics show that racialized children, and in particular First Nations and African Canadian children, are significantly over-represented in CAS [Children's Aid Society] care and federal and provincial correctional institutions" (p. 3). As well, "Racialized and immigrant workers tend to be overrepresented in precarious, temporary types of employment and thus are more likely to lack dental insurance coverage" (p. 8).

In a follow-up to their study, Polanyi et al. (2018) in their report The *2018 Toronto Child & Poverty Report: Municipal Election Edition* outline a series of statistics that further situates and contextualizes that "the highest rates of child poverty are among indigenous, racialized and newcomer families"(p. 6):

- 84% of Indigenous families with children in Toronto live in poverty
- One-third of racialized children (33.3%) in Toronto live in low-income families, while in comparison 15.1% of non-racialized children live in poverty

- Greater proportions of racialized children live in poverty, and child poverty rates are unacceptably high among children who are West Asian (59.5%), Arab (58.8%), Black (43.6%) and Latin American (36.1%)
- Poverty rates are much higher for children from racialized groups compared to non-racialized groups for each generation. For example, among children who were born in Canada and whose parents were born in Canada (3rd generation or more), the poverty rate for racialized children is twice that of non-racialized children (22.8% vs. 10.7%).
- First-generation newcomer children have extremely high rates of poverty, including staggering rates within the Arab (70.5%), West Asian (68.3%), Korean (57.5%) and Black (48%) communities.
- Children who are of West Asian (44.4%) and Black (42.1%) backgrounds have very high poverty rates even when they were born in Canada and have parents who were born in Canada (3rd generation or more). (p. 6)

These statistics are alarming; the intersection of poverty and systemic racism places Indigenous, racialized, and newcomer families at a great disadvantage. It is significant to recognize how these processes work as a collective to impact the embodied and lived experiences of racialized identities within particular communities as it applies to accessibility to opportunities for upward social mobility. The dynamics of the school-community interface is largely influenced by these socio-political and economic factors impacting student learning. This is particularly significant in the early years as it impacts motivation and engagement with their schooling experiences (James, 2012; Ontario Ministry of Education, 2014).

Most recently, a United Way report released May 2019 titled *Rebalancing the Opportunity Equation* identifies the Greater Toronto Area (GTA) as the "income inequality capital of Canada" (United Way, 2019, p. 8). The report goes on to further explain that "the GTA labour market is increasingly characterized by precarious work; there is a lack of affordable places for people to live; and people continue to face systemic discrimination in the economy and everyday life" (p 8). The report identifies particular identities and social groups who are systemically disadvantaged when it comes to access to opportunities for upward social mobility:

> Young people, immigrants, racialized people, and women are seeing that their circumstances—the things about themselves that they cannot control

(such as their age, immigration status, whether or not they belong to a racialized group, their gender, and even their postal code)—are barriers to their success in today's GTA. (p. 8)

The report supports its claims by pointing out, "In the GTA, it doesn't matter how long you've been in Canada—the fact that you weren't born here means that you are earning less" (p. 10).

The report further explains,

Immigrants, regardless of their years of residency in Canada, have become poorer over time. The average income of longstanding immigrants, who have been in Canada for more than 20 years, has not increased in 35 years, whereas the average income of the Canadian-born population has increased steadily over that time period. (p. 10)

The other key finding of the report is that, "the racial divide in the GTA has reached a historic high" (p. 12). The report explains:

Racialized groups have become poorer over time. Incomes for racialized groups have not increased in 35 years and the income-gap between racialized and white groups has increased. For every dollar a white person in Toronto earns, a racialized person in Toronto earns 52.1 cents. (p. 12)

What all these aforementioned studies point out via their findings supported with statistics is that the racialized experience is unique within Canadian society, and one that is plagued with navigating systemic barriers on a consistent basis across numerous sectors ranging from child care and employment to education and housing. It is significant to avoid pathologizing individuals for their circumstances and instead from an equity lens examine how we can improve the social conditions systemically in different ways and across different sectors to provide access to quality opportunities for marginalized social groups which consequentially can lead to betterment of their lives and their communities. The problem is that through a neoliberal market-driven view of education, responsibility is often exclusively judged through an individualistic lens emphasizing the student's decisions and choices irrespective of the exploitative and inequitable institutional practices and policies that create the social conditions that present limited choice(s) to individuals (Eizadirad & Portelli, 2018).

Returning to standardized testing as an accountability tool, Bower and Thomas (2013) emphasize how the current administration of standardized tests leads to reproduction of social classes without anyone being held accountable or responsible for shortcomings of the education system. They argue that

> Standardized testing provides a technology for stratification as it allows administrators and politicians to wash their hands of any responsibility for endemic social inequality. It does this not by sorting students on the basis of merit but by reproducing existing class inequalities, by privileging elite cultural capital as well as positivistic and rationalistic forms of knowledge. (p. 172)

Bower and Thomas (2013) expand on Froese-Germain's (2001) argument about how "standardized testing provides a technology for stratification" (p. 172) by further intensifying educational inequity through test bias and misuse of test scores. Froese-Germain (2001) identifies three major negative consequences of standardized testing that disadvantages racialized students and those from lower SES:

- Language bias that centers the hegemonic language as the means for testing particularly disadvantaging those whose first language is not English,
- Content that ignores cultural experiences, perspectives, and knowledge of children from racial and ethnic minorities, low-income families, and inner-city and rural children,
- The individual dimension of problem solving referring to the different learning styles (not different abilities), often associated with such factors such as race, ethnicity, income level, and gender not considered in test design with the assumption being that all individuals perceive information and solve problems in the same way. (p. 116)

Disadvantages constructed by externally administered standardized tests have real-life implications and consequences on the lives of racialized students and their families both in school and outside of school within their community. Implications of the "structural violence" (Hori, 2013, p. 4) enacted in schools through the use of standardized tests and its domino effect of streaming students into non-academic fields has contributed to

The over-representation of socioeconomically marginalized and racially excluded youths in the prison, the over-representation of socioeconomically marginalized and racially excluded youth in non-academic, special education, skill-oriented and essential curriculums in Secondary schools, and the under-representation of socioeconomically marginalized and racially excluded students in gifted and academic curriculums in Secondary schools. (Hori, 2013, p. 42)

It is significant to question how these patterns of "over-representation" of racialized bodies in non-academic fields began, what processes it involves, and why such patterns have persisted over time and continue to exist today. Specifically, what role do educational institutions, and their policies and practices such as the use of standardized tests, play in perpetuating and/or disrupting such existing inequities?

Overall, under neoliberalism, education as a field is embedded with inequities driven by market ideologies which lead to the reproduction of the status quo benefiting the affluent at the expense of exclusion and oppression of others—the socio-economically marginalized members of society (Apple, 1978; Dei, 2000; McNeil, 2000). As Kohn (2000) puts it, the focus of many current policies is on "standards of outcome rather than standards of opportunity" (p. 39). When institutions face criticism about their inequitable practices, they resort to emphasizing individualism, which translates into glorifying one success story with the theme of "if you work hard enough you can overcome anything." Yet, for every working-class and minoritized/racialized student who is saved by an education initiative which invests in individuals, such as scholarship creation, there are hundreds if not thousands of others who become victims of the vicious cycle of inequality of opportunity (Kohn, 2000; Masood, 2008; Sharma, 2009). We never get to hear "unsuccessful" stories, as they are silenced and forgotten.

Institutional dysfunction is largely responsible for the perpetuation of living conditions permeated with inequality of opportunity that creates a socio-stratified and hierarchical society (Apple, 1978). Within Canadian society, racialized identities and communities are placed at a particular disadvantage. As Garrison (2009) points out, "Closing gaps in intellectual performance—that is, in equalizing outcomes—will not solve the problem of what are now unsustainable social inequalities because these social inequalities do not have their origin in intellectual difference" (p. 105). These inequalities are rooted in the social, cultural, political, and economic spheres which trickle down to impact learning and achievement within schools at the micro level. Yet, neoliberal subjectivity connects destiny to individual decision-making. Dominant discourse and its meta-narratives promote stereotypical ideologies that attempt to freeze identities in time and space. For example, the poor are judged as responsible for their living conditions because they are lazy and prefer being on social assistance programmes rather than finding a job and working hard. Neoliberalism simplifies complex social issues and places blame on individuals while masking and silencing discussion about exploitative social practices of institutions driven by market ideologies. As a result, poverty is not examined as a systemic issue directly and indirectly linked to inequitable access to resources and opportunities such as lack of meaningful permanent full-time employment with benefits. It's time to change gears and shift the conversations and discussions towards a collective equity lens with a focus on how to change policies and practices systemically to meet the needs of all citizens instead of a selective few.

REFERENCES

Anyon, J. (1980). Social class and the hidden curriculum of work. *Journal of Education, 162(1)*, 67–92.

Apple, M. (1978). Ideology, reproduction, and educational reform. *Comparative Education Review, 22(3)*, 367–387.

Au, W. (2010). *Unequal by design: High-stakes testing and the standardization of inequality*. London: Routledge.

Block, S., & Galabuzi, G. (2011). Canada's colour coded labour market: The gap for racialized workers. Wellesley Institute and Canadian Centre for Policy Alternatives. Retrieved from http://www.wellesleyinstitute.com/wp-content/uploads/2011/03/Colour_Coded_Labour_MarketFINAL.pdf

Bourdieu, P., & Passeron, J. (1977). *Reproduction in education, society, and culture*. Beverley Hills, CA: Sage.

Bower, J., & Thomas, L. (2013). *De-testing + de-grading schools; Authentic alternatives to accountability and standardization*. New York, NY: Peter Lang Publishing.

Brown, R. (2009). *Making the grade: The grade 9 cohort of fall 2002: Overview*. Research Report, Toronto: Retrieved from http://www.tdsb.on.ca/Portals/research/docs/reports/MakingTheGrade2002-07Overview.pdf

City of Toronto. (2018). Neighbourhood improvement area profiles. Retrieved from https://www.toronto.ca/city-government/data-research-maps/neighbourhoods-communities/nia-profiles/

Colour of Justice Network. (2007). Colour of poverty. Retrieved from http://www.learningandviolence.net/lrnteach/material/PovertyFactSheets-aug07.pdf

Colour of Poverty and Colour of Change. (2019). Fact sheets. Retrieved from https://colourofpoverty.ca/fact-sheets/

Curtis, B., Livingstone, D. W., & Smaller, H. (1992). *Stacking the deck: The streaming of working-class kids in Ontario schools* (Vol. 24). Toronto: James Lorimer & Company.

Dei, G. J. S. (2000). Towards an anti-racism discursive framework. In G. Dei & A. Calliste (Eds.), *Power, knowledge and anti-racism education: A critical reader*. Toronto, ON: Fernwood Publishing Co.

Dei, G. J. S. (2008). Schooling as community: Race, schooling, and the education of African youth. *Journal of Black Studies, 38*(3), 346–366.

Dei, G. J. S., Holmes, L., Mazzuca, J., McIsaac, E., & Campbell, R. (1995). *Drop out or push out. The dynamics of Black students' disengagement from school.* Toronto, Canada: Ontario Institute for Studies in Education.

Eizadirad, A. (2016). Is it "bad" kids or "bad" places? Where is all the violence originating from? Youth violence in the City of Toronto. *Review of Education, Pedagogy, and Cultural Studies, 38*(2), 162–188.

Eizadirad, A. (2017). The university as a neoliberal and colonizing institute; A spatial case study analysis of the invisible fence between York University and the Jane and Finch neighbourhood in the City of Toronto. *Journal of Critical Race Inquiry, 4*(1), 25–53.

Eizadirad, A., & Portelli, J. (2018). Subversion in education: Common misunderstandings and myths. *International Journal of Critical Pedagogy, 9*(1), 53–72.

Froese-Germain, B. (2001). Standardized testing + High-stakes decisions = Educational inequality. *Interchange, 32*(2), 111–130.

Gardener, D. A. K. (2017). *EQAO Preparation and the Effects on In-Classroom Instruction.* Master of Teaching research paper, Department of Curriculum, Teaching and Learning, University of Toronto, Toronto, ON.

Garrison, M. (2009). *A measure of failure: The political origins of standardized testing.* Albany, NY: State University of New York Press.

Hori, M. M. (2013). *The Toronto District School Board & Structural Violence.* Mahad. M. Hori.

Hulchanski, J. D. (2007). *The three cities within Toronto: Income polarization among Toronto's neighbourhoods 1970–2005.* Toronto, ON: Cities Centre Press, University of Toronto. Retrieved from http://www.urbancentre.utoronto.ca/pdfs/curp/tnrn/Three-Cities-Within-Toronto-2010-Final.pdf

James, C. E. (2012). *Life at the intersection: Community, class and schooling.* Halifax, NS: Fernwood Publishing.

Kearns, L. (2011). High-stakes standardized testing and marginalized youth: An examination of the impact on those who fail. *Canadian Journal of Education, 34*(2), 112–130.

Kearns, L. (2016). The construction of 'illiterate' and 'literate' youth: The effects of high-stakes standardized literacy testing. *Race Ethnicity and Education, 19*(1), 121–140.

Kohn, A. (2000). *The case against standardized testing: Raising scores, ruining the schools.* Portsmouth, NH: Heinemann.

Ladson-Billings, G. (1994). *The dreamkeepers: Successful teachers for African-American children.* San Francisco: Jossey-Bass.

Lewis, S. (1992). Report of the advisor on race relations to the Premier of Ontario, Bob Rae. Retrieved from https://archive.org/details/stephenlewisrepo00lewi

Masood, O. (2008). *At risk: The racialized student marked for educational failure.* (Unpublished doctoral dissertation). University of Toronto, Toronto, ON.

McIntosh, P. (1988). White Privilege: Unpacking the Invisible Knapsack. Retrieved from http://hd.ingham.org/Portals/HD/White%20Priviledge%20Unpacking%20the%20Invisible%20Knapsack.pdf

McMurtry, R., & Curling, A. (2008). *The review of the roots of youth violence.* Toronto, ON: Ministry of Children, Community and Social Services. Retrieved from http://www.children.gov.on.ca/htdocs/English/professionals/oyap/roots/index.aspx

McNeil, L. (2000). *Contradictions of school reform; Educational costs of standardized testing.* New York, NY: Routledge.

Nagy, P. (2000). The three roles of assessment: Gatekeeping, accountability, and instructional diagnosis. *Canadian Journal of Education/Revue canadienne de l'éducation, 262–279.*

Nezavdal, F. (2003). The standardized testing movement: Equitable or excessive? *McGill Journal of Education, 38*(1), 65–78.

Ontario Ministry of Education. (2014). *How does learning happen? Ontario's pedagogy for the early years: A resource about learning through relationships for those who work with young children and their families.* Toronto: Queen's Printer for Ontario. Retrieved from http://www.edu.gov.on.ca/childcare/HowLearningHappens.pdf

Paradkar, S. (2017, May 5). The Yonge St. riot of 1992... or was it an uprising?: Paradkar. *Toronto Star.* Retrieved from https://www.thestar.com/news/gta/2017/05/05/the-yonge-street-riot-of-1992-or-was-it-an-uprising-paradkar.html

Pinto, L. E. (2016). Tensions and fissures: The politics of standardised testing and accountability in Ontario, 1995–2015. *The Curriculum Journal, 27*(1), 95–112.

Polanyi, M., Wilson, B., Maddox, R., Ekra, M., Kerr, M., & Khan, A. (2018). *2018 Toronto child & family poverty report: Municipal election edition.* Retrieved from http://www.torontocas.ca/sites/torontocas/files/2018_Child_Family_Poverty_Report_Municipal_Election_Edition.pdf

Polanyi, M., Wilson, B., Mustachi, J., Ekra, M., & Kerr, M. (2017). *Unequal city: The hidden divide among Toronto's children and youth. 2017 Toronto child and family poverty report card.* Retrieved from http://torontocas.ca/sites/torontocas/files/CAST%20Child%20Poverty%20Report%20Nov%202017.pdf

Racial Justice Report Card for Ontario. (2014). Retrieved from http://yourlegal-rights.on.ca/sites/all/files/COPC%20Provincial%20Racial%20Justice%20 Report%20Card%20_2014_.pdf

Ricci, C. (2004). The case against standardized testing and the call for a revitalization of democracy. *Review of Education, Pedagogy, and Cultural Studies, 26*(4), 339–361.

Sattler, P. (2012). Education governance reform in Ontario: Neoliberalism in context. *Canadian Journal of Educational Administration and Policy, 128,* 1–28.

Sharma, M. (2009). *Inner city students: Stamped, labeled and shipped out! Deficit thinking and democracy in an age of neoliberalism.* (Unpublished master's thesis). University of Toronto, Toronto, ON.

Toplak, M., & Wiener, J. (2000). A critical analysis of Grade 3 testing in Ontario. *Canadian Journal of School Psychology, 16*(1), 65–85.

United Nations Statistics Division. (2018). *Country profile: Canada.* World Statistics Pocketbook. Retrieved from http://data.un.org/en/iso/ca.html

United Way. (2019). *Rebalancing the Opportunity Equation.* Retrieved from https://www.unitedwaygt.org/file/2019_OE_fullreport_FINAL.pdf

Volante, L. (2006). An alternative vision for large-scale assessment in Canada. *Journal of Teaching and Learning, 4*(1), 1–14.

Volante, L. (2007). Educational quality and accountability in Ontario: Past, present, and future. *Canadian Journal of Educational Administration and Policy, 58,* 1–21.

Williams, C., Jones, D., & Bailey, R. (2013). From the margins: Building curriculum for youth in transition. Ministry of Justice & Youth Association for Academics, Athletics and Character Education. Retrieved from http://yaaace.com/wp-content/uploads/2013/06/From-the-Margins-Building-Curriculum-for-Youth-in-Transitions.pdf

Symbiotic Relationship Between Curriculum, Tyler Rationale, and EQAO Standardized Testing

The relationship between subject-specific curriculum content and imple-mentation of standardized testing to assess mastery of learning content is facilitated by the Tyler Rationale, referring to the central questions Ralph Tyler identified as significant for effective curriculum development and its philosophical underpinnings. The theorization of this relationship is explored and described as symbiotic (Ydesen, 2014), referring to the notion that all three components need each other to survive, thrive, and legitimize one another; the curriculum and the Tyler Rationale facilitate the justification and need for one another and create the socio-cultural and political niche to legitimize use of Education and Quality Accountability Office (EQAO) standardized testing as a tool for accountability purposes.

Pinar, Reynolds, Slattery, and Taubman (1995) in their foundational book titled *Understanding Curriculum: An Introduction to the Study of Historical and Contemporary Curriculum Discourses* provide a holistic interdisciplinary analysis of how over time the meaning of the word *curriculum* has changed and reconceptualized based on different schools of thought and societal expectations. Their timeline of curricu-lum examination begins with an early historical focus on curriculum development as a field and transitions to explore more modern use of curriculum in dominant discourses in the twentieth century (Pinar et al., 1995). Pinar et al. (1995) argue that "curriculum reconceptual-ization" (p. 17) has occurred in more recent years where curriculum is deconstructed from specific theoretical vantage points and disciplines

A. Eizadirad, *Decolonizing Educational Assessment*,
https://doi.org/10.1007/978-3-030-27462-7_5

including but not limited to understanding "curriculum as historical and political text" and now more than ever the importance of "understanding curriculum as racial text" (p. 23).

Although Pinar et al. (1995) explore curriculum as other "texts," I agree with them on the importance of examining "curriculum as racial text" in the context of schooling in North America, specifically Ontario, where neoliberal market-driven ideologies about education exclusively place blame on individuals for underachieving including performance on standardized tests and consequentially contribute to an over-representation of racialized bodies in non-academic fields (Block & Galabuzi, 2011; Hori, 2013; Pinto, 2015; Portelli & Sharma, 2014). Under the current celebratory multiculturalism meta-narratives and its associated equality paradigms, there is a disregard for the salience of race in defining social order in society (Giroux, 2003). Centring "curriculum as racial text" as the entry point to analyse the experiences of racialized children and parents provides the medium to map in what ways EQAO standardized test impacts their identity, family, school, and the larger surrounding community in which they live and whether such narratives support or oppose the dominant narrative disseminated by EQAO about the benefits and effectiveness of EQAO standardized tests for accountability outcomes. This is particularly important at a time where neutrality and colour-blindness is promoted as part of the normalized school culture and implementation of educational policies (Giroux, 2003; Portelli & Sharma, 2014). Understanding curriculum as racial text involves critically questioning the power dynamics in implementation of curriculum and standardized testing and making visible the processes involved in perpetuation of subtle racism within schools enacted through educational policies and practices (Dei, 2008; James, 2012; Knoester & Au, 2017; Kumashiro, 2004; Lopez, 2003; McLaren, 2015; Noguera, 2003). We have to constantly ask, who does the current enactment of curriculum and standardized testing policies and practices benefit and which identities does it oppress and marginalize, and more importantly in what ways and at what costs?

HISTORICAL OVERVIEW OF WHAT CONSTITUTES AS *CURRICULUM*

Before examining how the development of the Ontario curriculum was largely influenced by the Tyler Rationale and its philosophical underpinnings, we must first briefly examine the operationalization and use of the word *curriculum* from a historical perspective and changes within the field of Curriculum Studies over time. Egan (1978) examines the historical root of the word *curriculum* and outlines changes in its meaning over time and how it was used in the field of curriculum development for different purposes. Egan (1978) explains that *curriculum* is "a Latin word carried directly over into English" (p. 10), rooted in the Latin word *currere* literally meaning being "a running," "a race," "a course" which can be interpreted as "the course to be run" (p. 10). From this perspective, *curriculum* is the content that students study in a course which is considered important to master, and by end of "the course" students are expected to demonstrate mastery of knowledge and understanding of the content presented to them. Important questions that arise from viewing *curriculum* as a "course to be run" are "What should the curriculum contain?" and "What is the best way to organize these contents?" (Egan, 1978, p. 11). Egan (1978) argues it was not until many decades later that societies began considering the significance of "How should things be taught?" (p. 12), which led to a transitional shift towards considering teacher pedagogy rather than an absolute focus on content when developing curriculum. This symbolized a monumental shift from obsession with *what* questions to *how* questions. Transition to "How should things be taught?" led to exploring curriculum in relation to various factors ranging from the way the classroom space is set-up to considering specific needs and interests of students relative to their preferred learning styles and other variables that individualized learning to maximize teaching and learning effectiveness. This is exemplified through the metaphor of the teacher role being changed from "*teacher as master*" to "*teacher as facilitator*" (Egan, 1978, p. 14).

Philosophical Underpinnings of the Tyler Rationale and Its Role in Development of the Ontario Curriculum and Use of Standardized Testing in Schools

Ralph Tyler is well known for his contribution to the field of *Curriculum Development* for the central questions he identified as significant for effective curriculum development in his book titled *Basic Principles of Curriculum and Instruction* published in 1949. His work is referred to by many scholars as "the Bible of curriculum making" (Pinar et al., 1995, p. 33) due to its profound impact in establishment of the field of Curriculum Development as a discipline. The questions identified by Ralph Tyler became known as the *Tyler Rationale* within the field of Curriculum Studies and Curriculum Development. Tyler outlines four important questions:

1. What educational purposes should the school seek to attain? [Objectives]
2. What educational experiences can be provided that are likely to attain these purposes? [Design]
3. How can these educational experiences be effectively organized? [Scope and Sequence]
4. How can we determine whether these purposes are being attained? [Evaluation]. (Kliebard, 1970, pp. 259–260)

Tyler's questions have been used as a step-by-step guide to develop curriculum content in a linear manner that begins with outlining learning objectives and ends with assessing mastery of the learning content often via assessment methods such as standardized tests. As Hunkins and Hammill (1994) state,

> Tyler gave us a techno-speak that enabled us to be part of the modernism of this century. In a very real sense, the Tyler Rationale gave us slogans and shared ideals and views of curriculum and its creation. We could share common visions; we could communicate with a shared language. (p. 8)

Tyler's vision was influential in establishing the field of Curriculum Development as a discipline but as Eizadirad, Martinez, and Ruminot (2016) argue, Tyler's approach towards curriculum development was aligned with a positivist and technocratic approach coinciding "with the paradigm of social functionalism which views education as scientific, observable, and a measurable phenomenon; a process that is quantifiable" (p. 67). It is important to note that although this might not have been Tyler's vision and intent to align his rationale with a positivist and technocratic approach, this is what pursued historically. According to the positivist paradigm rooted in psychology, the learning process is prompted by a rationale curriculum that is linear and captured in a quantifiable manner structured in learning objectives, observable behaviours, and a system of evaluation (Tyler, 1949). Hunkins and Hammill (1994) point out that Tyler's Rationale towards curriculum development quickly became very popular due "to the very reasonableness and workability of the rationale, regardless of one's context" (p. 7). They go on to expand:

It could all be mapped out in linear fashion. In a sense, all we had to do was connect the dots and the outline of the program would become evident. Then our task was just to color within the lines and the curriculum would be covered. (p. 8)

The Tyler Rationale serves as a step-by-step instruction guide to develop an efficient curriculum for a given course. This begins with selecting content and defining objectives, followed by selecting, creating, and organizing learning experiences in terms of their scope, depth, and sequence, and finally evaluating mastery of the content presented as part of the curriculum through student assessments such as standardized testing or other methods.

The evaluation process, which is the last step of the Tyler Rationale, is also known as the checking step for mastery of content. Tyler (1969) states, "evaluation needs to be conducted to find out the extent to which students are actually developing the patterns of behavior that the curriculum was designed to help them learn" (p. 32). This is where the justification for the use of tests, including EQAO standardized tests for accountability purposes, arises as a technocratic evaluation apparatus with a focus on outcomes via test scores to check the extent to which students have mastered the curriculum content (Eizadirad, 2018).

The Tyler Rationale and its philosophical underpinnings were at the core of designing and developing the Ontario subject-specific curriculum documents produced by Ministry of Education beginning in the 1990s where standardization was the hallmark of educational reforms being introduced and implemented by the government. According to the Ontario Ministry of Education website (2018c), "The Ministry of Education is responsible for the development of curriculum. School boards and schools are responsible for the implementation of curriculum" (para. 1). The website further states,

> Curriculum policy documents identify what students must know and be able to do at the end of every grade or course in every subject in Ontario publicly funded schools. Curriculum documents are made up of three components:
>
> - The front matter provides critical foundational information about the curriculum itself and about how learning connects to Ministry of Education policies, programs, and priorities.
> - The curriculum expectations (overall and specific expectations) are the knowledge and skills that students are expected to demonstrate in each subject at each grade level by the end of the grade.

- Additional supports, glossaries and overviews are included to provide further guidance and information to support the implementation of the curriculum. (Ontario Ministry of Education, 2018c, para. 3)

Grey (2017) explains how due to political pressure to produce better student achievement results on international comparison tests, the Ontario government responded by establishing "higher standards through the development of common curricular outcomes across schools district and regions" (p. 7). This resulted in publication of *Common Curriculum Grades 1–9* document by Ontario Ministry of Education in 1995. Shortly after in 1997, the Common Curriculum document was replaced with subject-specific curriculum documents titled the *Ontario Curriculum Grades 1–8*. Grey (2017) outlines, "the new curriculum promised to be more dynamic and efficient than the previous one" (p. 7). The Ontario Curriculum Grades 1–8 (1997) states the intention of the new curriculum is to explicitly outline "the required knowledge and skills for each grade set high standards and identify what parents and the public can expect children to learn in the schools of Ontario" (p. 3). The document further states,

The provisions of detail will eliminate the need for school boards to write their own expectations, will ensure consistency in curriculum across province, and will facilitate province-wide testing. Province-wide testing will be helpful to students who change schools, and will help parents in all regions to have a clear understanding of their child's progress. (p. 3)

Hence, the need for Ontario's large-scale standardized testing was justified under accountability purposes to fill the need for quantifiable results as a means to demonstrate to the public that students are mastering the curriculum content and therefore schools are offering high-quality education. Mastery of content by students was judged via standardized tests and their quantifiable scores. Standardized tests were introduced and implemented by establishment of EQAO in 1996 as an independent testing agency.

EQAO functions as a technocratic assessment apparatus, justifying the need for quantifiable outcome-based results to demonstrate to the public the quality of education offered by schools. According to the Education and Quality Accountability Office (EQAO) website (2018a), under "*About the Agency*," they state:

EQAO is an independent agency that creates and administers large-scale assessments to measure Ontario students' achievement in reading, writing and math at key stages of their education. All EQAO assessments are developed by Ontario educators to align with *The Ontario Curriculum*. The assessments evaluate student achievement objectively and in relation to a common provincial standard. (para. 1)

The trilateral symbiotic relationship between the Ontario curriculum, the Tyler Rationale, and the use of EQAO standardized tests becomes clear through the above description which justifies the use of "large-scale assessments" for measuring student achievements (the Tyler Rationale) relative to the "Ontario curriculum" and its prescribed overall and specific expectations to be achieved by end of each grade. In order to legitimize the assessment process in the eyes of the public as reliable and trustworthy, EQAO emphasizes it is an "independent agency" and that assessments are done "objectively" for accountability purposes relative to a "common provincial standard." Furthermore, the EQAO website (2018b) explicitly outlines various beneficial *Accountability Outcomes* for taxpayers, students, parents, and teachers associated with the implementation of EQAO standardized tests in schools.

For Taxpayers
- Increase, through a base of clear and reliable information, public ability to make judgements about the quality of education available across Ontario.
- Report on the success of our students measured against accepted, understandable standards in order to evaluate and improve learning.
- Ability to analyse student achievement in Ontario in relation to national and international standards.
- Improve public understanding of the ways in which students' knowledge and skills are assessed.
- Report to the general public on the state of Ontario's schools, with data on achievement, and the contextual factors that influence student learning.

For Students
- Provide students with clear and timely information on their progress.
- Reinforce student successes and identify areas where attention is needed.

- Provide information and direction which give students insight to plan for their future.
- Demonstrate to students that the knowledge and skills required of them are consistent across the province.
- Strengthen students' involvement in continuous learning and improvement.

For Parents
- Make parents increasingly aware of content taught and standards expected in our schools.
- Create opportunities for timely intervention to support student improvement.
- Clarify expectations for students' academic performance at key ages and stages through which parents can evaluate their children's progress.
- Give parents information they can use when talking to teachers about their children's progress.

For Teachers
- Help teachers to ascertain students' knowledge and skills, so they may intervene appropriately to foster improvement.
- Recognize the importance of the teacher's daily observations and records in both good teaching and good classroom assessment.
- Model and publicize excellent assessment practices which can serve as examples for daily classroom evaluation and help teachers improve their assessment skills.
- Provide common language and examples of student achievement to ensure straightforward reporting.
- Address public criticism of the education system by providing teachers with clear and credible data on student achievement and strategies for improvement. (EQAO, 2018b, para. 1–4)

By listing exclusively positive benefits associated with administrating EQAO standardized tests, EQAO seeks to legitimize implementation of standardized tests in schools by emphasizing "accountability outcomes" for taxpayers, students, parents, and teachers (EQAO, 2018b).

Overall, based on the historical analysis provided throughout this chapter, there is evidence of a trilateral symbiotic relationship between the Ontario curriculum, the Tyler Rationale, and EQAO standardized testing. The theorization of this relationship is symbiotic as all three components need each other to function as a cohesive entity providing the niche for the rise of outcome-based education in Ontario implemented under accountability discourse. The market-driven model of education, largely influenced by the Tyler Rationale and its philosophical underpinnings led to the introduction of subject-specific curriculum documents in Ontario in mid-1990s which outlined overall and specific expectation to be achieved by each student by end of each grade.

The rise of quantifiable outcome-based education, supported by the Tyler Rationale and introduction of subject-specific curriculum documents for each grade in Ontario schools, created an environment that homogenized the needs of all students under a one-size-fits-all approach and contributed to perpetuation of inequitable educational practices. The assumption was that standardized tests would provide quantifiable indicators to judge the quality of education offered by schools calculated by how students did on EQAO administered standardized tests. The implementation of the Tyler Rationale in developing curriculum documents created an environment where technocracy, neoliberalism, and racism flourished in the educational system leading to inequitable practices that expected all students to be achieving at a certain level by the end of each grade regardless of their socio-economic status and lived circumstances such as access to opportunities, support, and social services. If students did not achieve at an expected level, they were judged for being incompetent and potentially labelled as "at risk."

REFERENCES

Block, S., & Galabuzi, G. (2011). Canada's colour coded labour market: The gap for racialized workers. Wellesley Institute and Canadian Centre for Policy Alternatives. Retrieved from http://www.wellesleyinstitute.com/wp-content/uploads/2011/03/Colour_Coded_Labour_MarketFINAL.pdf

Dei, G. J. S. (2008). Schooling as community: Race, schooling, and the education of African youth. *Journal of Black Studies, 38*(3), 346–366.

Egan, K. (1978). What is curriculum? *Curriculum Inquiry, 8*(1), 65–72.

Eizadirad, A. (2018). Legitimization and normalization of EQAO standardized testing as an accountability tool in Ontario: Rise of quantifiable outcome-based education and inequitable educational practices. *OISE Graduate Student Research Conference Journal, 1*(1), 6–18.

Eizadirad, A., Martinez, X., & Ruminot, C. (2016). Comparative analysis of educational systems of accountability and quality of education in Ontario, Canada and Chile: Standardized testing and its role in perpetuation of educational inequity. *Interfaces Brasil/Canadá, 16*(2), 54–88.

Giroux, H. (2003). Spectacles of race and pedagogies of denial: Anti-Black racist pedagogy under the reign of neoliberalism. *Communication Education, 52*(3-4), 191–211.

Grey, M. K. (2017). *Perpetuating inequities in Ontario schools: A large-scale practice of assessment.* Master of Teaching research paper, Department Curriculum, Teaching and Learning, University of Toronto, Toronto, ON.

Hori, M. M. (2013). *The Toronto District School Board & Structural Violence.* Mahad. M. Hori.

Hunkins, F. P., & Hammill, P. A. (1994). Beyond Tyler and Taba: Reconceptualizing the curriculum process. *Peabody Journal of Education, 69*(3), 4–18.

James, C. E. (2012). *Life at the intersection: Community, class and schooling.* Halifax, NS: Fernwood Publishing.

Kliebard, H. M. (1970). The Tyler rationale. *The School Review, 78*(2), 259–272.

Knoester, M., & Au, W. (2017). Standardized testing and school segregation: Like tinder for fire? *Race Ethnicity and Education, 20*(1), 1–14.

Kumashiro, K. (2004). *Against common sense: Teaching and learning toward social justice.* New York: Routledge.

Lopez, R. G. (2003). The (racially neutral) politics of education: A critical race theory perspective. *Educational Administration Quarterly, 39*(1), 68–94.

McLaren, P. (2015). *Life in schools: An introduction to critical pedagogy in the foundations of education.* New York, NY: Routledge.

Noguera, P. A. (2003). Schools, prisons, and social implications of punishment: Rethinking disciplinary practices. *Theory into Practice, 42*(4), 341–350.

Ontario Ministry of Education. (1997). *The Ontario curriculum grades 1–8, 1997.* Toronto: Queen's Printer for Ontario. Retrieved from http://www.edu.gov. on.ca/eng/curriculum/elementary/subjects.html

Ontario Ministry of Education. (2018a). *Independent review of assessment and reporting.* Toronto: Queen's Printer for Ontario. Retrieved from http://www. edu.gov.on.ca/CurriculumRefresh/student-assessment.html

Ontario Ministry of Education. (2018b). *Ontario's graduation rate.* Toronto: Queen's Printer for Ontario. Retrieved from http://www.edu.gov.on.ca/eng/

Ontario Ministry of Education. (2018c). *The Ontario curriculum: Elementary.* Toronto: Queen's Printer for Ontario. Retrieved from http://www.edu.gov. on.ca/eng/curriculum/elementary/common.html#display

Pinar, W., Reynolds, W., Slattery, P., & Taubman, P. (1995). *Understanding curriculum: An introduction to the study of historical and contemporary curriculum discourses.* New York: Peter Lang Publishing, Incorporated.

Pinto, L. E. (2015). Fear and loathing in neoliberalism; School leader responses to policy layers. *Journal of Educational Administration and History, 47*(2), 140–154.

Portelli, J., & Sharma, M. (2014). Uprooting and settling in: The invisible strength of deficit thinking. *LEAR Ning Landscapes, 8*(1), 251–267.

Tyler, R. W. (1949). *Basic principles of curriculum and instruction* [Twenty-ninth impression, 1969]. Chicago, IL: The University of Chicago Press.

Tyler, R. W. (1969). *Basic principles of curriculum and instruction.* Chicago: University of Chicago Press.

Ydesen, C. (2014). High-stakes educational testing and democracy—Antagonistic or symbiotic relationship? *Education, Citizenship and Social Justice, 9*(2), 97–113.

CHAPTER 6

EQAO Results and School Rankings

For all Education Quality and Accountability Office (EQAO) assessments, questions are linked to the Ontario curriculum expectations and include a range of multiple choice, true and false, and open-ended response questions. For EQAO tests in the primary division, children write the tests in late May or early June, near end of the school year in Grade 3, and receive their results in late September or early October the following school year at the start of Grade 4 (EQAO, 2011). Pinto (2016) explains that "completed tests are sent to EQAO for marking by 1700 markers hired and trained by EQAO" (p. 99). Each student receives an Individual Student Report (ISR) which "describes his or her achievement on the test" (EQAO, 2012, p. 8) ranging from Level 1 being below grade expectations to Level 4 being above grade expectations in relation to the Ontario provincial curriculum standards. According to EQAO (2011), "these are the same achievement levels teachers use in the classroom and on reports cards to evaluate a child's progress" and "the provincial standard is a Level 3 which corresponds to a B– or B+" (EQAO, 2011, p. 2). If students meet or exceed the Level 3 achievement level, it is inferred they have mastered and demonstrated most or all of the required skills expected of them by the end of Grade 3 (EQAO, 2011).

In September along with each student receiving their ISR outlining their personalized achievement levels in the domains tested, each school receives a detailed report about overall achievement of their students in grades tested and a compiled report outlining their respective school

© The Author(s) 2019
A. Eizadirad, *Decolonizing Educational Assessment*,
https://doi.org/10.1007/978-3-030-27462-7_6

district results (EQAO, 2011). Being an educator with the Toronto District School Board and having spoken to many principals over the years, EQAO results and score improvements are a major area of focus as part of the School Improvement Plan (SIP) developed at the start of the school year in September by school administrators and teachers targeting specific numeracy and literacy goals. Each school within the Toronto District School Board (TDSB) has to develop and comply with a Board Improvement Plan for Student Achievement and Well Being (BIPSA) (TDSB, 2015). As part of BIPSA, when schools start in September, administrators and staff are responsible for establishing professional learning teams, update evidence of needs in different areas for the School Improvement Plan, and deconstruct EQAO data from the previous year. In October, schools continue to develop their School Improvement Plans with a specialized focus on numeracy and literacy. As a strategy, in early October specific students are identified in Grades 3 and 6, known as marker students, to be the focus of attention by the teachers with the collective goal of moving those specific students at least one level higher in their EQAO scores by providing them with extra help and support. The goal is to help the identified marker students improve but also to increase the overall EQAO achievement scores of the school since all children in Grades 3 and 6 are expected to participate in writing the EQAO test.

Throughout the school year each student's abilities and competencies are monitored by teachers. If teachers strongly feel that a student is functioning below grade level consistently, they can initiate the process of getting them assessed to qualify for an Individual Education Plan (IEP). According to the TDSB *Special Education in Ontario* document (2017), an IEP "is a written plan describing the special education program and/ or services required by a particular student. It identifies any accommodations and special education services needed to assist the student in achieving his or her learning expectations" (p. 153). An IEP outlines "learning expectations that are modified from or alternative to the expectations given in the curriculum policy document for the appropriate grade and subject or course" (p. 153). Students with IEPs who write the EQAO test are given the same accommodations and/or modifications outlined in their IEP relative to their unique needs. Examples of accommodations are extra time, writing in a less crowded or quieter space, and having a teacher transcribe and write oral responses of a student to questions on the EQAO test.

The Fraser Institute: Ranking of Schools and Correlation with Property Values

According to Eizadirad et al. (2016), "Despite the fact that many initiatives are being implemented to respond to students' needs rather than to test needs, the efficiency of the educational system including its plans, programs, resources and technical efforts are still indirectly evaluated predominantly through EQAO test results" (p. 90). This is exemplified by the importance given to The Fraser Institute school rankings which ranks schools each year based on their student performance on EQAO scores. The Fraser Institute "provides a detailed report on how each school is doing in academics compared to other ranked schools. It also shows whether the school's results are improving, declining, or just staying steady over the most recent five years" (Fraser Institute, 2018, para. 1). Many parents, particularly affluent parents from higher socio-economic backgrounds, use public ranking of schools to judge the quality of education offered by schools and select which schools to enrol their children in (Ricci, 2004; Morgan, 2006; Hori, 2013; Kempf, 2016; Pinto, 2016; Knoester & Au, 2017). The emphasis on school rankings places immense pressure on schools, particularly administrators and specific grade teachers whose students write the EQAO test, to improve their school's test results. It induces socio-emotional stress on teachers and administrators to demonstrate and produce improved results as often the school's identity and quality of education offered is judged through EQAO test results. This can lead to teaching to the test and narrowing of the curriculum by focusing more on subjects that are tested at the expense of marginalization to the Arts and Health and Physical Education (Miller, 2000; Portelli & Konecny, 2013). The pressure to get improved EQAO results, by any means necessary, can create a highly stressful learning environment within schools. Even though at the absolute level the Grade 3, 6, and 9 EQAO tests are considered low-stakes, within the public sphere those school rankings carry with it heavy weight and much currency to the extent that it impacts property values within the surrounding community.

Gardener (2017) outlines that "the Fraser Institute is an independent and registered charity public policy think tank established in 1974" and "the formation of the institute was to study, measure and broadly communicate government policies that affect the quality of life for Canadians" (p. 19). The Fraser Institute website (2018) states it "ranks schools using objective, publicly-available data such as average scores on province-wide tests" (para. 2). As Gardener (2017) further explains, "data for the [Fraser Institute] Report Card is based on seven indicators, all of which are province-wide tests of literacy and mathematics administered by the province's Education Quality and Accountability Office" (p. 19). The ranking formula does not take into account each school's unique student population in terms of demographics and contextual factors "such as those students with Individual Education Plans or students who are English Language Learners" (Gardener, 2017, p. 20). Morgan (2006) also raises the point that there is opposition and resistance from teacher unions against publication of school ranking based exclusively on EQAO test scores as it "creates a competitive environment in Ontario's education system" and it "pits both schools and school boards against one another" (p. 134), creating a competitive atmosphere that is not conducive to the learning needs of students.

EQAO test scores have gained so much currency in ranking and judging schools that increases or decreases in property values in neighbourhoods are highly correlated to school rankings (Morgan, 2006; ETFO, 2010; Pinto, 2016). The Fraser Institute produces two separate lists of rankings: one for elementary schools and another one for high schools (https://www.fraserinstitute.org/school-performance). Kohn (2001) argues, "Don't let anyone tell you that standardized tests are not accurate measures. The truth of the matter is they offer a remarkably precise method for gauging the size of the houses near the school where the test was administered" (p. 349). Real estate agents selling properties often emphasize school rankings to attract homebuyers which feeds into the cycle of parents making inferences about the quality of education offered at a school based on EQAO scores (Hori, 2013; Pinto, 2016; Kempf, 2016; Langlois, 2017). This greatly disadvantages and marginalizes schools that are ranked low on the list because it can contribute to lower student enrolment and less funding since "school funding is tied to school enrolment and if enrolment falls, then the money allocated to the schools under the per-pupil funding formula also falls" (Morgan, 2006, p. 134).

Monetary Costs of Administrating EQAO Standardized Tests

The cost of administrating EQAO tests annually is approximately $32 million dollars (EQAO, 2012), which equates to $17 per student. According to Kempf (2016), "when calculated to reflect only students in those grades [who participate in writing the test], rather than all of the province's 2,031,195 students, the province spends almost $60 per student per test" (p. 18). The EQAO document (2012) *The Power of Ontario's Provincial Testing Program* outlines,

> EQAO's budget is equivalent to 0.15% of the average per-pupil funding allocation by the Ministry of Education and represents a drop in the education bucket. It is a minimal and appropriate cost to perform an independent check on the use of tax dollars in our publicly funded education system. (p. 19)

EQAO uses the phrase "check on the use of tax dollars" which aligns with the market-driven economical view of education as technocratic, measurable, and quantifiable through standardized testing. This perspective heavily emphasizes outcome-based education based on quantifiable indicators such as scores on standardized tests. The assumption is that the pulse and heartbeat of the education system in terms of its quality and effectiveness can be measured through results from EQAO standardized tests.

TEACHER UNIONS OPPOSING STANDARDIZED TESTING

Ontario provincial teacher unions, the Elementary Teachers' Federation of Ontario (ETFO) and the Ontario Secondary School Teachers' Federation (OSSTF), have publicly criticized and opposed the practice of EQAO standardized testing in schools. ETFO "is the professional and protective organization representing 78,000 teachers, occasional teachers and educational professionals employed in Ontario's public elementary schools" (ETFO, 2018, para. 1). OSSTF consists of approximately 60,000 members including "teachers, educational assistants, continuing education teachers and instructors, psychologists, secretaries, speech-language pathologists, social workers, plan support personnel, attendance counselors, and many other education professionals" (OSSTF, 2018, para. 1). Both unions, since the introduction of EQAO standardized tests in Ontario schools, have taken a political stance opposing the practice. They communicate their stance by distributing educational memos, documents, and various texts to their members and the public outlining negative impacts of standardized testing on teaching and student learning and the negative consequences that arise from ranking schools based on EQAO scores.

ETFO in 2010 produced a video titled "Is EQAO Failing Our Children?" (https://www.youtube.com/watch?v=w3VqK4i4fFg) (ETFO, 2010). The video is approximately 10 minutes long and described by ETFO "as their most popular video ever" (ETFO, 2010, para. 1). Within the video various scholars, researchers, teachers, and parents express their concerns about the harmful impacts of EQAO standardized testing at the macro institutional level and at the micro-level within schools, classroom environments, and on administrators, teachers, and the students. Some of the criticisms of EQAO standardized testing include teaching to the test, diminishing of teachable moments and interconnectivity of subjects across various domains, narrowing of the curriculum to areas being tested, impact on property values and student enrolment, and high stress placed on administrators, teachers, and students. What is missing in the video based on the perspectives represented are voices of children, particularly racialized children in elementary schools and how EQAO standardized tests impacts their identities and communities. As mentioned earlier, this exploratory study seeks to examine the experiences, opinions, and concerns of racialized children and parents regarding how the EQAO standardized test impacts their identity, family, school, and the larger surrounding community in which they live. A key feature and entry point to this analysis is "understanding curriculum as racial text" (Pinar et al., 1995, p. 23), specifically how race influences students experience with EQAO and whether or not these narratives support or oppose the dominant narrative disseminated by EQAO about the benefits and effectiveness of EQAO standardized tests for accountability outcomes.

In May 2015, in a document sent out to ETFO members by the union providing central collective bargaining updates, there was a subsection titled "EQA-NO: Members Share Their Thoughts About Standardized Testing" (ETFO, 2015, p. 2). At the time, there was labour unrest and teacher contract negotiations were not going smoothly with the Liberal government. The document updated members that EQAO testing at the elementary level, which is typically administered in the month of June, was "cancelled in public school boards during this school year due to job action by ETFO members" (ETFO, 2015, p. 1). The document further described the reasoning for ETFO teachers not administrating the EQAO tests:

> As educators, we know that genuine learning is driven by two things: students' natural curiosity and our ability to harness that curiosity in the classroom. Genuine learning is, by definition, not standardized. It is risky, complex, unpredictable and original. That's why standardized testing regimes

like EQAO don't ultimately help students succeed—it's impossible to measure and attach a meaningful number to the quality of our students' original thoughts and personal growth. (ETFO, 2015, p. 2)

Following the aforementioned statement, there was a list outlining shortcomings of EQAO standardized testing as expressed by ETFO members:

- It subtracts from valuable instruction time.
- It provides minimal useful feedback to classroom teachers.
- It leads to a neglect of non-verbal ways of learning, like music and art.
- It channels instructional resources to literacy and numeracy at the expense of other curriculum areas.
- It penalizes students who think in non-standard ways.
- It gives control over delivery of the curriculum to Ministry bureaucrats rather than educational practitioners.
- It assumes that what students need to know ten years from now is already known and can be tested.
- It reduces teacher creativity and the appeal of teaching as a profession.
- It disadvantages large numbers of students based on language, culture, ethnicity, race and social class.
- It creates unnecessary stress and negative attitudes toward learning.
- It blocks instructional innovations that can't be evaluated by a test score. (ETFO, 2015, p. 2)

Overall, both elementary and secondary teacher unions in Ontario continuously oppose the practice of EQAO standardized testing. In solidarity, both unions express that EQAO standardized testing is not an effective use of financial resources by the government, and that classroom-based assessment by teachers over the period of the school year from September to June is the most effective source of information about student learning. The unions further argue that the information gathered by EQAO standardized tests over a one-week period of testing is not representative of the students' holistic abilities and competencies as it is only a snapshot of the learning that takes place within an entire school year.

References

Education Quality and Accountability Office. (2011). *EQAO tests in elementary school: A guide for parents.* Toronto: Queen's Printer for Ontario. Retrieved from https://www.rainbowschools.ca/wp-content/uploads/2016/04/EQAO_ParentGuide_PrimaryJunior2011.pdf

Education Quality and Accountability Office. (2012). *The power of Ontario's provincial testing program*. Toronto: Queen's Printer for Ontario. Retrieved from http://www.eqao.com/en/assessments/communication-docs/power-provincial-testing-program.PDF

Eizadirad, A., Martinez, X., & Ruminot, C. (2016). Comparative analysis of educational systems of accountability and quality of education in Ontario, Canada and Chile: Standardized testing and its role in perpetuation of educational inequity. *Interfaces Brasil/Canadá, 16*(2), 54–88.

Elementary Teachers' Federation of Ontario. (2010). EQAO testing. Retrieved from http://www.etfo.ca/defendingworkingconditions/issuesineducation/pages/eqao%20testing%20-%20advice%20to%20members.aspx

Elementary Teachers' Federation of Ontario. (2015). ETFO bargaining bulletin: Central collective bargaining updates published by ETFO.

Elementary Teachers' Federation of Ontario. (2018). ETFO. Retrieved from http://www.etfo.ca/Pages/Home.aspx

Fraser Institute. (2018). *School performance*. Retrieved from https://www.fraser-institute.org/school-performance

Gardener, D. A. K. (2017). *EQAO Preparation and the Effects on In-Classroom Instruction*. Master of Teaching research paper, Department of Curriculum, Teaching and Learning, University of Toronto, Toronto, ON.

Hori, M. M. (2013). *The Toronto District School Board & Structural Violence*. Mahad. M. Hori.

Kempf, A. (2016). *The pedagogy of standardized testing: The radical impacts of educational standardization in the US and Canada*. New York: Springer.

Knoester, M., & Au, W. (2017). Standardized testing and school segregation: Like tinder for fire? *Race Ethnicity and Education, 20*(1), 1–14.

Kohn, A. (2001). Fighting the tests: A practical guide to rescuing our schools. *Phi Delta Kappan, 82*(5), 349–357.

Langlois, H. (2017). *Behind the snapshot: Teachers' experiences of preparing students in lower socioeconomic status schools for the Ontario Secondary School Literacy Test*. Master of Teaching research paper, Department Curriculum, Teaching and Learning, University of Toronto, Toronto, ON.

Miller, J. P. (2000). *Education and the soul: Toward a spiritual curriculum*. New York: SUNY Press.

Morgan, C. (2006). A retrospective look at educational reforms in Ontario. *Our Schools, Our Selves, 15*(2), 127–141.

Ontario Secondary School Teachers' Federation. (2018). *About us*. Retrieved from https://www.osstf.on.ca/about-us.aspx

Pinar, W., Reynolds, W., Slattery, P., & Taubman, P. (1995). *Understanding curriculum: An introduction to the study of historical and contemporary curriculum discourses*. New York: Peter Lang Publishing, Incorporated.

Pinto, L. E. (2016). Tensions and fissures: The politics of standardised testing and accountability in Ontario, 1995–2015. *The Curriculum Journal, 27*(1), 95–112.
Portelli, J., & Konecny, P. C. (2013). Neoliberalism, subversion, and democracy in education. *Encounters on Education, 14,* 87–97.
Ricci, C. (2004). The case against standardized testing and the call for a revitalization of democracy. *Review of Education, Pedagogy, and Cultural Studies, 26*(4), 339–361.
Toronto District School Board. (2015). *2015–2017 school improvement plan for student achievement& well-being (k-grade 12+).* Toronto. Retrieved from http://schoolweb.tdsb.on.ca/Portals/humbervalley/docs/SchoolImprovement Plan.pdf
Toronto District School Board. (2017). *Special education in Ontario.* Toronto. Retrieved from http://www.edu.gov.on.ca/eng/document/policy/os/on schools_2017e.pdf

CHAPTER 7

Understanding the Research Approach and the Data

In this chapter I explain in depth the theoretical lens used to approach the research, collect the data, and conduct the analysis based on the responses of the children, parents, and educators interviewed.

METHODOLOGY AND RESEARCH PARADIGM: CRITICAL THEORY AND CRITICAL RACE THEORY

As a researcher concerned with "redressing oppression and committed to social justice" (Brown & Strega, 2005, p. 11), I use Critical Theory (Brown & Strega, 2005; Creswell, 2007; Denzin & Lincoln, 2000; Lather, 1986) as my research methodology and paradigm to explore the power dynamics embedded in Education Quality and Accountability Office (EQAO) test preparation and administration in elementary schools and its consequential impact on racialized Grade 3 students, parents, and educators. I utilize Creswell's (2007) definition of a paradigm which is, "[T]he philosophical stance taken by the researcher that provides a basic set of beliefs that guides action. It defines, for its holder the nature of the world, the individual's place in it, and the range of possible relationships to that world" (p. 248).

I adopt Brown and Strega's (2005) definition of Critical Theory as a conceptual framework which defines Critical Theory as "theories that view knowledge in social constructionist terms as rooted in subjective experiences and power relations" (p. 68). From this vantage point, lived experiences are

© The Author(s) 2019
A. Eizadirad, *Decolonizing Educational Assessment*,
https://doi.org/10.1007/978-3-030-27462-7_7

a form of valuable knowledge which can provide insights into how educational policy is enacted in elementary schools within specific power relations impacting children, parents, and educators differently in their respective schools and communities given their identities. This social constructionist approach with an emphasis on the connection between subjective experiences and power relations aligns with what Lather (1986) calls "research as praxis," where research inquiry is characterized by "negotiation, reciprocity, and empowerment" (p. 257). Describing differences between "research as praxis" and positivist methodological inquiries, Lather (1986) points out,

> Rather than the illusory "value-free" knowledge of the positivists, praxis-oriented inquirers seek emancipatory knowledge. Emancipatory knowledge increases awareness of the contradictions hidden or distorted by everyday understandings, and in doing so it directs attention to the possibilities for social transformation inherent in the present configuration of social processes. (p. 259)

This exploratory qualitative research study seeks to be emancipatory in nature, for participants in the study as well as the readers, to the extent it increases awareness about the experiences, opinions, and concerns of racialized children, parents, and educators regarding how the EQAO standardized test impacts their identity, family, school, and the larger surrounding community in which they live.

The research approach for conducting this qualitative study is unique because it goes beyond simply crunching and interpreting statistics in a simplistic, linear, and quantitative manner and instead works with a more holistic, complex, in-depth approach "capable of grasping the messy complexities of people's lives, especially the lives of those on the margins" (Brown & Strega, 2005, p. 11) from an interdisciplinary lens led by voices of racialized children and parents who are often marginalized within the school system due to systemic barriers (Dei, 2008; James, 2012; Kumashiro, 2004; Lopez, 2003; McLaren, 2015). Brown and Strega (2005) distinguish differences between doing research on the marginalized versus doing research with the marginalized by explaining:

> Research from the margins is not research on the marginalized but research by, for, and with them/us. It is research that takes seriously and seeks to trouble the connections between how knowledge is created, what knowledge is produced, and who is entitled to engage in these processes. It seeks to

reclaim and incorporate the personal and political context of knowledge construction. It attempts to foster oppositional discourses, ways of talking about research, and research processes that explicitly and implicitly challenge relations of domination and subordination. (p. 7)

At the core of this study is the interconnection of "the personal and the political" led by voices of racialized children, parents, and educators "from the margins" as it relates to the use of EQAO standardized testing in elementary schools. The goal is to complexify understanding of EQAO standardized testing discourses from multiple perspectives by fostering "oppositional discourses" including the pros and cons of standardized testing and its short- and long-term effects.

Central to this inquiry process is a critique of the power relations and processes associated with preparation, administration, implementation, and legitimization of EQAO standardized testing in elementary schools. I use the works of Kincheloe and McLaren (2002) who emphasize "critical social theory is concerned in particular with issues of power and justice and the way that the economy, matters of race, class, and gender, ideologies, discourses, education, religion and other social institutions and cultural dynamics interact to construct a social system" (p. 90). Similarly, Brown and Strega (2005) describe the characteristics of critical research by stating:

Critical research rejects the ideas of value-free science that underpin both qualitative and quantitative approaches to research. Instead, it positions itself as about critiquing and transforming social relations. Critical researchers view reality as both objective and subjective: objective in terms of the real forces that impinge on the lives of groups and individuals, and subjective in terms of the various individual and group interpretations of these forces and the experiences they engender. (p. 9)

This study acknowledges that each experience of the participants interviewed, as children, parents, and educators, is unique and needs to be contextualized relative to their identities and their social locations within the realm of the schools and the communities they are situated within.

Kincheloe and McLaren (2002) outline a series of characteristics that define Critical Theory. One of the main characteristics and goals of Critical Theory is critical enlightenment. According to Kincheloe and McLaren (2002),

Critical theory analyzes competing, power interests between groups and individuals within a society, identifying who gains and who loses in a specific situation. In this context, to seek critical enlightenment is to uncover the winners and losers in particular social arrangements and the process by which such power operates. (pp. 90–91)

As an extension of critical enlightenment, this study explores through semi-structured interviews how EQAO preparation and administration privileges certain identities and knowledges while simultaneously oppressing and marginalizing other identities. Some of the important factors examined as part of the analysis include gender, race, socio-economic status, and spatial locations of neighbourhoods.

Another major characteristic of Critical Theory is critical emancipation. According to Kincheloe and McLaren (2002):

Those who seek emancipation attempt to gain the power to control their own lives in solidarity with a justice-oriented community. Here, critical research attempts to expose the forces that prevent individuals and groups from shaping the decisions that crucially affect their lives. (p. 91)

Critical Theory works towards critical emancipation by centring "subaltern voices" (Spivak, 1988, p. 66) of the marginalized at the core of its analysis relative to how power is enacted in schools at the systemic institutional level. Building on the works of Antonio Gramsci, Spivak develops the term "subaltern" to refer to oppressed subjects or social groups or more generally those of inferior rank in a given society. Critical Theory works to identify systemic barriers by listening to voices and concerns expressed by marginalized and racialized identities to engage in dialogical conversations from multiple perspectives about how to challenge and change oppressive policies and practices and their harmful effects. Critical emancipation explores the impact of hierarchical power relations on specific identities by asking new questions from new perspectives within a "dialogical framework" (Freire, 1970, p. 17). Freire (1970) explains in *Pedagogy of the Oppressed*:

In order to understand the meaning of dialogical practice, we have to put aside the simplistic understanding of dialogue as a mere technique. Dialogue does not represent a somewhat false path that I attempt to elaborate on and realize in the sense of involving the ingenuity of the other. On the contrary, dialogue characterizes an epistemological relationship. Thus, in this sense, dialogue is a way of knowing and should never be viewed as a mere tactic to involve students in a particular task. We have to make this point very clear. I engage in dialogue not necessarily because I like the other person. I engage in dialogue because I recognize the social and not merely the individualistic character of the process of knowing. In this sense, dialogue presents itself as an indispensable component of the process of both learning and knowing. (p. 17)

Within a framework that recognizes dialogue as "an indispensable component of the process of both learning and knowing," many silenced and unanswered questions pertaining to the effects of EQAO standardized testing on racialized children, parents, and educators need to be raised and discussed as a means of arriving at new understandings. Asking new questions from multiple competing perspectives will lead beyond binaries and linear modes of thinking, such as whether EQAO standardized testing is good or bad, to engaging in higher critical thinking that inquires what social groups are privileged and who is oppressed, and more specifically in what ways. This allows us to further understand "curriculum as racial text" (Pinar, Reynolds, Slattery, & Taubman, 1995, p. 23) in the context of today's classrooms in Ontario.

The third major characteristic of Critical Theory is a reconceptualized critical theory of power: hegemony. This refers to the works of Antonio Gramsci and his concept of hegemony (Gramsci, 1995, 2000). According to Kincheloe and McLaren (2002), Gramsci understood that

Dominant power is not always exercised simply by physical force but via social-psychological attempts to win people's consent to domination through cultural institutions such as the media, the schools, the family, and the church. The hegemonic field, with its bounded socio-psychological horizon, garners consent to an inequitable power matrix—a set of relations that are legitimated by their depiction as natural and inevitable. (p. 93)

From a reconceptualized critical theory of power, this study critiques how standardized testing is normalized and legitimized through "people's consent" as a dominant tool to measure accountability in schools. More specifically, contextual factors are examined such as various social, cultural, and political conditions that created the niche that harnessed "people's consent" to enact mandatory standardized testing in Grades 3, 6, 9, and 10 administered by EQAO. For Gramsci, hegemony is characterized by "the combination of force and consent" (Gramsci, 2000, p. 423) and is socio-culturally constructed through a dynamic process that unconsciously and consciously influences social relations through normalization and legitimization of a narrow set of ideologies as "common sense" often told from the perspective of the dominant class and those in positions of authority.

For the purpose of this book, hegemony is defined using Weiner's (2014) definition derived from the works of Gramsci:

> The term hegemony applies to the process whereby ideas, structures, and actions come to be seen by the majority of people as wholly natural, preordained, and working for their own good when in fact these ideas, structures, and actions are constructed and transmitted by powerful minority interests to protect the status quo that serves these interests so well.
>
> The subtle cruelty of hegemony is that over time it becomes deeply embedded, part of the natural air we breathe. One cannot peel back the layers of oppression and identify a group or groups of people as the instigators of a conscious conspiracy to keep people silent and disenfranchised. Instead, the ideas and practices of hegemony become part and parcel of everyday life—the stock opinions, conventional wisdom, or commonsense ways of seeing and ordering the world that people take for granted. (p. 40)

Hegemony provides a lens to critique current normalized and legitimized standardized testing policy in elementary schools, and the processes involved, where all Grade 3 students attending publicly funded schools in Ontario participate in writing the EQAO test to demonstrate accountability to the general public. Central to this analysis is how individuals and social groups accept this practice without critically questioning its motives and whose interests it serves which consequentially legitimizes standardized testing as a "commonsense" approach to demonstrating accountability.

Madison (2012) makes an important point that "The central feature of Gramsci's notion of hegemony is that it operates without force. We give consent because we are interpolated and prescribed to believe that the interest of the power bloc is really our interest. It becomes our worldview, and through hegemony we are in complicity with our own subordination" (p. 65). Weiner (2014) concurs with Madison by emphasizing,

> [H]egemony, although correctly associated with domination and oppression, is effective in normalizing power relations—social, economic, sexual, cultural—at the level of imagination because it offers people a significant degree of comfort and familiarity. In short, hegemonic thinking can feel good, in spite of its oppressive thrust, because it protects thinkers from

appearing strange or different on one hand, while on the other it keeps them unaware of how their conformity in thought and practice might be working against their own or group interests. When being different (thinking against the grain of accepted ideas attitudes, and/or interests) in and of itself exposes a person to ridicule, imprisonment, or some other form of social exclusion, then for many the natural "choice" is to stay within acceptable conventions, even if to do so is to become complicit in one's own dehumanization. (pp. 40–41)

With majority of children, parents, and educators interviewed as participants self-identifying as racialized, Critical Race Theory (CRT) is also used as a relevant conceptual framework to examine and interpret the data collected via semi-structured interviews. W. E. B. Du Bois in 1903 pointed out that "the problem of the Twentieth Century is the problem of the color line" (p. 9). It could be argued that the problem of the twenty-first century continues to be the "color line" now referred to as race and racism. Du Bois in his book *The Souls of Black Folk* laid the foundational framework which gave birth to Critical Race Theory (CRT). CRT centres the lived experiences of those who have been historically marginalized and oppressed, including individuals and groups, at the core of its analysis in the process questioning how social injustices are perpetuated, institutionalized, and normalized through construction of a racial hierarchy. CRT questions the meta-narratives that perpetuate the status quo and the hegemony that provides power, privilege, and voice to certain groups at the expense of suffering, marginalization, and silencing to others. As Trevino, Harris, and Wallace (2008) emphasize:

> At its core, CRT is committed to advocating for justice for people who find themselves occupying positions on the margins—for those who hold "minority" status. It directs attention to the ways in which structural arrangements inhibit and disadvantage some more than others in our society. It spotlights the form and function of dispossession, disenfranchisement, and discrimination across a range of social institutions, and then seeks to give voice to those who are victimized and displaced. CRT, therefore, seeks not only to name, but to be a tool for rooting out inequality and injustice. (p. 8)

One of CRT's main premises is that racism is prevalent in society and not an exception (Delgado & Stefancic, 2000). Comparing the present and the past, Lopez (2003) states that "The only difference between racism today and of the past is that modern-day racism is more subtle, invisible, and insidious" (p. 82). CRT attempts to support this stance by naming racism and putting a face to it by recognizing and giving importance to the voices and narratives of the oppressed and their lived experiences. These lived experiences are analysed through multiple and interdisciplinary vantage points taking into consideration macro and micro perspectives as a means of providing a historical, social, political, and cultural context to the narratives.

I use Knoester and Au's (2017) definition of Critical Race Theory which they outline as "a conceptual framework useful in understanding how racism operates, including within institutions such as schools, by paying careful attention to the differential resources and opportunities available to students of different races, as opposed to the more common form of racial theorizing, focusing on individual acts of hatred or racism" (p. 4). From this vantage point, each interview with the child and their parents is treated as a unique case study offering a window into the complexities of how they are impacted by EQAO standardized tests in terms of both preparation and administration. The participants' lived experiences, told through their voices, are contextualized and critiqued relative to the dominant narrative told by EQAO about the usefulness and effectiveness of EQAO standardized tests. As Lopez (2003) indicates, a key characteristic of Critical Race Theory (CRT) "is the privileging of stories and counter-stories particularly the stories that are told by people of color. CRT scholars believe there are two differing accounts of reality: the dominant reality that 'looks ordinary and natural' to most individuals, and a racial reality that has been filtered out, suppressed, and censored" (p. 84).

From a CRT perspective, one has to ask, how is racism embedded within the DNA and social fabric of our educational institutions via its neutral policies and practices such as the practice of EQAO standardized testing, yet appearing undetectable to the naked eye without critical analysis? Knoester and Au (2017) deconstruct how to identify subtle racism within educational institutions by explaining:

> [A] key tenet of Critical Race Theory is that such inequality is regularly obscured under the guise of race-less or race-neutral laws and policies and is instead framed around individual equality as expressed through concepts such as meritocracy—that success is purely the result of individual hard work and not the function of social, historical, or institutional processes. Thus, within a Critical Race framework, it becomes important to consider issues

surrounding segregation, desegregation, and re-segregation of schools as part of a larger conversation about white material advantage and the material disadvantage of communities of color, often under the guise of non-race specific and sometimes rhetorically anti-racist policies. (p. 4)

Overall, this study uses Critical Race Theory as a paradigm to interrogate and critique data collected via semi-structured interviews led by voices of racialized Grade 3 children, parents, and educators about their experiences with EQAO tests relative to the dominant normalized and legitimized narrative told by EQAO. The objective of the study is to explore, critique, validate, and challenge from multiple perspectives in a dialogical manner the hegemonic discourse that legitimizes the use of standardizing testing in elementary schools for the purpose of efficiency and accountability. As Madison (2012) emphasizes, the application of Critical Theory to studying social issues "takes us beneath surface appearances, disrupts the status quo, and unsettles both neutrality and taken-for-granted assumptions by bringing to light underlying and obscure operations of power and control" (p. 5).

METHODS

Creswell (2007) explains that "Qualitative research begins with assumptions, a worldview, the possible use of a theoretical lens, and the study of research problems inquiring into the meaning individuals or groups ascribe to a social or human problem" (p. 37). For this study, semi-structured interviews with eight Grade 3 children and their parents were conducted, mostly racialized, to capture the depth and details of their subjective embodied experiences preparing and writing the EQAO standardized test. My methods approach combined formal and informal observations as part of audio and video recording of the semi-structured interviews to bring to life the lived realities and experiences of the participants interviewed and how they are impacted by EQAO preparation and administration. While the formal part of the interview involved children and parents responding to various questions pertaining to before, during, and after writing the EQAO test, my informal observations included making note of the mood of the child and parents, ways the child might be influenced by the presence of their parent(s) or the videographer, and when participants would make pauses in their responses. Other non-verbal communication noted as part of my informal observations included body language and tone of voice. This assisted in more accurately analysing participants' responses when rewatching and transcribing the interviews. Pole and Morrison (2003) point out, critical theorists are not "concerned with presenting a distanced, scientific and objective account of the social world, but with an account that recognizes the subjective reality of the experiences of those people who constitute and construct the social world" (p. 5). Therefore, the subjective interpretation of the children and their parents about their experiences matter and should be a central part of the discussion about seeking to better understand the appropriateness and effectiveness of EQAO standardized testing in elementary schools for accountability purposes. Yet, within the operation of school boards and day-to-day functioning of schools, the hierarchical power dynamics and relations often marginalize and silence voices of racialized children and parents deeming their negative experiences as exceptional cases and not the norm for those participating in writing EQAO tests. Children and parents' voices on school matters such as effectiveness of EQAO standardized testing are typically not an integral component of policy development and enactment in schools. Yet, as Lather (1986) importantly remind us:

> For praxis to be possible, not only must theory illuminate the lived experience of progressive social groups; it must also be illuminated by their struggles. Theory adequate to the task of changing the world must be open-ended, nondogmatic, informing, and grounded in the circumstances of everyday life; and, moreover, it must be premised on a deep respect for the intellectual and political capacities of the dispossessed. (p. 262)

Agreeing with Lather's (1986) stance on effective research praxis as "grounded in the circumstances of everyday life," this qualitative study uses a variety of open-ended questions as part of the semi-structured interview with the participants to capture the complexities associated with preparing and writing the Grade 3 EQAO standardized test.

INSTRUMENT OF DATA COLLECTION: SEMI-STRUCTURED INTERVIEWS

Semi-structured interviews were the main medium for data collection for this exploratory qualitative research study. Semi-structured interviews were audio and video recorded to capture body language and facial expressions of the participants as these are important unconscious means of communicating, particularly as it applies to children who are still developing and maturing physically, socially, emotionally, and cognitively. Another reason for video recording of interviews is to work with the footage to create a short film for a more general audience in the near future. Being able to video record the interviews provided the advantage of rewatching the interviews as part of transcription, interpretation, and analysis of the data. It also provided visual cues to contextualize and deconstruct interviewee's responses relative to their mood, tone of voice, facial and body expressions, and influence of parent(s) and researcher being present. My conventions for the transcription included transcribing the entire interview word by word from start to finish without alterations. Round brackets were used to describe respondent's non-verbal communication reflecting how respondents spoke in relation to sounds, facial expressions, and pauses. Periods were used to punctuate end of thoughts relative to the question asked as well as minor pauses in the flow of the conversation with long responses. I started new sentences with the start of each new question. Commas were used to capture short pauses with specific length being described within the parenthesis to help contextualize interpretation and analysis. Connected codes were italicized to assist me in identifying themes.

Glesne (2015) uses the analogy of "interviewing as the process of getting words to fly" (p. 67) to describe the dynamic process between interviewer and interviewee(s). Glesne (2015) explains, "As the interviewer, you are not a research machine, but you do 'pitch' questions at your respondents with the intent of making words fly" (p. 67). Glesne (2015) uses a sports analogy, particularly "pitching" in baseball, to emphasize the importance of asking appropriate relevant interview questions that can elicit in-depth and insightful responses from the participants being interviewed. I would add to Glesne's (2015) baseball analogy of "pitching" the visual imagery of fishing; questions become what you put on your "hook" to fish or in other words to engage the interviewee(s) and get them to open up about their experiences, opinions, emotions, and values as part of a meaningful reciprocal dialogue between the interviewer and the interviewee(s). Madison (2012) emphasizes that

> The ethnographic interview opens realms of meaning that permeate beyond rote information or dining the "truth of the matter." The interviewer is not an object, but a subject with agency, history, and his or her own idiosyncratic command of a story. Interviewer and interviewee are in partnership and dialogue as they construct memory, meaning, and experience together. (p. 28)

This ethnographic perspective is in contrast to positivist paradigms of research where the interviewer is a photographer who seeks to capture information in the form of a freeze frame image of an object. From an ethnographic interview (Madison, 2012), the interviewer and the interviewee are in a dynamic dialogical interaction; dance partners trying to find the right rhythm through engaging in relevant and appropriate discussions, which symbolically can spark movement and new insights about the complexities of the social phenomena under examination. The objective of the ethnographic interviewer is to represent a moving "subject" in time and space in a complex manner that takes into consideration relevant personal and political factors as well as spatial power dynamics.

One of the major strengths of using semi-structured interviews to collect data is that it provides flexibility for conversations to go in multiple directions based on unique identities of the interviewees including their personal values, opinions, beliefs and lived experiences. It also provides the time to go in depth in discussing complex topics, issues, or questions that each interviewee finds more relevant and significant to their unique lives accompanied with follow-up questions by the interviewer where necessary. As well, the interview can go in unexpected directions not anticipated by the interviewer. Singh (2016) points out, "semi-structured interview gives the participant an opportunity to bring up issues that the researcher may not have previously considered, thereby adding to the depth of the research" (p. 38).

Galletta (2013) points out that "the semi-structured interview provides a repertoire of possibilities" (p. 24). The interviewer can ask various types of questions as part of the semi-structured interview which can include "behaviour or experience questions, opinion or value questions, feeling questions, knowledge questions, sensory questions, and background/demographic questions" (Madison, 2012, p. 28). I included all of the aforementioned types of questions when designing the semi-structured interview questions for this study. The order and sequence in which the interview questions are asked are just as important. Galletta (2013) explains that "the arrangement of questions may be structured to yield considerable and often multi-dimensional streams of data" (p. 24). As a result, I created two separate lists of questions: one for parents and another one for the child. Questions were worded using age-appropriate language and structurally organized relative to time: before, during, and after writing the Grade 3 EQAO standardized test (see Appendices E and F).

Participant Selection, Criteria, and Sample Size

Wolfer (2007) explains that "Qualitative research is aimed at a more in-depth understanding of a research issue" and that "this type of research usually involves small sample sizes because the researcher is not interested in generalizing to a wider population, but instead focused on a more detailed exploration of the topic" (p. 13). From a Critical Theory perspective, Brown and Strega (2005) emphasize that "the goals for anti-oppressive research are very different as involving people is done more for community building, empowerment, and a better understanding than for goals of representativeness or validity" (p. 269). This is the case with this exploratory qualitative research study as its main research objective is "a more detailed exploration" and in-depth understanding of the experiences of racialized Grade 3 children, parents, and educators with EQAO standardized testing.

Galletta (2013) points out that "Qualitative research does not involve random sampling of participants in the statistical sense" (p. 33). Similarly, discussing sampling in anti-oppressive research, Brown and Strega (2005) explain,

> Sampling in anti-oppressive research is seldom random. Sampling is a power-laden decision and seen as one of many political acts in research. In this, ideally, an outsider researcher is never the sole source of invitations to participate. Ideally it is a community of participants/insider researchers who do the inviting/including. (p. 269)

Galletta (2013) outlines a list of significant questions researchers should ask themselves when recruiting participants for one's qualitative research involving the use of semi-structured interviews as a medium for data collection. These questions are

- What individuals are most likely to offer responses relevant to your research question?
- Where might there be gaps in locating diverse perspectives and experiences as it relates to your research question?
- How will you fill in those gaps? (p. 33)

I utilized Galletta's (2013) questions as a guide to purposefully recruit participants based on a range of differences so that their responses would help "fill in those gaps" relative to "diverse perspectives and experiences."

I began the participant recruitment process in September 2016 by out-lining my selection criteria. The main criteria required to be considered a potential research participant was that the child had to be in Grade 3, self-identify as racialized, attending a publicly funded school in Ontario, and participating in writing the EQAO standardized test. My goal was to interview between five and ten racialized Grade 3 students and their par-ents; a combination of male and females attending schools in the Greater Toronto Area. I intended to recruit children who attended different schools located spatially in different neighbourhoods to capture a range of different perspectives and experiences. Being racialized was an important selection criterion as there were no studies that I found that focused on experiences of Grade 3 children as told by their voices in relation to how they experienced EQAO. Similar to Singh (2016), I purposefully chose a smaller sample size to focus in depth and "on the nuances that are preva-lent in the data collected as well as the areas in which there are silences and pauses in order to capture the individual experience" (p. 38).

According to Wolfer (2007), purposeful sampling is appropriate "when researchers want to focus on specific cases for further in-depth examina-tion" (p. 209). A sample size of five to ten children and their parents made the study manageable, feasible, and allowed time for "in depth examina-tion." I recruited participants through my community networks via educa-tion and sports differing in gender, race, and socio-economic status to get different responses "in terms of their socioeconomic perspectives and demographic compositions" (Tollefson, 2008, p. 175) reflecting the diversity in today's classrooms in Ontario. I stopped the interviews at eight participants as I reached data saturation and the themes began to repeat themselves (Singh, 2016). The credibility of the data was enhanced through multiple data collection techniques, known as triangulation, to identify emerging themes and findings.

RECRUITMENT OF PARTICIPANTS; ETHICS, INFORMED CONSENT, AND CONFIDENTIALITY

Parents and their children who met the selection criteria were contacted through purposeful sampling based on my community connections and networks. Similar to Tollefson (2008), "in order to facilitate the creation of a safe environment for genuine dialogue, free from the politics and his-tory of any given site, my goal was to ensure that all participants came from different schools" (p. 175). If I was not able to reach my target number of five to ten children from different schools and neighbourhood areas, via my own community networks in education and sports, the next step in the action plan was to use referrals and word of mouth to recruit more participants. But, I was able to recruit eight children and their parent(s) as participants via purposeful sampling within my own community networks.

As a means of being conscious to not exploit vulnerable populations such as racialized children and their parents as well as those from a lower socio-economic status, I approached research participants by describing my research project and its objectives in detail using age-appropriate language. I provided the parents and the child each with separate information letters. I specifically used child-friendly language in the information letter for the children to better assist them in understanding what the research project entailed and what was required of them as a participant. This reflected my perspective and ontology from a Critical Theory paradigm that the child should be part of the decision-making process as reality is subjective and co-constructed within different contexts.

The information letters explained the overview and purpose of the research project, the degree of involvement expected of the participants in terms of time and type of activity, any potential risks or harm the participants may experience, and how the data will be used. If the parent(s) and the child both agreed to participate in the research after reviewing the information letters and having had the opportunity to ask questions, we proceeded to the next set of forms. This step involved signing an informed consent form separately by the parent(s) and the child face to face with the researcher. The child, through their willingness to participate voluntarily and with proxy consent from their parents, signed the permission to interview and the consent form which stated:

- With full knowledge, I agree of my own free will, to participate in this study.
- I agree to have my interview audio and video recorded.
- I agree to the use of anonymous quotations in any thesis or publication that comes of this research.

The parent(s) completed a separate form agreeing to the same identical aforementioned statements above.

Overall, all research participants through intentional purposeful sampling were approached for voluntary participation in the research study and were given information letters and informed consent forms to read, complete, and sign confirming their participation. I reminded participants at various intervals that they can opt out of the study at any time without any penalties, even after completion of the interview. I also offered to provide a translator, if requested, to mitigate language barriers for those who English was not their primary language spoken at home. The option of having a translator available was mentioned on multiple occasions including during the administration of information letters, informed consent forms, and the semi-structured interview, but all participants respectfully declined.

Identifiable data such as the name of the child, the school they attend, and name of their parents were given pseudonyms to ensure anonymity and confidentiality. I explained to participants that the perceived risks of being part of this qualitative research study are minimal as they are mainly engaging in a semi-structured interview at a mutually agreed-upon location. I expressed although they may feel uncomfortable having their comments from the interview analysed and published in academic journals or books, all identifying information will be removed to protect their identity and no one will be able to connect and know who they are as participants in the study.

The Interview: Location and Duration

Madison (2012) makes an important point that "as a qualitative researcher, you must consider how you enter the terrain of your subjects in ways that are appropriate, ethical, and effective" (p. 24). As a researcher, I wanted to create the least disruption to the lives of the participants given their busy family, school, and work schedules. I wanted to be accommodating and make the process as convenient as possible for the participants as they were giving up time in their busy schedules to be part of the research study without any monetary compensation. Therefore, a mutually agreed-upon location was chosen by the research participants to conduct the semi-structured interview. Six of the participants selected their home and the other two selected a school near their home as the most convenient place to conduct the interview. I travelled to the mutually agreed-upon locations with my videographer who assisted me in audio and video recording the interviews. The strength of this approach was that it allowed me to transcribe the interviews at a later point by rewatching the interviews and I would get access to visuals of participants' non-verbal cues to help me contextualize and interpret their responses. I had to work proactively to ensure my videographer was available on the same day and time as the family which was going to be interviewed. To minimize the presence of the videographer being interpreted as intrusive, parents and children were notified well in advance as part of the informed consent about the recording of the interview so they would not be surprised. The day before the interview, I called the family being interviewed to confirm time and location as well as remind them of the interview being recorded. Although initially I thought perhaps recording the interview, along with the equipment such as the microphone, might be interpreted as intrusive by the children, surprisingly it was received by interest and fascination. Numerous children asked questions about the microphone during sound checks. The camera and the microphone became a hands-on tool which seemed to engage the children and the parents as part of the interview process. The children were very enthusiastic about being recorded by the camera solo during the middle segment of the interview where the presence of the parent(s) was removed to minimize their influence on children's responses. I ensured semi-structured interviews with the child and the parent(s) were given as much time needed to gather in-depth details to the open-ended questions asked. Participants were provided with multiple opportunities to ask questions before, during, and after the interview. Overall, the interviews ranged from 45 to 60 minutes in duration.

DATA ANALYSIS

I use Green et al.'s (2007) framework for data analysis which describes four key stages to generating qualitative evidence as part of a research study. The four stages include "data immersion, coding, creating categories, and identifying themes" (p. 547). The first step is data immersion and it involves capturing the information from the semi-structured interviews in a detailed and holistic manner. This means going beyond simply transcribing the participant's responses. It involves making note of "the details that make up the interview context including hesitations, confidence in answering questions, the tone of participants as well as the shared experiences of researcher and participants" (Green et al., 2007, p. 547). Video recording of the interviews provided the opportunity to rewatch the interviews multiple times and make note of body language and tone of voice of participants when responding to the questions. Video recording of interviews would be more of a concern if researcher has no prior rapport or relationship with the interview participants. Given that I had prior rapport and a certain level of trust established with all the participants through my community connections via teaching and sports, the concern of being recorded as being intrusive was somewhat minimized.

The second stage of data analysis is coding the responses after transcription. It involves "the process of examining and organising the information contained in each interview and the whole dataset. It forces the researcher to begin to make judgements and tag blocks of transcripts" (Green et al., 2007, p. 548). Coding requires "effectively conducting a detailed, taxonomic process of sorting and tagging data" (Green et al., 2007, p. 548). I went through the participants' responses line by line and began focused coding (Clarke & Braun, 2017) and tagging the data relative to participants' identities, occupation, school demographics, neighbourhood location, and various other significant factors such as race, gender, and socio-economic status. This was a malleable process led by voices of the children and parents. I summarized the information in a chart to make the data more manageable to facilitate identification of categories and themes.

The third stage of data analysis is creation of categories and it involves grouping codes and tags by relevance and relatable connections to "categorise the ways in which research participants speak about aspects of the issue under investigation" (Green et al., 2007, p. 548). Green et al. (2007) explain, "Analytic categories are 'saturated' when there is sufficient information for the experience to be seen as coherent and explicable" (p. 548). Therefore, codes are strategically grouped based on interconnections and their ability to explain a cohesive interpretation of a series of data (Clarke & Braun, 2017). After transcription of all interviews, I reread the transcripts multiple times and grouped the identified codes into categories based on reoccurring themes expressed by participants relative to their experiences preparing and writing the Grade 3 EQAO standardized test. I further separated the emerging codes based on whether the content was expressed by the children or the parents.

The final stage of data analysis is identification of themes. It is important to acknowledge that, "A theme is more than a category. The generation of themes requires moving beyond a *description* of a range of categories; it involves shifting to an *explanation* or, even better, an *interpretation* of the issue under investigation" (Green et al., 2007, p. 548). This final step in the analysis brings together all previously explained stages to holistically produce what is known as thematic analysis (TA) (Clarke & Braun, 2017). Clarke and Braun (2017) operationalize thematic analysis as "a method for identifying, analyzing, and interpreting patterns of meaning ('themes') within qualitative data" (p. 297). They distinguish the difference between codes and themes by explaining:

> Codes are the smallest units of analysis that capture interesting features of the data (potentially) relevant to the research question. Codes are the building blocks for themes, (larger) patterns of meaning, underpinned by a central organizing concept—a shared core idea. Themes provide a framework for organizing and reporting the researcher's analytic observations. The aim of TA [thematic analysis] is not simply to summarize the data content, but to identify, and interpret, key, but not necessarily all, features of the data, guided by the research question. (p. 297)

CREDIBILITY, DEPENDABILITY, AND TRANSFERABILITY

According to Brown and Strega (2005), "Qualitative researchers see social reality as subjective, and their research practices involve observing and interpreting the meanings of social reality as various groups and individuals experience them" (p. 9). Recognizing "social reality as subjective," I used purposeful sampling to recruit research participants for semi-structured interviews. I selected participants who attend different schools and spatially live in different neighbourhoods to capture various lived experiences reflecting diversity of children and parents that make up today's classrooms in Ontario (Tollefson, 2008). In describing differences in quantitative and qualitative approaches to doing research, Creswell (2007) points out, "Instead of using quantitative terms such as 'internal validity,' 'external validity,' 'generalizability,' and 'objectivity,' the qualitative researcher may employ terms such as 'credibility,' 'transferability,' 'dependability,' and 'confirmability'" (p. 18). Using Critical Theory, specifically CRT, as my research paradigm for this exploratory qualitative study, I agree with Creswell (2007), and pursue to establish "credibility, transferability, dependability, and confirmability" as key measuring sticks for evaluating the depth and breadth of the identified research findings. In the following subsections, each of the aforementioned terms will be described in detail and further explained in how I achieved each relative to the purpose and objective of the study.

Credibility, transferability, dependability, and confirmability are inter-connected under the umbrella term "trustworthiness" of the data col-lected (Tollefson, 2008). Prior to going more in depth in discussing each of these terms, it is important to acknowledge epistemological assump-tions associated with the Critical Theory paradigm which recognizes all "knowledge as partial, multiple, situated, and subjugated" (Brown & Strega, 2005, p. 66). From this theoretical stance, "knowledge is under-stood as situated by one's social location as a result of privileges and oppression that one has experienced" (Brown & Strega, 2005, p. 66). Therefore, a key focus point of the data collected, via the semi-structured interviews, is capturing the details of the participants' lived experiences of preparing and writing the Grade 3 EQAO standardized test. As a researcher, I was not interested in judging or categorizing the participants' experiences as right, wrong, or ideal, but more interested in capturing the detailed complexities involved in each unique experience relative to the identity of each participant and other relevant factors. It was significant to document both the parents and children's perspectives as they each have a unique interpretation of their subjective experiences relative to their iden-tities and the power relations embedded within their respective schools and communities. Kincheloe and McLaren (2002) reaffirm the impor-tance of considering power relations when deconstructing lived experi-ences from a Critical Theory lens. They go on to state, "Critical research traditions have arrived at the point where they recognize that claims to truth are always discursively situated and implicated in relations of power" (p. 118).

In order to establish trustworthiness through credibility, I recruited participants through purposeful sampling. Purposeful sampling is a non-probability sampling technique whose main purpose is not random selec-tion of participants but rather conscious selection of participants as key figures who can provide insightful new perspectives towards examining a social issue or topic. Wolfer (2007) explains, "just because it [purposeful sampling] can't be generalized to a broad population doesn't' mean that the sample doesn't produce useful information" (p. 207). With respect to all the participants interviewed, I had prior rapport with either the parent(s) or the child directly through connections in the teaching community and/ or involvement via sport initiatives. As an accepted member, as an insider to a certain extent, it allowed me as a researcher to engage in more honest, open, genuine dialogical conversations with the participants as part of the semi-structured interview. This rapport and prior relationship with the participants facilitated the blurring of dichotomized binaries and its associated hierarchical power relations between the researcher and the researched (Giroux, 2007; Smith, 1999). This was exemplified by many participants feeling comfortable to invite and welcome the videographer and me into their homes to conduct the interviews. Overall, as a researcher I felt my presence was less likely perceived as a threat and the pressure on research subjects to put on a performance to appeal to my role as a researcher was somewhat minimized by having prior rapport with them.

Other strategies used to ensure credibility of the data included the use of triangulation, participant member-checks for accurate interpretation of their responses, and video recording of interviews to capture facial expressions, body language, and tone of voice for more accurate data analysis and interpretation. These strategies are not exhaustive in nature but work complementary with each other to holistically establish and increase credibility and trustworthiness of the data. Triangulation is known as using different approaches and techniques for gathering data. Key feature of triangulation is that it cross-examines events and experiences from multiple perspectives to ensure findings are credible and dependable (Wolfer, 2007). Creswell (2007) refers to triangulation as using "multiple sources of data" (p. 38). Creswell (2007) explains,

> Qualitative researchers typically gather multiple forms of data, such as interviews, observations, and documents, rather than rely on a single data source. Then the researchers review all of the data and make sense of them, organizing them into categories or themes that cut across all of the data sources. (p. 38)

One of the primary reasons for video recording the interviews was the importance of visually capturing body language, facial expressions, and tone of voice of participants as these are important unconscious indicators of communication. Being able to video record the interviews and rewatch it and compare it to notes I made during the interview assisted in more accurately interpreting the interviewee's responses relative to factors such as their mood and influence of parent(s) and the researcher being present. I recognized sometimes children looked at their parents for validation of their responses, particularly when the questions were more complex or sometimes parents tried to guide their children's unclear responses or long pauses by assisting them in finishing their thoughts. As a means of neutralizing the parental presence on the responses of the children, I divided the interview into three parts. I began the interview with the parent(s) and the child together responding to a series of questions. For the second part of the interview, I removed the parent(s) and had the child individually respond to a series of questions. I concluded the interview with the parent(s) rejoining the interview with the child. This approach to conducting the interview was important as I wanted to capture different perspectives associated with subjective experiences of preparing and writing the Grade 3 EQAO standardized test. Creswell (2007) explains, "In the entire qualitative research process, the researchers keep a focus on learning the meaning that the participants hold about the problem or issue, not the meaning that the researchers bring to the research or writers from the literature" (p. 39). Therefore, as a researcher I recognized each voice has a unique story to tell which can lead to new understandings and insights.

In order to further ensure credibility with the data collected, I conducted member-checks with the participants after completion of interviews by consulting them about my interpretation of their statements and the emerging themes. This provided an opportunity for the participants to give input, critique assumptions made by the researcher, and provide new perspectives on factors unnoticed. This was an important step in the research process from a Critical Theory paradigm as the researcher and participants co-construct reality through a collaborative approach that takes into consideration unequal power relations and tries to neutralize its impact to the extent possible. Member-checks also assist in ensuring that researcher's bias does not confound the lens of interpretation and that the voices of participants lead the discussions and findings.

Dependability in qualitative research is referred to as the reliability of the research findings and the processes involved in arriving at the findings. I concur with Tollefson (2008) that

> In a qualitative paradigm, my goal is not to isolate and control variables, ensuring that my results will be replicable in other settings. It is rather to make sure that outside readers would concur that, given the data collected, the results make sense—they are consistent and dependable. The question then is not whether findings will be found again but *whether the results are consistent with the data collected* [italics in the original]. (p. 186)

To ensure dependability as a process and outcome for this exploratory qualitative study, I began by explicitly locating myself to the participants in terms of positionality to the research topic under examination. I provided contextual information about my lived experiences and what has contributed to my gravitation towards studying the impact of standardized testing professionally and academically. Providing information about researcher positionality is vital in allowing participants and readers to judge the dependability and reliability of the study "because it forces us to acknowledge our own power, privilege, and biases just as we are denouncing the power structures that surround our subjects" (Madison, 2012, p. 8).

Locating self as a researcher relative to the research topic is a significant component of anti-oppressive research methodologies where "neutrality and objectivity do not exist in research since all research is conducted and observed through human epistemological lenses" (Brown & Strega, 2005, p. 97). Emphasizing the importance of "reflexivity" as an integral part of the research process contributing to increased reliability, Brown and Strega (2005) point out,

> By inviting researchers to consider politics of location as a serious form of enquiry, to map the ways in which we are socially and historically constituted, intertwined, and intersect with(in) the world and in relationship to subjects of our research, reflexivity requires a resistance to theoretical generalizations and monolithic truth claims. (p. 136)

From a Critical Theory stance, power embedded within relationships between the researcher and the researched have to be taken into consideration when interpreting data through reflexivity. Reflexivity requires a constant effort to find interconnections between relationships and how they are anchored by power relations in specific contexts. Madison (2012) call this "reflexive ethnography": it is a "turning back" (p. 8) on ourselves as researchers.

Pierre Bourdieu is considered one of the founders and advocates of reflexive sociology. Bourdieu and Wacquant (1992) in their book titled *An Invitation to Reflexive Sociology* explain that "Social science is reflexive in the sense that the knowledge it generates is 'injected' back into the reality it describes" (p. 37). Hence, they argue theoretical underpinnings from research should have practical implications in the lives of those researched in a manner that is empowering and emancipatory. Similarly, Paulo Freire (1970) argues that it is through "conscientization," (p. 67) a process of developing critical awareness about one's social reality through reflection and action, that objects come to see themselves as subjects beholding agency and having capacity to make a change at the micro and macro level.

Bourdieu and Wacquant (1992) outline three types of biases that "may blur the sociological gaze" (p. 39) of the researcher. These include:

a. Social origins and coordinates of the individual researcher including class, gender, ethnicity, etc.
b. Position that the analyst occupies, not in the broader social structure, but in the microcosm of the academic field; must consider relevant fields of power.
c. The intellectualist bias which entices us to construe the world as a spectacle, as a set of significations to be interpreted rather than as concrete problems to be solved practically. (p. 39)

Reflexive sociology not only entails critiquing one's own researcher bias and positionality of power and privilege but also going further to critique the larger gaze of one's academic field and its associated hegemonic theoretical claims for "truths" in interpreting and analysing data. As Bourdieu and Wacquant (1992) advocate, it is significant to break away from constructed categories that are normalized and legitimized truths within a discipline perpetuated by its "experts," and work towards analysing data from an interdisciplinary holistic lens that at times is conflicting, messy, and complex.

Transferability of a qualitative study is referred to as its external validity (Tollefson, 2008). Findings from this study contribute to filling in the research gap in the field of standardized testing on racialized and minoritized children in elementary schools. Findings from the data generate fruitful discussions from multiple perspectives that are beneficial to parents and professionals working with children in numerous capacities. The target audience includes educators in schools and community settings, administrators, parents, caregivers, early childhood educators, child and youth care workers, social workers, and researchers. Brown and Strega (2005) point out, "Research that results in social change, particularly in relation to the material realities of the participants, is considered the primary criteria of validity as long as it is emancipatory in nature" (p. 51). Transferability of findings from this study is not concerned with what positivist paradigms call "generalizability" to the larger population through random sampling, but rather what Tollefson (2008) calls "case-to-case transfer" (p. 186); that having described the processes involved in detail such as purposeful sampling and reflexivity "outside readers can determine for themselves whether my findings are of any use in their context" (p. 187).

Significance and Limitations

Although there has been research on standardized testing in Ontario, majority of the studies have been conducted at the secondary level (Hori, 2013; Kearns, 2016; Kempf, 2016; Klinger, Rogers, Anderson, Poth, & Calman, 2006; Lock, 2001; Masood, 2008; Singh, 2016; Spencer, 2006). Hence, there is a lack of research focusing on experiences of racialized Grade 3 children, parents, and educators with EQAO preparation and administration at the elementary level. Therefore, this exploratory qualitative research study seeks to arrive at news insights and understandings by providing various opportunities for the interview participants to express the extent to which EQAO preparation and administration impacts their identities and lived experiences relative to the school they attend and the community in which they live.

My research findings are relevant as they come at a critical time when on September 6, 2017, Premier of Ontario at the time Kathleen Wynne, announced the creation of a panel of experts to review and "explore ways to more effectively assess whether students in kindergarten through Grade 12 are learning the skills they need for their futures, in both the workplace and as citizens" (Gordon, 2017, para. 3). Part of this process involves "looking at the role, relevance and timing of standardized tests administered by the province as well as what parents read on their children's report cards" (Gordon, 2017, para. 4). Gordon (2017) further reports "the shakeup comes at a time of growing concern that the [education] system is too focused on EQAO tests which critics say don't broadly reflect the many skills that students need to keep learning—such as creativity and critical thinking" (para. 5). Interestingly, according to the *Public Attitudes Toward Education in Ontario 2015: The 19th OISE Survey of Educational Issues*, under the subsection "The Impact of Testing," Hart and Kempf (2015) report that "A majority [of the public and parents] think tested subjects get a lot more (37%) or somewhat more (30%) attention than subjects not tested" (p. 3). As well, "majority of the public (57%) and parents (56%) agree that if a school has good scores on province wide tests for reading, writing, and mathematics, parents should assume the school is doing a good job overall" (Hart & Kempf, 2015, p. 4).

As mentioned earlier, we are currently at a critical juncture in education, particularly with respect to the practice of EQAO testing, socially and politically. There is tension between the provincial government and EQAO with respect to whether or not to cancel the Grade 3 EQAO standardized testing as advised by the Premier's education advisors or maintain it as argued by EQAO. The concerns with the use of standardized testing in terms of its relevance and effectiveness intersects and interconnects with equity concerns associated with the achievement gap outlined in the Toronto District School Board (TDSB) report published in December 2017 titled *Enhancing Equity Task Force: Report and Recommendations* (TDSB, 2017). The TDSB *Enhancing Equity Task Force* report includes suggestions on how to create more equitable practices in the education system in various areas to address the needs of marginalized and racialized students who are underachieving. Some practical examples include investing in alternative programmes and access to resources to gain better results on EQAO scores and improvements in student achievement. Yet, although the TDSB report seeks to minimize the achievement gap, it does not critique or question the effectiveness of EQAO standardized tests as tools to measure student learning and achievement. The assumption is that EQAO standardized testing is an effective tool and the focus needs to be on improving the outcomes.

What the announcement by Premier Kathleen Wynne and the TDSB *Enhancing Equity Task Force* report emphasize is the importance of re-evaluating many current practices in education including the effectiveness of EQAO standardized testing and exploring alternative solutions to measuring accountability and improving student achievement for different social groups. This study can be part of the larger discussion about finding alternative assessment models to support racialized Grade 3 children and their parents with pressures arising from performing well on EQAO standardized tests. The findings can have larger implications for administrators and policymakers when it comes to introducing new policies, practices, and initiatives or revising current ones to support student learning from an equity lens. As Brown and Strega (2005) emphasize,

> Recognizing that knowledge is socially constructed means understanding that knowledge doesn't exist "out there" but is embedded in people and the power relations between us. It recognizes that "truth" is a verb; it is created, it is multiple: truth does not exist, it is made. Therefore, in anti-oppressive research, we are not looking for a "truth"; we are looking for meaning, for understanding, for the power to change. (p. 261)

A multi-level approach to analysing the responses of participants from the interviews goes beyond simply crunching numbers and interpreting data in a simplistic linear manner. It combines qualitative data in a dynamic, dialogical, mixed methods manner to bring to life the lived experiences of racialized children and parents impacted by EQAO standardized testing contextualized through a CRT lens that highlights internal and external challenges of the school-community interface. This interdisciplinary and holistic approach to doing anti-oppressive research allows for historicizing and contextualization of racialized children and parents' subjective experiences and it avoids homogenization of all experiences into one metanarrative.

Limitations of this study are its small sample size and that majority of families interviewed can be described as middle-class with both parents working. From an intersectionality perspective, although majority of the parents are racialized, many of them work within the education system, and can be described as middle-class based on incomes earned. This does not mean that the data collected cannot yield significant new insights and understandings about standardized testing and its impact on racialized Grade 3 children and parents, but it is important to keep these factors in mind when contextualizing the findings in relation to specific power relations. Working with different demographics and a larger sample size are areas to be considered for future research as they hold potential to shed more light into the complexities and power relations that normalize and legitimize standardized testing in elementary schools as a tool for measuring accountability.

References

Bourdieu, P., & Wacquant, L. J. (1992). *An invitation to reflexive sociology*. Chicago: University of Chicago press.

Brown, L., & Strega, S. (2005). *Research as resistance: Critical, indigenous, and anti-oppressive approaches*. Toronto, Canada: Canadian Scholars' Press.

Clarke, V., & Braun, V. (2017). Thematic analysis. *The Journal of Psychology, 12*(3), 297–298. https://doi.org/10.1080/17439760.2016.1262613

Creswell, J. W. (2007). *Qualitative inquiry and research design: Choosing among five approaches* (2nd ed.). Thousand Oaks, CA: Sage.

Dei, G. J. S. (2008). Schooling as community: Race, schooling, and the education of African youth. *Journal of Black Studies, 38*(3), 346–366.

Delgado, R., & Stefancic, J. (2000). *Critical race theory: The cutting edge*. Philadelphia: Temple University Press.

Denzin, N., & Lincoln, Y. (2000). Introduction: The discipline and practice of qualitative research. In *Handbook of qualitative research*. London: Sage Publications.

Freire, P. (1970). *Pedagogy of the oppressed*. New York: The Continuum International Publishing Group Inc.

Galletta, A. (2013). *Mastering the semi-structured interview and beyond: From research design to analysis and publication*. New York: NYU Press.

Giroux, H. (2007). Where are we now? In P. McLaren & J. Kincheloe (Eds.), *Critical Pedagogy: Where Are We Now?* New York: Peter Lang Publishing Inc..

Glesne, C. (2015). *Becoming qualitative researchers: An introduction*. Boston, MA: Pearson.

Gordon, A. (2017, September 6). Ontario to launch review of how students are tested. *Toronto Star*. Retrieved from https://www.thestar.com/news/gta/2017/09/06/ontario-to-launch-review-of-how-students-are-tested.html

Gramsci, A. (1995). *Further selections from the prison notebooks*. Minneapolis: University of Minnesota Press.

Gramsci, A. (2000). *The Gramsci reader: Selected writings, 1916–1935*. New York: NYU press.

Green, J., Willis, K., Hughes, E., Small, R., Welch, N., Gibbs, L., et al. (2007). Generating best evidence from qualitative research: The role of data analysis. *Australian and New Zealand Journal of Public Health, 31*(6), 545–550.

Hart, D., & Kempf, A. (2015). *Public attitudes toward education in Ontario 2015: The 19th OISE survey of educational issues*. OISE, University of Toronto. Retrieved from https://tspace.library.utoronto.ca/bitstream/1807/76898/2/Final_Report_-_19th_OISE_Survey_on_Educational_Issues_2015.pdf

Hori, M. M. (2013). *The Toronto District School Board & Structural Violence*. Mahad. M. Hori.

James, C. E. (2012). *Life at the intersection: Community, class and schooling*. Halifax, NS: Fernwood Publishing.

Kearns, L. (2016). The construction of 'illiterate' and 'literate' youth: The effects of high-stakes standardized literacy testing. *Race Ethnicity and Education, 19*(1), 121–140.

Kempf, A. (2016). *The pedagogy of standardized testing: The radical impacts of educational standardization in the US and Canada*. New York: Springer.

Kincheloe, J. L., & McLaren, P. (2002). Rethinking critical theory and qualitative research. In Y. Zou & H. Trueba (Eds.), *Ethnography and schools: Qualitative approaches to the study of education* (pp. 87–138). Lanham, MD: Rowman & Littlefield.

Klinger, D., Rogers, W., Anderson, J., Poth, C., & Calman, R. (2006). Contextual and school factors associated with achievement on a high-stakes examination. *Canadian Journal of Education, 29*(3), 771–797.

Knoester, M., & Au, W. (2017). Standardized testing and school segregation: Like tinder for fire? *Race Ethnicity and Education, 20*(1), 1–14.

Kumashiro, K. (2004). *Against common sense: Teaching and learning toward social justice*. New York: Routledge.

Lather, P. (1986). Research as praxis. *Harvard Educational Review, 56*(3), 257–278.

Lock, C. (2001). *The influence of a large scale assessment program on classroom practices.* (Unpublished doctoral dissertation). Queen's University, Kingston, ON.

Lopez, R. G. (2003). The (racially neutral) politics of education: A critical race theory perspective. *Educational Administration Quarterly, 39*(1), 68–94.

Madison, D. (2012). *Critical ethnography: Methods, ethics, and performance.* Thousand Oaks, CA: SAGE Publications.

Masood, O. (2008). *At risk: The racialized student marked for educational failure.* (Unpublished doctoral dissertation). University of Toronto, Toronto, ON.

McLaren, P. (2015). *Life in schools: An introduction to critical pedagogy in the foundations of education.* New York, NY: Routledge.

Pinar, W., Reynolds, W., Slattery, P., & Taubman, P. (1995). *Understanding curriculum: An introduction to the study of historical and contemporary curriculum discourses.* New York: Peter Lang Publishing, Incorporated.

Pole, C., & Morrison, M. (2003). *Ethnography for education.* Maidenhead: Open University Press.

Singh, S. (2016). *Critical discourse analysis: The impact the Ontario Secondary School Literacy Test has on ESL teachers' teaching practices and work environments.* Doctor of Education thesis, Faculty of Graduate Studies, University of Calgary, Calgary, Alberta.

Smith, L. (1999). *Decolonizing methodologies: Research and indigenous peoples.* London: Zed Books Ltd.

Spencer, B. (2006). *The will to accountability: Reforming education through standardized literacy testing.* (Unpublished doctoral dissertation). University of Toronto, Toronto, ON.

Spivak, G. C. (1988). Can the subaltern speak? Reflections on the history of an idea. In C. Nelson & L. Grossberg (Eds.), *Marxism and the interpretation of culture* (pp. 21–78). London: Macmillan.

Tollefson, K. (2008). *Volatile knowing: Parents, teachers, and the censored story of accountability in America's public schools.* Lanham, MD: Lexington Books.

Toronto District School Board. (2017). *Enhancing equity task force: Report and recommendations.* Toronto. Retrieved from http://www.tdsb.on.ca/Portals/0/community/docs/EETFReportPdfVersion.pdf

Trevino, J., Harris, M., & Wallace, W. (2008). What's so critical about critical race theory? *Contemporary Justice Review, 11*(1), 7–10.

Weiner, E. (2014). *Deschooling the imagination: Critical thought as social practice.* Boulder, CO: Paradigm Publishers.

Wolfer, L. (2007). *Real research: Conducting and evaluating research in the social sciences.* Boston, MA: Pearson Education Inc.

CHAPTER 8

Invisible Scars and Traumatizing Effects of Standardized Testing: Voices of Grade 3 Children, Parents, and Educators

EQAO provides many documents on their website (http://www.eqao. com/en/) available for the public to download to inform them about the agency, its goals, objectives, and findings from EQAO student achievement results. Within the recently EQAO-produced document titled *Highlights of the Provincial Results* (2017) for the 2016–2017 school year, there is a sub-section which outlines the overall objective of EQAO tests. It states,

> EQAO's tests measure student achievement in reading, writing and mathematics in relation to *Ontario Curriculum* expectations. The resulting data provide accountability and a gauge of quality in Ontario's publicly funded education system. By providing this important evidence about learning, EQAO acts as a catalyst for increasing the success of Ontario students. (p. 4)

This exploratory qualitative research study with its focus on Grade 3 EQAO standardized testing within Ontario schools seeks to further explore and examine the extent which narratives told from the perspective of racialized children, parents, and educators interviewed support or oppose the dominant narrative disseminated by EQAO about the benefits and effectiveness of EQAO standardized tests for "accountability outcomes."

The main research question explores, "What are the experiences, opinions, and concerns of racialized children, parents, and educators regarding how the EQAO standardized test impacts their identity, family, school and the larger surrounding community in which they live?" Voices of the

© The Author(s) 2019
A. Eizadirad, *Decolonizing Educational Assessment*,
https://doi.org/10.1007/978-3-030-27462-7_8

children and parents interviewed can shed light on how to make education more equitable in a manner that would meet the unique needs of racialized children and parents given their circumstances and neighbourhood living conditions. By examining participants' voices and experiences, we can better understand and further explore the short- and long-term effects of institutional policy enactment related to preparation and administration of EQAO standardized tests in elementary schools.

The interviews with the participants were conducted between June and August 2017 at mutually agreed locations through purposeful sampling involving my community connections via teaching and sports. Children interviewed wrote the EQAO test in their respective schools from May 23 to June 5, 2017. It was important to interview the children shortly after having written the test to capture more clearly and with more depth details about their experiences as waiting longer to conduct interviews had the potentiality of them forgetting details about their experiences. Overall, I interviewed five male and three female children as participants along with their respective parent(s). Each student attended a different public school geographically. Hence, no two students attended the same school. Each interview ranged between 45 and 60 minutes in duration. Questions asked were organized thematically focusing on before, during, and after writing the EQAO standardized test. Interviews were conducted at a mutually agreed-upon location that was convenient for the participants: six were conducted at participant's homes and two at a nearby school.

BIOGRAPHICAL SKETCH OF PARTICIPANTS

In the following subsection, some background information about each interview and participant is provided including some of the conversations that took place. The conversations presented in this section are descriptive in nature and without analysis. The objective is to provide some biographical information about the children and their parent(s) in order to get to know them better in terms of their identity, personalities, and circumstances. Pseudonyms are given to the participants to ensure confidentiality.

Laila

Laila was born in January 2008 and at the time of the interview was ten years old. She self-identifies as female and a visible racialized person. She has a white mother who is an elementary school teacher and an African father who is a businessman that travels frequently. Laila was born in Canada and speaks English and French. She attends a Catholic public school located in the southwest downtown region of Toronto which offers classes from Kindergarten to Grade 6. The school is located within a neighbourhood associated with affluent higher socio-economic status. It is a uniformed school where students have to wear a combination of white and navy blue garments. Laila does not like having to wear a uniform to school as she cannot choose whatever she wants when getting ready for school. On the other hand, her mother thinks uniforms are great as it makes getting ready for school easier with fewer decisions to be made in the mornings. Laila is enrolled in the French Immersion programme and as a result only had to write the Mathematics component of the Grade 3 EQAO standardized test. Laila has a female teacher and there are approximately 20 students in her class. Laila's favourite subjects are art, gym, and science and her least favourite subject is writing. When asked what she likes about school, she stated, "the fact that I have many friends." When asked what she doesn't like about school, she stated "I feel at times I am being more excluded compared to other years." I was able to recruit Laila as a research participant having previously taught at a school where her mother was also a teacher. The interview took place at Laila's place of residence which is a house with her mother present.

Deshaun

Deshaun was born in May 2008 and at the time of the interview was nine years old. He self-identifies as male and a visible racialized person having parents that are from Jamaica and Saint Vincent and the Grenadines. His mother is a chef and his father is unemployed. Deshaun was born in Canada and only speaks English. He attends a public school in the northwest region of Toronto which offers classes from Kindergarten to Grade 5. The school is located within a neighbourhood associated with low socio-economic status. Deshaun has a female teacher and there are approximately 20 students in his class. His favourite subject is math and his least favourite subject is reading because "it takes too long." Deshaun's hobbies and interests are riding his bike and scooter, playing outside, and going to the park to play games. When asked what he likes about school, he responded "that I get recess and I get to learn." When asked whether he likes his teacher he responded, "a little bit." Deshaun explained that "Her voice could be better. She yells a lot because the students keep fooling around." In response to what she likes about the school Deshaun attends, his mother stated, "I like that they are very adamant about the children being there present and not late for school. I like the fact that they have meetings that involve the community and they have fundraisers. I like that they have Future Aces program there, breakfast club, and after school programs." I was able to recruit Deshaun as a research participant having previously known his mother through community events in their neighbourhood associated with sports. The interview took place at Deshaun's place of residence which is a government subsidized housing complex provided by Toronto Community Housing Corporation. The interview was conducted on the balcony with his mother present.

Jordan

Jordan was born in December 2008 and at the time of the interview was nine years old. He self-identifies as male and a visible racialized person born to second-generation Canadian Caribbean parents. He lives with his mother and step-father; they recently got married. Jordan's mother works with the school board as an Education Resource Facilitator (ERF) at an elementary school and his step-father works as an elementary school teacher. They work at different schools. Jordan was born in Canada and speaks English and a little bit of French. He attends a public school in the southeast region of Toronto which offers classes from Kindergarten to Grade 5. He changed schools at the start of Grade 3. In response to why they changed schools, his mother explained,

> He particularly had a rough time when he first started school. He was actually in the French Immersion program to begin with, and he wasn't doing well, not because of the program itself, but he was having a lot of behavioural difficulties. We decided to take him out hoping that maybe that was why he was frustrated taking both French and English. He started to do a bit better, but we found once he is in the school he is at now, which is a smaller school, more of a community where everyone knows you and all the teachers know all the students, he is doing a lot better and he hasn't had as much difficulties in school compared to when he was in a much larger school.

Jordan's current school is located within a neighbourhood associated with mixed socio-economic status; certain pockets within the neighbourhood are high socio-economic status whereas other pockets are low socio-economic status. Jordan is in a split Grade 2/3 class which has both Grade

2 and Grade 3 students learning together in one class. He has a female teacher and there are approximately 24 students in his class. His favourite subject is computers and his least favourite subject is art. In response to why he doesn't like art, Jordan stated, "Because you get dirty sometimes, and sometimes if you make a mess, most of the class is so tired to clean up, we don't wanna clean up." When asked about his experiences at the two different schools, Jordan responded "I like my new school. I like how we have three recesses and the third recess is longer. In my old school we would have computer lab for a short amount of time. At my new school we have computer lab for a long time, for a whole period until lunch." I was able to recruit Jordan as a research participant having previously known his step-father through community events in their neighbourhood associated with sports. The interview took place at Jordan's place of residence which is a house with his mother and step-father present.

Kobe

Kobe was born in December 2008 and at the time of the interview was nine years old. He self-identifies as male and a visible racialized person born to second-generation Canadian parents who have Caribbean and English roots. His mother is an elementary school principal and his father is a newly promoted middle school vice-principal. They work at different schools. Kobe was born in Canada and speaks English and some French. Kobe has an older brother as a sibling who is currently in high school. Kobe attends a public school in the west region of Toronto which offers classes from Kindergarten to Grade 8. The school is located within a neighbourhood associated with upper-middle to high socio-economic status. When asked what he likes about school, Kobe stated, "I like my friends. Everyone seems pretty friendly. I like the teachers and I like gym!" In response to what he dislikes about school, Kobe stated, "I like to play a lot of stuff at home which I can't play with at school like board games and car games." Kobe's favourite subject is gym and his least favourite subject is language, specifically writing. Kobe's hobbies and interests are soccer, basketball, baseball, and badminton. In response to what they like and dislike about the school Kobe attends, his mother stated, "Because he is a French Immersion student he has two teachers. One day he gets the English teacher and the next day he has the French teacher. His French teacher is strong in terms of engagement and types of assessment she does. The English teacher I didn't find as strong. They sort of have a disjointed math program, so I think it is ok but I wouldn't rave about it." Kobe's father expanded by stating, "One of the things we found is that the reading program is really weak, like it took them at least six or seven months to be able to identify what level he [Kobe] was reading at. Long time!" I was able to recruit Kobe as a research participant having previously known his father through a community grassroots non-profit educational organization we were both involved with in the Jane and Finch community. The interview took place at Kobe's place of residence which is a house with his mother and father present.

Madison

Madison was born in August 2008 and at the time of the interview was nine years old. She self-identifies as female and white being born to Canadian parents. She was born in Canada and speaks English and some French. Madison lives with her mother in a single-parent household and has an older sister as a sibling who is two years older than her. Her mother is divorced and works as a self-employed consultant. Madison attends a public school located in Oakville which offers classes from Kindergarten to Grade 8. The school is located within a neighbourhood associated with upper-middle class to high socio-economic status. Madison is in a split Grade 2/3 class which has both Grade 2 and Grade 3 students learning together in one class. She has a female teacher and there are approximately 24 students in her class. When asked what she likes and dislikes about Madison's school, her mother stated,

> I thought Madison's teacher was very caring and interested in doing the right things for her students. They had a split grade so a 2/3 split grade. That's the second year in a row that Madison has been in a split grade and I think that can cause challenges in terms of, you know, learning and getting through the curriculum. I think the school tries to teach the curriculum. I know they have an EA [Educational Assistant] in the class to help with the class size and the challenges they have.

Madison has an Individual Education Plan (IEP). I inquired how long Madison has had an IEP and what kind of accommodations she receives. Her mother explained, "She has had it for a little over a year. It changed a bit this year. We've found some things that work a little bit better. She got her own computer this year for dictating." She went on to explain,

Madison does a lot more self-directed learning than most of the other students so she spends a lot of time on the computer and they've given Madison her own computer with a dictation device so she can do her journals and what not. Also some ear phones for external noise. Bright lights bother her too.

Madison's favourite subject is math. Her least favourite subjects are language, art, and gym because as she explains, "I'm not really … like … I am not an artist and I don't like going to gym because it's always so loud and every single time I go to gym I always get a headache before I go there because everybody in my class is like really loud." When asked what she likes about school Madison stated,

> I like having a lot of friends and playing with them and I like umm having indoor recesses because it's really fun and because me and my friend we always play this Penguin game and it's like Connect 4 and it's really fun. I like learning about math because math is my favourite strength in school and umm I like it because it's my favourite thing and I like counting money and I like making patterns and we do puzzles.

When asked about her hobbies and interests Madison stated,

> Mostly going on the computer playing Dreambox and sometimes Scratch. I normally play ball or like basketball and soccer but I've been roofing lots of them so we barely have any balls. Outside of school, I like playing with my bike and with my babysitter because she is so much fun. Oh ya and I got a new skateboard and I'm starting to learn how to do that!

I was able to recruit Madison as a research participant having previously known her mother through community events in their neighbourhood associated with sports. The interview took place at Madison's place of residence which is a house with her mother present.

Malcolm

Malcolm was born in December 2008 and at the time of the interview was nine years old. He self-identifies as male and a visible racialized person as his mother is Trinidadian and his father is Nigerian. He lives with his mother and step-father. His mother is an eye-specialist assistant. His step-father is Jamaican and an elementary school teacher. Malcolm was born in

Canada and speaks English and a little bit of Spanish. He has a one-year old sister as a sibling. He attends a public school in the west region of Toronto which offers classes from Kindergarten to Grade 5. Malcolm's school is located within a neighbourhood associated with middle-class socio-economic status. Malcolm has a male teacher. His favourite subject is math "because it's easy." His least favourite subject is science. When asked what he likes about school, Malcolm explained, "It's fun and they have games that we can play and they have math that I like." Expanding on what he does not like about school, Malcolm stated, "Most people they don't do what the teacher says. Sometimes I actually tell them to stop so we can play a game or something." Malcolm's hobbies and interests are playing video games, taking care of his sister, and playing the piano. In response to what's his opinion of the school Malcolm attends, his step-father stated,

> This year his teacher is a male teacher. It's the first time his teacher is a male from a South Asian background. His teacher was very interested in Malcolm. He always wanted to figure out what Malcolm is doing and why he is doing things so he was in contact with us as the parents very often almost on a weekly basis. The teacher also called us during report card time so this year is very good. He was very involved and it seems like he really cares about Malcolm's education and he helped him a lot with his grades and it was reflected when he got his report card.

I was able to recruit Malcolm as a research participant having previously known his step-father through community events in their neighbourhood associated with teaching and sports. The interview took place at a nearby school site with his step-father present.

Christopher

Christopher was born in April 2008 and at the time of the interview was nine years old. He self-identifies as male and a visible racialized person. His mother is Ecuadorian and works as a dental assistant and his father is Jamaican. He lives with both his parents and has a younger brother and an older sister as siblings. Christopher was born in Canada and speaks English and a little bit of Spanish. He attends a public school in the northwest region of Toronto which offers classes from Kindergarten to Grade 5. Christopher's school is located within a neighbourhood associated with mixed socio-economic status; certain pockets within the neighbourhood are middle class whereas other pockets are affiliated with lower socio-economic status. Christopher has a female teacher and is in a split 3/4 class which has both Grade 3 and Grade 4 students learning together in one class. There are approximately 21 students in his class. His favourite subject is math and his least favourite subject is language. When asked what he likes about school, Christopher stated, "We get to play and then we get games and teachers who help us and all that." Expanding on what he dislikes about school, Christopher stated, "We don't get nap time like in Kindergarten." Christopher's hobbies and interests are playing basketball and playing with his younger brother. In response to what she likes about Christopher's school, his mother stated, "I like that they have a strong community and I like that the staff, they try to communicate as much as possible with the parents, so it's very high communication." I was able to recruit Christopher as a research participant having previously taught him in an alternative summer school programme he was enrolled in. The interview took place at a nearby school site with his mother present.

Chantel

Chantel was born in July 2008 and at the time of the interview was nine years old. She self-identifies as female and a visible racialized person born to second-generation Canadian parents with Caribbean roots. She was born in Canada and speaks only English. She has a younger brother as a sibling. Chantel lives with her mother in a single-parent household. Her mother is unemployed and a stay-at-home mother, but in the summer she worked seasonally as a camp counsellor in downtown Toronto. Chantel attends a public school located in North York area of Toronto which offers classes from Kindergarten to Grade 6. The school is located within a neighbourhood associated with high socio-economic status. Chantel is in a split 2/3 class which has both Grade 2 and Grade 3 students learning together in one class. There are approximately 30 students in her class. She has a female teacher and it's the same teacher she had in Grade 1. Chantel has an Individual Education Plan which was initiated at the beginning of Grade 3 by her current teacher. When asked what she likes and dislikes about Chantel's school, her mother stated,

> It's a good school. Her teacher really cares about her education. Her Grade 2 teacher didn't really. Not to say she didn't care but she didn't really take an interest, but nonetheless, she's been there for the last 3 years. So yea, it's

a good school. The community is more of a richer school. We live around a lot of rich people so they help a lot in the community. They give back to the school and as a single mother if I can't do something for them then the school is more than welcome to help with all of that.

Contrasting Chantel's Grade 2 and Grade 3 teachers, Chantel's mother expressed,

Her Grade 2 teacher did not really focus the way her Grade 3 teacher does. Chantel was having trouble with certain things in Grade 1 and that teacher tried to get me involved with her education, because I'm like so for education, so she tried to get me to help so I assumed that because she was really good at keeping up with that her next teacher would be too. Her Grade 2 teacher never really spoke to me about Chantel's education. I would always ask her how Chantel is doing and she would just say she's fine, that's it. She would never tell me any details or whatever, so when the report cards came home, it never made any sense, whereas in Grade 3 I am getting weekly updates from her teacher.

Chantel's favourite subject is gym. Her least favourite subject is math. Her hobbies and interests are watching television, playing soccer, doing cartwheels around the house, skipping, and playing with her younger brother. I was able to recruit Chantel as a participant having previously taught Chantel in an alternative summer school programme she was enrolled in. The interview took place at Chantel's place of residence which is a government subsidized housing complex provided by Toronto Community Housing Corporation with her mother present.

THEMES AND FINDINGS

After transcribing the interviews, I identified eight findings based on the reemerging themes. Themes were separated based on whether it was the children or parents' perspective as well based on timing relative to before, during, and after writing the EQAO test. The eight reemerging themes are:

- Fear of failure
- Relevance of the test
- Importance of the tests
- Timing of the test
- Type of feedback provided and when it is given

- Assessment for improvement
- Impact on teacher pedagogy and delivery of the curriculum
- Limited definition of success

In the remainder of this and the next chapter, these themes are explained thoroughly under various findings. Directly following the explanation of each finding, various major affiliated components are discussed which include implications and recommendations. Although the findings and implications are presented separately, it is significant to note they are holistically interconnected and impact each other directly and indirectly through a domino effect.

Finding #1

Most children experienced high intensity socio-emotionally induced stress and anxiety subjectively attributing it to fear of failure and poor performance. The level of stress and anxiety was so severe in some cases that the child could not sleep the night before the test or refused entering the classroom on test day to participate in writing the EQAO test.

One of the most reoccurring themes that emerged from the interviews with the Grade 3 children was the induced stress and anxiety they experienced from the socio-emotional impact of preparing for the EQAO test from the start of the school year to when they had to write it in late May or early June. Children recognized the importance of the test as constant references were made to it starting from September by teachers and administrators in their respective schools to ensure they were prepared for the EQAO test. Common preparation techniques experienced by children interviewed were doing practice questions in class with reference to EQAO expectations, completing EQAO booklets from previous years as practice, and receiving informational school letters intended for their parents emphasizing importance of the children being available to participate in writing the EQAO test. The informational letters also outlined various tips to assist parents in ensuring their child is optimally ready to partake in the test. Examples of suggestions for the parents included packing healthy snacks and ensuring children go to bed early the night before the testing.

When asked what was different in Grade 3 compared to Grade 2, Deshaun explicitly stated "The EQAO test." When I further probed by asking how does the EQAO test make it different, Deshaun explained,

"It's because we didn't have something that hard in Grade 1 or 2." Similarly, in response to the same question about differences in Grade 3 compared to Grade 2, Kobe stated that "nothing was different except for the EQAO." Kobe further explained, "I have never done a test that big, like that long." These responses indicate that the children felt that the EQAO standardized test was a major event they participated in. From their subjective viewpoints, the EQAO test in its length, format, structure, and time allocated to prepare for it was drastically different compared to their other routine experiences in school.

Although students were reminded by their teachers and school administrators, and at times by their parents, that the EQAO test did not impact their report card marks or advancement to Grade 4, the emphasis that was placed on the importance of the test in terms of constant reference to it and the amount of time dedicated to preparing for it, created the unintended consequence of placing extensive pressure on the children to do well. Children expressed they felt that the EQAO test was an indicator, similar to a thermometer, of how smart they were and to what extent they had mastered the curriculum content they had learned up to that point in their life in Reading, Writing, and Mathematics. Children further explained they felt pressured to do well to justify their identity as smart, worrying that if they did poor they are judged by their peers and it would be representative of their families, teacher, school, and community. Hence, most students stated being highly anxious and even scared about writing the test due to fear of failure. In one extreme case, Jordan would not enter the class on the first day of EQAO testing to participate in writing the test because he was feeling scared and nervous. The school administrators had to call Jordan's mother to speak to him over the phone to calm his nerves and reassure him that he is not going to be judged regardless of how he does. Jordan's mother explained the incident;

> On the first day he wouldn't go to class and the school ended up having to call me to help out the situation. It did help. It was just reassuring him not to worry too much and just do his best. As the week went on, he did start to loosen up and not be so worried or stressed about it.

After hearing reassuring words from his mother, Jordan felt somewhat comfortable enough to walk into the classroom willingly and participate in writing the EQAO test. When asked about the reasoning for not wanting to enter the classroom, Jordan stated,

I felt nervous and scared. I didn't know if it's gonna go on my report card or not. I felt it's gonna go on my report card so I didn't wanna go to class cause if I got most of my answers wrong, I would have to do Grade 3 all over again.

Similarly, I asked other children how they felt during EQAO testing week, particularly on the first day of testing. Christopher stated, "The first day of the test I felt very nervous." When asked to rate the intensity of his emotions on a scale of one to ten, with one being not nervous at all and ten being extremely nervous, Christopher expressed an eight. Another child who expressed experiencing severe anxiety and anxiousness was Madison who has an IEP. As part of her IEP accommodations, she often engages in self-directed learning with help from an Educational Assistant (EA) in the classroom. Madison receives her own computer from the school which has a dictation program that assists her in writing and doing her homework such as journal responses. She is also allowed to wear headphones in class to tune out external noise as loud noises and bright lights give her headaches. In regard to how she felt about the EQAO test, Madison stated, "I felt like (pause) really really really worried and um (pause) I kinda felt like a little bit frustrated with all the pressure I had to do, like, I never had to do that much work in one day."

Madison expresses that compared to other routine activities she does in the classroom, she "never had to do that much work in one day," having to complete various EQAO booklets within a limited allocated time. She explained this drastically differs from her routine experience in school where she learns at her own pace as a form of accommodation. I followed up by asking Madison who is putting pressure on her to do well on the test. Madison stated, "One of my (pause) Ms. Alvi, cause she's telling me you have to do this and that, and all at the same time, and I can't, like I can't do all that at the same time." Madison was frustrated with the change in her routine schedule and the expectations that she had to complete a certain amount of work within a limited allocated time. Madison's mother put things into perspective by further explaining Madison's identified exceptionalities and the support services she receives from the school and her teachers;

> I think Madison gets lots of flexibility at school in terms of, you know, if she needs to stop doing something, she can do something different. She does a lot of self-directed learning. So to have to actually sit and do something that is different, I think there is a lot of pressure there.

In order to better understand the magnitude of pressure Madison felt, I asked her to rate her level of anxiousness having to write the EQAO test on a scale of one to ten, with one being not anxious at all and ten being extremely anxious. She expressed loudly, "10 out of 10!" I followed up by asking Madison's mother to explain what she observed in Madison in terms of changes in emotions or behaviours leading up to EQAO testing week. At this point in the interview, Madison eagerly wanted to jump in and respond to the question first before her mother. Madison expressed,

> So I've been having a lot of emotions to the EQAO (pause) like I've been having a lot of problems with it, because I was really worried because I was not sure if I am going to be passing it or not. Like (pause) I am not used to getting so much work in one day because we have to do it until 5th period and we only have one period off but after when I was done, I felt much better.

Madison's mom further expanded and contextualized her response by explaining,

> Madison worries so we work through some anxiety pieces there. When something is a little bit different, you know, it really affects her so she thought about it a lot at nighttime and worrying about it coming up. I think because of how much prep work they did with her to umm help her be successful in her testing (pause) umm it became, you know, a big deal at the school and it became a big deal to Madison too. She worried about it a lot at nighttime.

With regard to administration of EQAO tests, Madison and other students with similar exceptionalities associated with writing difficulties are often taken out of their regular classroom and placed into a separate room where they work one on one with another teacher or EA to complete the EQAO test booklets. With Madison, the EA read out the questions to her, followed by Madison responding orally and her EA transcribing and writing her responses into the EQAO booklet for her. Madison explained this process was very frustrating as she was worried and nervous about communicating clearly.

When asked, how is the EQAO test similar or different to other things she does in school, Madison said, "I couldn't understand why it's here [on the test] when I haven't done it yet." It appeared that the entire experience from the preparation to the lead up and administration of the test, on multiple levels, was traumatizing for Madison as it had caused her to experience severe intense negative emotions such as anger, frustration, and sadness associated with worrying about doing poorly on the test and fear of failure and being judged as not smart. This was exemplified when I asked Madison how she felt after finishing writing the EQAO test, which she quickly with enthusiasm and a big smile stated, "I felt happy that it was over and that I didn't have to do it anymore!"

Other Grade 3 children interviewed had similar responses in describing their emotions leading up to the test and during the week EQAO tests were administered. When asked how she felt emotionally on a scale of one to ten, with one being not nervous at all and ten being extremely nervous, Chantel who also has an IEP, responded "a 9 because I thought I was gonna fail." Once again, the negative emotions experienced were associated with fear of failure and the imaginative perceived consequences that can arise from doing poorly. This can be attributed to the EQAO test being highly emphasized and extensively made references to throughout the school year by teachers and administrators starting from September. This is not to infer that all teachers and administrators are in favour of the test, but they work within the power dynamics affiliated with standardized testing policy enactment which gives importance to school EQAO results. This translates into pressure placed upon teachers and administrators to improve EQAO test scores to avoid being labelled as a "bad" school that offers poor-quality education. Hence, even though children are reminded by their teachers and parents that their performance on EQAO tests does not impact their report card marks or advancement to Grade 4, the atmosphere around the importance of the test contributes to children feeling extremely pressurized, anxious, nervous, and scared about doing poorly and failing.

I wanted to go beyond simply identifying the emotions felt by the children as they prepared and participated in writing the EQAO test. I was also interested in what they thought of the test in terms of its format, structure, and relevance as often their voices are not heard in a meaningful constructive manner as part of policy development due to their young age. I asked Chantel what she liked about the EQAO test, which she responded by stating, "Um … nothing!" causing her mother and her to burst into laughter. As a follow-up, I asked what she didn't like about the test which she stated, "Everything. It was everything. I don't like EQAO because it's boring. All you ever do is sit there with a pencil and answer questions." In gauging the relevance of the test, I asked Christopher to rate the effectiveness of the test in helping him as a student on a scale of one to ten which he expressed, "To be honest, a 2, because it's not like it's gonna go on your report card or something." With Christopher, because he recognized it did not impact his report card mark, he perceived the EQAO test as less relevant. I wondered whether his perception of the lack of influence of the test on his report card mark had any impact on how much effort he put into completing the test. Similarly, I asked Kobe how the test helped him and if so in what ways, which he responded, "Not really." Malcolm described the test as "boring." When asked what he would change about the test if he had the power to do so, Malcolm expressed, "Umm I would change a few things like I would actually make it more fun and more colourful so they could do the test quickly and they don't get bored doing it."

From the above aforementioned responses from the children describing the EQAO test, it can be inferred that most did not find the EQAO test engaging or highly relevant in helping them. Descriptive words such as "bored" and "boring" were commonly used by many of the children interviewed to refer to length and format of the test which is predominantly multiple choice, true or false, and short answer questions. Laila expressed that although she was excited about doing the test, those feelings changed quickly once she began the test. Laila explained, "It [feelings of excitement] died after a few minutes, (pause) after like 30 minutes, because it got harder and harder every question I did." Laila's excitement diminished quickly due to difficulty of the questions on the EQAO test which consequentially impacted her self-confidence. Her sense of excitement was replaced with feeling nervous, anxious, and worried about doing poorly and failing.

Implications

Responses of the Grade 3 children interviewed in terms of what they expressed as negative socio-emotionally induced stress, anxiety, and fear of failure associated with writing the EQAO test confirms and aligns with what The National Center for Fair and Open Testing (FairTest) identifies as negative harmful effects of using standardized testing on young children impacting their "healthy development and learning" (FairTest, 2017, p. 1). Examples of negative physical and psychological impacts expressed by the interviewed children included losing sleep by worrying about doing poorly, experiencing overwhelming anxiety and nervousness demonstrated by crying and needing reassurance from loved ones such as parents to enter the classroom to take the EQAO test, feeling excluded by being taken out of the regular classroom to prepare for and write the EQAO test, and fear of failure and being labelled as "dumb." Majority of the children perceived writing the EQAO test as a significant event compared to their other routine academic experiences in school due to constant references made to it and the amount of pressure they felt to do well on the test. Regardless of what the children were told about the non-impact of the test on their marks and advancement to Grade 4, majority of them did not believe it, demonstrated by their fear of failure and their own subjective perceived consequences associated with doing poorly on the test such as having to do Grade 3 all over again.

The socio-emotional impact of preparing and writing the Grade 3 EQAO test does not stop as soon as the last EQAO booklet is completed and the pencil is requested to be placed down once the allocated time has finished. We are naive to assume that is the case since events in life that arouse severe negative emotions typically have long-lasting impact later into life (Curtis, Livingstone, & Smaller, 1992; Eizadirad, 2016; James, 2012; Ontario Ministry of Education, 2014). With respect to young children, Ontario Ministry of Education document (2014) *How Does Learning Happen? Ontario's Pedagogy for the Early Years* emphasizes, "positive experiences in early childhood set the foundation for lifelong learning, behaviour, health and well-being" (p. 10), and "high-quality early childhood programs recognize the connection between emotional well-being and social and cognitive development and the importance of focusing on these holistically" (p. 11). Hence, the severe intense emotions experienced by racialized Grade 3 children writing the EQAO test in a highly pressurized environment can have a negative impact on their social and emotional development, particularly in the early years. EQAO standardized tests function under homogenizing assumptions focusing exclusively on outcomes. The assumption is that all children should attain a certain level of achievement by the end of Grade 3 regardless of their unique identities and individualistic developmental needs and life circumstances.

The responses of children and parents interviewed, as a collective, expresses that there are more long-term effects associated with writing EQAO standardized tests. I label these long-term negative effects associated with preparing and writing externally administered standardized tests at a young age under the umbrella term *invisible scars and traumatizing effects of standardized testing*. Although it is easier to identify temporary physical displays of stress and anxiety experienced by children during

EQAO testing week and leading up to it, long-term socio-emotional, spiritual, and psychological impact of doing poorly on standardized tests is not visible until later as we actively listen to students' narratives about their experiences and explore the domino effect on their identity development and larger school experiences associated with their level of self-confidence, amount of effort they put into completing tasks, and overall level of engagement with school activities and initiatives.

One of the implications of placing such high importance on EQAO tests and doing well on them is the rise of test-taking anxiety amongst young children which can have a spill-over effect into the rest of their lives later on as they mature and attend high school and post-secondary institutions. If students do not feel great about themselves, in terms of their self-confidence as a result of doing poorly on a standardized test specially in the early years, it can lead to "a self-fulfilling prophecy on continuing lower achievement" (Ontario Teachers' Federation, 2011, p. 10) self-identifying as "dumb" or not as smart compared to their peers. This can occur at two stages: immediately after completion of the test based on their subjective self-perception of how they did on the test relative to how difficult they found the questions, and at the start of Grade 4 when they receive their EQAO results back and it does not align with how well they thought they did retrospectively and in comparison to their peers. Kobe's mother who is an elementary school principal states,

> Imagine, these kids get their results in Grade 4 and no one ever has a conversation about the results. So you have a child who might get a Level 1 who will now feel like "oh I am probably not very smart" and the parents might think that "my child is not very smart" depending on how they interpret it. That's not constructive, ever!

The negative psychological and emotional impact from receiving poor results on EQAO standardized tests can consequentially lead to lack of motivation, reduced effort in completing tasks, and simply not caring about school-related activities such as assigned homework. This can become part of a vicious cycle that perpetuates the "self-fulfilling prophecy" where the young child is labelled as "at risk" by the education system because they continuously fail to achieve the benchmark of excellence constructed by Ministry of Education standards. Russo (2012) makes an important developmental argument stating, "By placing unrealistic demands upon children who are not developmentally ready, we are asking teachers to spend most of their time attempting to push children in ways that may set them up to fail" (pp. 143–144). The problem may not be that the child is not knowledgeable, but rather that EQAO standardized test, as a medium and in its format, is not congruent with providing an effective avenue for all children relative to their developmental stage to optimally express what they know. As a result, "testing may make children feel 'dumb' especially when tested on materials that are developmentally inappropriate" (FairTest, 2017, p. 1). As Stiggins (2014), an assessment expert, argues "Branding them [children] with unflattering labels, as our assessment systems often do, is unwise, unfair, counterproductive, and harmful" (p. 9).

If schools are going to continue with the use of standardized testing on young children in elementary schools, we as caring and concerned adults in our various roles and capacities need to work towards mitigating the *invisible scars and traumatizing scars of standardized testing*. One approach is investment in mental health and mindfulness initiatives to help children express how they feel, process, and express their emotions constructively, and utilize positive coping mechanisms as outlets for stress, anxiety, and fear of failure induced from preparing and writing highly anticipated and publicized tests such as the Grade 3 EQAO test. We need a culture change beyond simply judging students' intellectual and academic competencies based on outcome-based standardized tests towards a more holistic interdisciplinary approach which takes into consideration their physical, social, emotional, spiritual, and psychological development. As Miller (2000) puts it, "In the mechanical school the focus is on testing and grades, often at the expense of learning. The learning in the soulful school, however, is holistic learning that integrates body, mind, emotions, and spirit" (p. 110). We need to strive to create more soulful schools to meet the needs of all children, particularly paying attention to the unique experiences of racialized children with standardized testing and its harmful effects.

Having documented some of the negative impacts of the Grade 3 EQAO standardized testing on children socio-emotionally, as expressed through their voices, the critical question we must further explore is whether the current way the Grade 3 EQAO test is prepared for and administered is helping children or hindering them in their holistic development and objective of achieving their full potential? More specifically, who is benefiting from the current EQAO standardized testing practices and who is marginalized and oppressed, and specifically in what ways? These questions will further be explored in the upcoming subsections of this chapter to gain a better understanding of the larger impact of EQAO test preparation and administration on other stakeholders in education.

Recommendations

I therefore recommend school boards and schools to immediately invest in mitigating the documented short- and long-term *invisible scars and traumatizing effects of standardized testing* by investing in more mental health and mindfulness initiatives. This will facilitate positive socio-emotional development in children from a young age and increase their emotional intelligence which includes children learning to acknowledge what emotions they are experiencing and why, how to process and express their emotions constructively, and how to use positive coping mechanisms as outlets to mitigate the stress, anxiety, and fear of failure associated with test-taking.

I therefore recommend school boards and schools to invest in creating more avenues and mediums, such as focus groups and online surveys, to engage children participating in writing EQAO standardized tests to express how they are socio-emotionally, spiritually, and psychologically impacted by the process before, during, and after writing the tests. The post-impact examination should have a special one-year time frame, particularly exploring the direct impact on children's identities when they receive their EQAO results in Grade 4.

I therefore recommend school boards and schools to invest in tracking cohort of students through longitudinal and intersectional studies administered by third-party external organizations to further explore the impact of standardized testing on young children relative to contextual factors including race, geography, gender, socio-economic status, teacher pedagogy, and access to support services. Data generated will provide more holistic insightful findings in terms of how specific identities are impacted by outcome-based EQAO standardized tests.

FINDING #2

Most parents expressed, based on changes they observed in emotions and behaviours of their child preparing and writing the Grade 3 EQAO test, that the test is more harmful than beneficial. All parents tried to counter and mitigate the test-induced anxiety, stress, and fear of failure in their child by using various strategies which included encouraging their child to try their best, having informal conversations with them about the non-impact of test results on marks and advancement to Grade 4, and doing practice questions in advance to familiarize them with types of questions on the test.

FINDING #3

Parents from higher socio-economic status had a better understanding of EQAO standardized testing and its purpose as a political accountability tool including how the test is administered and how the results are used. Whereas most parents preferred the Grade 3 EQAO test to be eliminated entirely, some parents including those who work within the educational system, were in favour of maintaining the test, but strongly felt it requires changes in its content and format to be effective and socio-culturally relevant to the identities, knowledge, skills, and lived experiences of racialized twenty-first century learners.

All parents interviewed expressed they observed higher levels of stress and anxiety in their child leading up to and during EQAO testing week. Most parents tried to counter and mitigate the test-induced anxiety, stress, and fear of failure in their child using various approaches which included encouraging their child to try their best, having informal conversations with them about the non-impact of test results on marks and advancement to Grade 4, and doing practice questions to familiarize them with types of questions on the test to reduce their test-taking anxiety. Most parents expressed that they feel the test is more harmful than beneficial.

In response to what were some of the mood, emotional, or behavioural changes they observed in their child during EQAO testing week and how they tried to support their child, here are what some of the parents expressed:

Chantel's mother:

She was more stressed out. Just the way she was acting at school. It was just more like she wasn't paying attention. She was worried about the wrong things and then like at home she was quiet.

Christopher's mother:

He was nervous I would say but at the end of the day I told him and reminded him to just do your best. It's just like any other test. I know at school they're already preparing them so they don't need another person over their head. So what I do is I ask how his day was, what he did, what he learned, and what he practiced. Basically that's it. I just leave it.

Madison's mother:

Well even just the way that, umm (pause), it just was very intimidating for Madison to have to umm (pause), just the way that her brain works like in terms of having to face all of that in one particular week and all the pressure. If the questions didn't go well, I think there was, you know, a sense of failure or not attaining something she was supposed to, even though at home we are ok with whatever.

Laila's mother who is also a teacher:

I think as a parent I wouldn't put so much emphasis on the test. I wouldn't stress the kids about it. I told Laila to do the best you can.

Malcolm's step-father who is also a teacher:

We had a few conversations about the test just talking about how you need to write these tests and it's not really that much (pause) and don't pressure yourself too much. Don't worry about it too much. Just do your best.

The aforementioned responses indicate that parents visibly observed a heightened level of stress and anxiety in their child from the pressure to do well on the EQAO standardized test associated with fear of failing or being labelled as "dumb" or "illiterate."

Although children were constantly reminded by their parents "not to worry" and "just do their best," they still felt highly nervous, anxious, and fearful of getting poor results. An important question to ask is where does this pressure to do well on EQAO standardized tests originate from and how is it placed on the children? The responses of the children and parents, as a collective, indicate the environment co-constructed by school administrators via the amount of time devoted to preparing for the test and the way EQAO is talked about amongst peers and older Grade 4 children contributes to Grade 3 children feeling intense pressure to do well and legitimize their identity. Grade 3 becomes the "EQAO year." Children fear that they will be judged by their peers, parents, teacher(s), and administrators, counter to what they have been told about the non-impact of the test in terms of its consequences.

The journey of placing high importance on the EQAO test begins in September at the start of Grade 3. All children interviewed expressed that their teacher(s) briefly explained to them at the beginning of the school year what the EQAO test is and when it will take place. Administrators also sent home an information letter conveying the same message to the parents. When parents were asked if they received any communication from the school about the EQAO test, they expressed:

Madison's mother: Yea, so we got a couple of notices saying that it was coming and the week it was going to happen to try to make sure that we were in school and available to participate and umm (pause) that's pretty much it. I mean we knew about it, umm (pause), just because the kids are coming home and talking about when it's gonna be and the prep that they were doing for it.

Malcolm's step-father: Yea throughout the entire year actually. We were in contact with the teacher and he talked about that it was an EQAO year. They notified us when the EQAO will take place and some of the things we can do. Also he would send homework home to help him prepare for the EQAO.

| Christopher's mother: | Yes, there was. It was for parents to come in to give them some information. Due to (pause), because I have two other kids, I've gone through it so I didn't go to it because it's mostly the same information. |

The parental approach to supporting their child and trying to mitigate the stress and anxiety associated with EQAO test-taking differed based on socio-economic status (SES). Parents from higher SES, some which worked in the school system, had a more comprehensive understanding about the EQAO test; what purpose it serves and awareness about the socio-political power dynamics associated with administration and use of EQAO test results. This can be attributed to having an insider role in the education system and recognizing the unique impact of EQAO standardized testing on various stakeholders within a hierarchical power structure.

In response to what is the EQAO test and why their child writes it, Kobe's father who is a school administrator in the capacity of a vice-principal stated,

I think the standard understanding is that it's a standardized test so that we, as parents and educators, can have some common understanding of where kids are at in comparison to other kids across the province in Reading, Writing, and Mathematics.

Similarly, Christopher's mother stated,

What I was told is that it's feedback for the government and for the school to see, umm (pause), where their education is standing, how high the language is or how high the math is, and hopefully with that information they can help out for the following year to improve.

Parents from higher SES were able to state the purpose of EQAO testing in a manner that aligns with the dominant narrative told by EQAO through its website and reproduction of various official documents available and accessible for download online (EQAO, 2018). According to EQAO (2017),

EQAO's tests measure student achievement in reading, writing and mathematics in relation to *Ontario Curriculum* expectations. The resulting data provide accountability and a gauge of quality in Ontario's publicly funded education system. By providing this important evidence about learning, EQAO acts as a catalyst for increasing the success of Ontario students. (p. 4)

In addition to having a better theoretical understanding of the purpose of EQAO testing, parents from higher SES were highly critical of the EQAO test and its effectiveness. Interestingly, they did not resort to removing their child from participating in writing the EQAO test as an act of resistance. Paradoxically, some parents who were highly critical of the effectiveness of EQAO tests took the initiative to do more preparation with their child, outside of what their child's teacher was doing, to further prepare their child for the test and help reduce test-taking anxiety and stress. These strategies included printing and photocopying previous years' test questions or modelling how to respond to questions similar to the format on EQAO tests which commonly asks to "show your work" and "explain your thinking." Jordan's mother, who works in the school system as an Educational Resource Facilitator providing various support services to students expressed that she reviewed questions at home with Jordan to better prepare him for the EQAO test. She explains, "In the beginning, he was definitely nervous. Even when we were doing review with him at home, he would get upset quickly." Similarly, Kobe's mother who is an elementary school principal photocopied practice booklets for Kobe on her own so he could work on them at home. I asked why she did this even though she was not in favour of the EQAO test which she stated,

One of the reasons we did the practice booklets is I knew the teacher wasn't doing it and as a principal lots of teachers do that to sort of alleviate anxiety. So I had Kobe write a practice test but then I gave him the answers so he can evaluate his answers and he could understand how he was being scored. So even though his answers were correct in many cases, he wouldn't get the highest score, unless he did particular things, so he learned what those things were. I have limited doubt he did better on the EQAO because of that. We did that a few times. Another thing we did was, he wrote positive affirmations about himself, and we put it in his pocket and prior to writing the test he said those things about himself. That was a strategy I used as a school principal as well because I read a lot of research on positive psychology and the impact of feeling good when you are about to write a test.

Being an insider who works in a position of authority as a principal in the school system, Kobe's mother understood getting answers correct on the EQAO test does not guarantee receiving a Level 4 score, especially with questions that indicate "show your work" or "explain your thinking." In order to achieve a Level 4 score, it is required for students to demonstrate the appropriate steps and processes involved in arriving at their answers. This demonstrated Kobe's mother's cultural capital (Bourdieu & Passeron, 1977; Kearns, 2016) associated with working in the education system and understanding the ins and outs and power dynamics of how EQAO booklets are marked and scored. From her perspective, the extra effort she put in preparing Kobe for the EQAO test was well intended to alleviate and mitigate the anxiety and psychological stress Kobe would experience writing a highly emphasized standardized test. I asked Kobe's mother, as a parent and an administrator, to what extent she felt the EQAO test helped Kobe in any capacity. She stated, "I think it [the EQAO test] definitely did not help him and I think had we not managed it the way we did, it would have done exactly the opposite by hurting him." According to Kobe' mother, her extra preparation efforts at home were intended to "manage" the negative harmful impacts of writing the EQAO test.

In wanting to hear other parents' perspectives, I asked others what they thought about the relevance of the Grade 3 EQAO test in helping their child. Laila's mother, who is also an elementary school teacher stated,

> I would say get rid of it [EQAO standardized testing] because it doesn't follow the way they are learning in school. In school they are learning very hands-on using manipulatives or you know lots of anchor charts and success criteria and stuff on the wall to refer to, yet, when you get to EQAO testing, everything comes down. It's all cleared off and you have no reference points so it kind of goes against the grain of what is actually taught.

Laila's mother expresses that as a teacher and a parent, she feels there are disconnects between how the elementary curriculum is typically delivered pedagogically throughout the school year compared to how the EQAO test is administered. Whereas typically throughout the school year children are allowed to ask for help, collaborate with peers, learn from making mistakes, co-construct success criteria, and have reference points in the form of pictures and posters in the classroom to guide their learning, this is not the case when EQAO tests are administered.

Jordan's mother expressed and echoed similar concerns to what Laila's and Kobe's mothers mentioned about the ineffectiveness of the EQAO test by stating:

I don't think it [EQAO testing] helps the children. I don't see any benefits. We were worried about him because we know he doesn't do well with that kind of stuff. Anytime you hear the word test, it makes kids, and everybody go kind of nervous. Even for me, I never did well on tests, and I don't think tests really reflect a child's abilities for the entire school year, especially this EQAO test. You have to evaluate kids in different elements. You have to evaluate them in their social element. Are they socializing with other kids? How do they respond to other kids and their teachers? And stuff like that as well as academics. I don't think it should be all academic based. That's not what schools are supposed to be. You have to look at everything as a whole. Doing these tests over three days doesn't show you how a child is. There are some kids that don't do well on tests. They can't. They have a lot of anxiety. They are stressed about it and they don't perform to the best of their abilities. Whereas if you sat down and had a conversation with them, they would probably give you a lot more information and do really well. I think teachers do a great job of trying to do that during the whole year, but I find when it's the Grade 3 and 6 EQAO testing, the teachers are not able to do their job as well as they would like to, because everything is so focused on EQAO testing and so it doesn't give teachers a lot of time to evaluate students in their entire element and give them the chance, you know, to show you that they do understand what they are doing in different ways. The test is not always the best way to find out if a kid can do what you are asking them to do. Students are getting labelled. You are breaking down kids and their self-esteem and that's not what we are supposed to be doing as educators.

Jordan's mother emphasizes that standardized tests do not appeal to the strengths of all children and their preferred learning styles because it doesn't "evaluate kids in different elements." Performing poorly on EQAO tests can make children feel bad about themselves and their abilities which can lower their self-esteem and confidence, particularly for racialized children who are facing systemic barriers within the education system (Dei, 2008; James, 2012). An image that visually exemplifies this point is the cartoon image of various animals lining up in front of a teacher sitting behind a desk with a caption stating, "For a fair selection, everybody has to take the same exam: Please climb that tree." This image demonstrates the irony that just because you use the same method to evaluate all students, it does not mean that it is fair. Not everyone will perform well because their strengths and competencies do not align with how they are being assessed in term of criteria to judge their potential.

In contrast to parents from higher SES, parents from lower SES had a limited understanding of what EQAO testing is and what purpose it serves. In response to what is EQAO testing, Deshaun's mother stated, "It's a nation wide math test. I took it when I was in Grade 3. I don't know if they do it in another grade. I just know that it's a math test." Deshaun's mother was not familiar that EQAO standardized tests assess children in domains of Reading, Writing, and Mathematics and that it is only a provincial test. Similarly, in response to the same question, Chantel's mother stated,

> I believe it's just on reading and writing I think. I remember taking it in Grade 9 and in Grade 6 and in Grade 3 or something like that, so I think it's every 3 years. I umm (pause), just think it's on reading and writing.

Both Deshaun and Chantel's mother make references to their own experiences writing the EQAO standardized tests when they were younger. These recollections are vague in terms of details remembering the specific domains assessed and for what purposes. In response to what the EQAO results are used for, Chantel's mom stated,

> Umm (pause) I don't know. Just to make sure everybody is at the level they're supposed to be. I mean they probably use it in studies for like, umm, I don't know. They probably just use it for some sort of study.

Deshaun's mother was also unaware when EQAO results are returned to students. She stated, "I think they should give the results right before the school year is finished. Like right on the last day of school."

Although somewhat less knowledgeable about details of EQAO standardized testing, parents from lower SES acknowledged that the EQAO test appeared important because of the way it was treated by administrators and teachers through the informational letters they received from the school, the informal and formal communication from their child's teacher, and the practice questions sent home as homework. Parents from lower SES lacked the cultural capital (Bourdieu & Passeron, 1977; Kearns, 2016) and the familiarity with how EQAO booklets are scored and the larger impact it can have on the perception of the school based on overall school scores. In describing how she knew EQAO scores were important to the school, Chantel's mom expressed, "It's different only because you're getting letters about it (laughs). I mean that's the only thing that makes me feel like it's really important because they send a letter home."

When asked whether the school had provided any communication regarding EQAO testing, Chantel's mom indicated "yes," but demonstrated confusion about the purpose of the test. She stated, "I don't really understand why we have to do it." I pursued this question further by asking how important it is for her child, Chantel, to do well on the EQAO test. She stated,

> Umm (pause) well I never thought about it until you asked me. But I noticed like with her, I think any sort of test is important just because she shows a bit of struggle with a lot of, with certain things, so any test for her specifically will be important.

Similarly, although Deshaun's mother did not have a clear understanding of the purpose of EQAO testing, she expressed it was "very important" because "it is then going to shape, I guess, how he [Deshaun] is viewed for his intellectual skills from now till when they do it again." For Deshaun's mother, the test was important because it validated Deshaun's intellectual knowledge, skills, and competencies and it would contribute to how Deshaun is viewed, perceived, and judged by his teachers and peers.

When asked if parents are impacted by EQAO standardized testing, Deshaun's mother stated,

> Yea, because if a child feels affected and they don't feel confident or they don't feel happy that they did well, it will then reflect on the parents, and the parents would feel ways for them.

Deshaun's mother expressed that parents are also impacted by EQAO testing because they are also judged based on the score their child receives.

When asked on a scale of one to ten about the relevance of the Grade 3 EQAO test in helping Christopher learn and improve, Christopher's mom stated:

> To be honest I would say zero because, like I said, it's only for the government and for the school and it doesn't count for his report card. So all the stress the kids go through and everything, I think it should, like that mark should somehow count as participation or be involved with their mark on their report card so the kids get a benefit out of it.

Christopher's mom further explained that her older daughter who is now 15 years old and attends high school experienced similar socio-emotional stress and anxiety writing EQAO tests in elementary school. She expressed,

To be honest (pause) my first daughter is fifteen years old now so I don't think it's necessary to stress out the kids with this. The kids are already stressed out and they're nervous and some of them can't sleep, but at the same time umm (pause) the only one who benefits is the government and the school. It's not even used as a mark on the report card. So for me as a parent, I don't think it's necessary because the teachers tell us don't stress the kids at home this or that, but at the same time, I see from both my kids that they got very stressed out.

Christopher's mom describes that both her children were highly stressed going through preparing and writing EQAO tests in elementary school, and that in retrospect she does not find the test relevant or helpful for the healthy development of her children. Similarly, Malcolm's step-father stated,

> For me personally, the EQAO test is not really that important. I think just him [Malcolm] learning the curriculum and how to act socially within different environments is more important than the EQAO test.

From the aforementioned responses, most of the parents feel the Grade 3 EQAO test is not a practical tool that effectively assesses the smartness of their child from a holistic lens. This was further acknowledged by Madison's mother in responding to how important it is for Madison to do well on the EQAO test as she stated, "It's not relevant at all. We don't judge, you know, our kids levels of anything based on test results or grades."

Whereas most parents preferred the Grade 3 EQAO test to be eliminated entirely considering it costs approximately $32 million dollars annually to administer it, some parents were in favour of maintaining the test but strongly felt it requires changes in its content and format to be socio-culturally relevant to the identities, knowledge, skills, and lived experiences of all students, particularly racialized children. Below are some of the parents' responses describing their advice to the government about what to do about EQAO tests:

> Kobe's father who is also a middle school vice-principal: I haven't thought through what would be a good replacement for it. I think they need to get rid of it number one. Because of the impact and the ways it plays out right now like the stress on teachers, the stress on parents, the judgment and evaluation that is placed on you know the schools and the communities based on a culturally biased and limited test in term of what data it gives us. It doesn't give you rich data, you know, even from a teaching and learning perspective, I think the way it plays out now it does way more harm than it

does good. Having said that, I do think we need to think about what kind of data we are going to use to test where kids are at and how we triangulate data to create a rich picture of where students are at in their learning.

Kobe's mother who is also an elementary school principal: I don't think we should have it either. I do think we should have some way where we demonstrate acquisition of knowledge for kids because that is what it's really about. So we do need to think, really critically, around how we want to demonstrate that students have actually learned. I don't think that EQAO does that, but we do need to think of a way where we can demonstrate that. I think the way in which EQAO is read, the way it is administrated, and the way in which it is taken up, it's problematic. So it goes back to, who is it for, really? The driver of education has to be the children and if EQAO is not anchored in that, then there is a problem.

Madison's mother: I would just eliminate it [EQAO testing]. I don't think it has a positive effect. I think that if we are going to put them in school and have teachers and a reporting system that should (pause), and we have the right people in place, the right teachers in place, you know, the right leaders in place that should be an accurate indication your kid being at the proper level. I don't think having a government dictated system that disrupts the school year is going to give us better results.

Jordan's mother who is also an Educational Resource Facilitator: I wouldn't say like get rid of tests like EQAO but I would like to see them modify it and do different things with it. Not so much in just three days but over the whole year, and maybe not emphasize so much that it's this one big test and it's so important. You need to bring it back to being for school purposes, and right now it's not for that. Right now, it's for so many other things than for the students and helping their learning and helping them improve. I think we've forgotten that. What are we here for? We are here for these kids and their future and we need to build them up and not break them down with tests like these. We also need to continue to grow as a community. I think we've lost sight and focus in what our purposes are in schools and I see it every day working in schools.

Malcolm's step-father who is also an elementary school teacher: Just to re-evaluate the test. Make sure the test is serving its purpose. I know it's there for a purpose but also look at the other end of it as well. Look at the social aspect of things within the school environment. Look at the teacher efficacy within the school environment. Look at the well-being within the school environment and use the test as well to judge the schools and judge the people in these schools operating these schools. Don't just look at the test and say the score is low so this school is not up to par. You have to look at other aspects as well and by doing that you are gonna improve the school environment and the school system.

The above responses as a collective indicate there are concerns from parents, including those who work in the education system, about the usefulness and the relevance of the data EQAO tests generate, how the data is interpreted by students, parents, the government, and the general public, and how it impacts children's development and self-perception at such a young age. The sentiment from the parents' responses is how EQAO tests are currently administered and how the data is utilized is more harmful than beneficial to healthy child development and improvement of student learning.

Implications

Hart and Kempf (2015) in their report titled *Public Attitudes Toward Education in Ontario 2015: The 19th OISE Survey of Educational Issues* express that, "Less than half of parents are satisfied either with schools' contribution to the physical development of students (41%) or their social and emotional development (45%)" (p. 2). This statistic complements and supports concerns expressed by interviewed parents about how EQAO tests assess children in limited domains and the pressure placed on them to do well is counter-productive to their socio-emotional development. Stiggins similarly (2014) points out,

> [L]ack of influence [of standardized tests] does not arise from the inappropriateness of the tests, but rather the insufficiency of the information they provide. We have relied on them too heavily when we should have been supplementing them with other applications of assessment that can provide the additional evidence needed to improve student learning. (p. 30)

Stiggins (2014) expresses concerns about the usefulness of data generated from standardized test results, similar to what the parents interviewed indicated.

At the core of the concerns raised by the parents and the educators interviewed is the ineffectiveness of EQAO relative to when and how the results are returned to children as well as how results are used by schools and the general public. Despres, Kuhn, Ngirumpatse, and Parent (2013) with specific reference to EQAO standardized testing in Ontario point out, "Standardized testing results are disseminated at the beginning of the following school year, reducing their effectiveness as an instrument for identifying and correcting weakness at the level of the individual student" (p. 10). Their report titled *Real Accountability or an Illusion of Success? A Call to Review Standardized Testing in Ontario* (2013) states, "The 1995 Commission noted that standardized testing would not be very useful to individual students because the results do not come quickly enough and when they do come, they do not include sufficient feedback, including an analysis of strengths and weaknesses" (p. 10). Children write the Grade 3 EQAO standardized test near the end of the school year in late May or early June. Upon returning from a two-month summer break, at the start of Grade 4 in late September or early October, children receive their results which does not include any descriptive feedback about how to improve. The results simply outline what numerical achievement level they have obtained in Reading, Writing, and Mathematics. It is a score ranging from NE which means "Not enough evidence to be assigned a Level 1" to Level 4 meaning "Exceeds provincial standard." Level 3 is the provincial standard that students are expected to be achieving at by the end of Grade 3. Jordan's mother raises an important concern when she states,

> When you get the results back, it's just a number. It's a number to who? They [the children] don't understand what this number means. It's not like a regular test, where you know, if you got the test back and you got a bad review, the teacher says let's look at this and why you got this answer wrong. It's not a test like that. When kids get the results, they don't understand if they did well or didn't do well.

Part of the argument of why EQAO standardized tests are ineffective is the limited data it provides in terms of descriptive feedback about what the child did well and where or in what areas errors were made. What further complicates the matter is the extensive time frame it takes for the children to get their results back. Children are receiving their results approximately three to four months after writing the test. Often times, not only have children drastically changed physically, emotionality, and intellectually from a developmental perspective over the several months, but they often do not remember the test content particularly after coming back from the summer break. Hence, achievement levels expressed on student's individual EQAO reports is left for students and their parents to be interpreted on their own without much guidance or support from the schools. Stiggins (2014) emphasizes that

> Problems arise if the communication of results is delayed for a long time. Students don't stop growing after they take the annual state test, so those test results that arrive weeks or even months after the test is administered no longer reflect students' achievement status. Timely feedback is important. (pp. 72–73)

Upon receiving test results, children often ask their peers how they did to compare one another's achievements. This sharing of one's achievement level amongst peers can be stressful and traumatizing, particularly if one has underachieved and did poorly. Peers joking or making fun of someone for their poor performance on a standardized test can be stressful and inscribe an identity on the child as "dumb" in that specific domain. This can have long-term effects on the child psychologically. For example, a child who does poor in reading might self-identify as a poor reader and consequentially avoid reading for enjoyment for not wanting to feel embarrassed by being judged or made fun of by others. Data collected as part of questionnaires administered to children who participate in writing the EQAO test at the Primary and Junior level indicate that "the number of students who read for enjoyment has dropped significantly over the last 10 years" (Ontario Teachers' Federation, 2011, p. 10). As Stiggins (2014) points out,

> Students constantly evaluate their own achievement too. They attend to adults' assessments of them, and they make key instructional decisions about how—indeed, whether—to continue with their own learning based on their own self-assessment and interpretation of the available evidence. The outcome can be hope or hopelessness, optimism or pessimism, an expectation of success or failure, regarding one's chances of future learning success. Depending on that internal judgement, students will either gain or lose confidence, increase or decrease engagement and effort, and experience learning success or failure. Their sense of themselves in the immediate learning context drives their subsequent actions. (p. 88)

Therefore, it is important to evaluate assessment techniques for their pros and cons and how it impacts students and their identities. There are different approaches to conducting student assessment with each serving a unique purpose. Ontario Teachers' Federation (2011) argues that "formative assessment (assessment for/as learning) more effectively promotes student learning than summative assessment (assessment of learning)" (p. 5). They explain that

Assessment for learning is continuous. It is used to monitor student performance, provide timely feedback and generally enhance the teaching-learning experience. It occurs during instruction to support the next stage of learning. (p. 5)

In 2010, Ontario Ministry of Education released a new policy document titled *Growing Success: Assessment, Evaluation, and Reporting in Ontario Schools* (Ministry of Education, 2010). Under a subsection titled "Fundamental Principles," the document explicitly states, "The primary purpose of assessment and evaluation is to improve student learning" (Ministry of Education, 2010, p. 6). It further outlines seven fundamental principles "to ensure that assessment, evaluation, and reporting are valid and reliable and that they lead to the improvement of learning for all students" (p. 6). These fundamental principles emphasize that assessment, evaluation, and reporting

- are fair, transparent, and equitable for all students;
- support all students, including those with special education needs, those who are learning the language of instruction (English or French), and those who are First Nation, Métis, or Inuit;
- are carefully planned to relate to the curriculum expectations and learning goals and, as much as possible, to the interests, learning styles and preferences, needs, and experiences of all students;
- are communicated clearly to students and parents at the beginning of the school year or course and at other appropriate points throughout the school year or course;
- are ongoing, varied in nature, and administered over a period of time to provide multiple opportunities for students to demonstrate the full range of their learning;
- provide ongoing descriptive feedback that is clear, specific, meaningful, and timely to support improved learning and achievement;
- develop students' self-assessment skills to enable them to assess their own learning, set specific goals, and plan next steps for their learning. (p. 6)

If the "primary purpose of assessment and evaluation is to improve student learning," (Ministry of Education, 2010, p. 28) then we should be investing more in "assessment for learning" and "assessment as learning" versus "assessment of learning," which is what EQAO standardized tests do. Fiore (2012) supports this stance stating, "One particular test or score does not paint a full, clear picture of a complex, developing child" (p. 5). As part of providing children with constructive and useful descriptive feedback to facilitate their positive healthy development, we must take into consideration more than just their age and what grade they are in. We must consider their socio-emotional intelligence, social skills, and level of maturity amongst other important factors impacting their motivation, engagement, and academic performance in schools and on standardized tests (People for Education, 2013). We need a shift towards understanding and demonstrating accountability in schools from a more holistic interdisciplinary lens. As Fiore (2012) explains, "The most appropriate assessment strategies and tools to promote children's learning and teacher effectiveness must coordinate with the most appropriate developmental period in order for maximum learning to occur" (p. 15).

Recommendations

I therefore recommend school boards and schools to work towards mitigating the short- and long-term effects associated with *invisible scars and traumatizing effects of standardized testing* on young children in elementary schools by providing workshops for parents with a focus on teaching parents mental health and mindfulness techniques to support their child in a holistic manner instead of placing more pressure on them to perform well on standardized tests. The workshops should be offered free of charge or kept at a minimal affordable cost. They should be offered at multiple time slots for accessibility purposes. Time periods to consider are before, during, and after school on weekdays and on weekends relative to the demographics of parents living in the community where the school is located. The focus of the workshops offered to parents should be on them learning how to read the mood of their child through their tone of voice and body language, and how they can support and facilitate an increase in their child's emotional intelligence. This includes helping parents understand and acknowledge specific emotions in their child, how to provide mediums for their child to express their emotions constructively, recognizing emotional triggers, and how to guide their child to use positive coping mechanisms as an outlet for test-induced stress, anxiety, and fear of failure.

A great example of a communication skill to teach parents as part of parental workshops offered is checking-in with the child about their experiences at school including those related to preparing for the EQAO standardized test. As Kobe's dad explains, in response to how he supports Kobe's learning throughout the school year:

> I think one of the things is just checking in with him about how he is feeling about school because his experience from a social-emotional perspective is gonna impact his academics as well. So, we just talk to him about what he likes about school, you know, his friends, if he likes his teachers, and those kinds of things. And then, you know, just checking in with him on a daily basis about what he did at school and if he has any homework and how we can support him with his homework.

This approach is effective as it goes beyond simply asking, "How was your day?" which often yields one-word decontextualized responses from the child such as "Good." Asking more specific open-ended questions allows for open dialogue and communication between parents and the child.

I therefore recommend, as a test trial for a year, EQAO administers Grade 3 EQAO tests in late September at the start of Grade 4 to address concerns associated with ineffective timing of when EQAO results are returned to children. If the objective is to assess students organically of their knowledge acquisition and mastery of content in the primary grades until end of Grade 3, it is optimal to select the start of Grade 4 to administer the EQAO test. This diminishes the opportunity for teachers to spend time prepping children and to teach to the test as a means of getting children to perform better and trying to increase their overall school scores. Upon administrating EQAO tests in late September, individual student results are to be scored and returned to the children by end of January of the same school year. This provides EQAO the same turnaround marking time they are utilizing right now which is about three to four months to mark and tabulate all individual and school results.

I therefore recommend EQAO to digitalize all marked EQAO booklets by scanning them and making them available to students and parents online via a secure website that allows them to log in with a personalized username and password to mitigate concerns about how individual EQAO results contains only raw achievement scores with limited descriptive feedback about children's strengths, weaknesses, and where errors are made. Once logged in securely, students and parents can download their individualized marked booklets and read more specific comments and suggestions as a form of descriptive feedback about how they did. This allows children and parents to visually see what questions they did well on, where errors were made, and how they can improve in various areas. Digitalizing EQAO marked booklets and making them accessible to students and parents online with more constructive descriptive feedback will cost money to be implemented, but in the long run, not only will it save money by the amount of paper it saves but it also makes the process more effective in supporting student learning and their improvement, which is one of the key goals of any type of educational assessment.

FINDING #4

Most children did not understand why they write the Grade 3 EQAO test and how the results are used.

In response to why they write the Grade 3 EQAO test, the children interviewed responded:

Deshaun: (long pause) I don't ... Math. To learn math better and to write paragraphs.
Kobe: (long pause) I don't know.
Chantel: I don't know. To get smart?

In response to what the results are used for, the children interviewed stated:

Laila: I don't know.
Kobe: I don't know.
Malcolm: I think that so that we can learn more so when we go to the next grade then we will be able to be more educated and be ready for it.

Based on the aforementioned responses, although some of the students are aware of the domains which they are assessed in by EQAO tests, most do not know what purpose the EQAO serves in the larger scheme of their schooling experiences and how the results are used.

Implications

The importance of the EQAO test as perceived by racialized children and consequences associated with doing poorly, both tangible and imaginable, creates a highly pressurized environment where children feel they are being judged for how smart they are even though they are confused about why they write the EQAO test and how the results are used. Jordan's mother explains why children become confused about the EQAO, its purpose, and how the results are used:

> There is pressure especially because it's their first year and the kids don't even know what it is. I think a lot of teachers say we are doing this test, but the kids actually have no idea what this test is until it actually gets closer to time. We start telling more and more about it and it kind of gives them a mixed message, because all year round you are pushing this test, and telling them you are going to do it, but when it comes time for the test, teachers tell you "Don't worry I don't want you to be nervous because this test doesn't count towards your grade. It's not going on your report card and you're still gonna pass Grade 3." So the kids are like "What's the point?" and then the kids are a little confused because they are like "Why do we even have to do this test? Why do I even have to try because you are saying it has no effect on me whatsoever?" I think it is giving kids a mixed message and it's giving the community a mixed message because you know, you try to tell your kids, you have to study and do well and try your best on all your tests, but then we have this big test and it's like don't worry.

Although children are somewhat aware of the importance of the test and the domains they are assessed in, they receive mixed messages about how much effort they should put into it. As Kohn (2000) points out, "there are students who take the tests but don't take them seriously" (p. 5). This lack of effort on behalf of students who might lack interest or motivation to do well on non-consequential standardized tests can lead to educators making assumptions about the competencies of the child. The child's poor achievement scores can be misinterpreted by educators due "to the insidious assumption that some children just can't learn—especially if the same kids always seem to show up below the median" (Kohn, 2000, p. 16). This feeds into perpetuation of a neoliberal deficit model of education (Sharma, 2009) where students are seen in complete control of their destiny based on decisions they make and the individual effort they put into completing their school work. Yet, as Portelli and Vilbert (2002) point out, "reducing complexities to a simple matter of defining common standards and measuring student achievement against them conveniently allows us to blame the individual—the student and/or the teacher—and ignore the larger social and political realities in which teachers, students, and schools are immersed!" (p. 13)

Recommendations

I therefore recommend schools to host "parent-student-teacher" meetings, in person or via alternative methods such as by phone or email, to explain to children and parents how to effectively interpret EQAO results in a constructive manner to improve student learning and mitigate the *invisible scars and traumatizing effects of standardized testing* associated with children's self-critique of themselves and parent's critique of their children based on EQAO scores. It is recommended "parent-student-teacher" meetings are conducted as soon as EQAO results are returned to children in late September or early October. As part of this conference meeting, the child, the parent(s), and the teacher should collaboratively co-construct an individualized personal action plan for the school year outlining short- and long-term goals for areas of improvement for the student along with plans on how to achieve those goals. This individualized personal plan produced based on Grade 3 EQAO results should be supplemented with other teacher observations and assessments throughout the year. The goals of the action plan should be monitored relative to its progress at various intervals throughout the school year, particularly leading up to when report card marks are finalized, to facilitate students getting descriptive feedback about their strengths and areas needing improvement to increase their marks. These "check-in" meetings on the progress of the goals should be revisited with the parent(s) and the child every three months. This can be done in person at the school through meetings or via alternative methods such as through email or over the phone to accommodate busy schedules of families.

FINDING #5

According to the parents, EQAO standardized testing relative to its structure, format, and administration does not align with "best practices" in education associated with meaningful teaching and learning in schools.

FINDING #6

Teacher pedagogy and delivery of the curriculum is negatively impacted by Grade 3 EQAO test preparation leading to teaching to the test. This is attributed to the pressure placed on teachers and administrators to increase their school scores, as schools are judged and ranked by external organizations such as the Fraser Institute based on overall performance of their students on EQAO tests.

Not only do children experience extensive amount of pressure to do well on EQAO standardized tests, but teachers and administrators also feel immense pressure to demonstrate improvement in school scores as EQAO results are used by some parents and external organizations to pass judgement on overall effectiveness of schools and the quality of education they offer. Although in Ontario, teacher pay is not associated with student performance on standardized tests, the testing culture and judgement of quality of education offered at schools based on overall EQAO scores create a highly pressurized environment to produce improvements impacting teacher pedagogy and delivery of the curriculum. In Ontario, there is a correlation between EQAO school scores and property values. Property values are higher for houses in close proximity to schools that have higher EQAO scores. This is reinforced by the Fraser Institute annual report which ranks all elementary and secondary schools based on their current and past overall EQAO scores (Fraser Institute, 2018). These rankings are published and made available online annually to the general public and receive extensive media attention upon its release.

Ranking of schools by the Fraser Institute has an impact on how schools and neighbourhoods are perceived; whether they are labelled as good or bad and consequentially the property values within the surrounding community and student enrolment. Many parents from higher SES who have the privilege of selecting where to purchase a house to live use school rankings as a guide to give their child access to a "good" quality education. As well, real estate agents use school rankings as a pull factor to promote and sell houses in affluent neighbourhoods which have schools with higher EQAO scores. Kobe's mom reaffirmed this by expressing:

> I think from a principal perspective, it's very much a political tool. So we have parents who will select schools based on EQAO scores. So I'll get calls as a principal, "tell me your scores," because they'll think it's a good school or not a good school. I think as a parent, you know, it's an indication of thinking your child is successful or not. That's how most parents seem to interpret it. I don't interpret it that way, but I know parents of Kobe's friends, they definitely do, and if their child doesn't do well, they feel like they're not doing well. And I know a lot of teachers feel it's a reflection of them as teachers.

Jordan's mother also reaffirmed the correlation between EQAO school test scores and property values by stating, "A lot of realtors look at the results, and stuff like that, which is kind of surprising because they're usually trying to sell homes and up the value of certain homes in certain areas which are schools that are doing well."

Kobe's mother further explained what she has observed as an administrator over the years about the negative pressure placed on teachers to get children to do well on EQAO tests:

> As a principal, the teachers were very stressed and often come to your office crying, because there is so much pressure on them as well. They would say, you know, "What would you like me to do to prep?" and I would say "I just want the kids to feel good." I want them to write positive affirmations about themselves. At first they thought, "Is this woman a lunatic?," but they saw the impact of the kids, you know, feeling good.

Kobe's mother was conscious of how EQAO standardized tests can label children if they end up doing poorly, so she tried to mitigate that by encouraging teachers to get children to write "positive affirmations" about themselves to gain more confidence for writing the test. Kobe's mother also explained how EQAO test scores impact many decisions made by administrators including which teachers are strategically selected to teach Grades 3 and 6, the grades where EQAO tests are administered. She emphasized,

> Because of the pressure and the impact of the results, I think schooling has changed in Grade 3 and 6 even in terms of how principals place teachers. They try to place their strongest teachers in those grades, where maybe that's not really where you need to put your strongest teachers if we're thinking about pedagogy or child development.

Kobe's mother expressed that, being a principal for over six years, there has not been a single year where she has not seen teachers breakdown crying due to the stress and anxiety affiliated with preparing students to do well on EQAO tests. She points out there is a clear connection that EQAO preparation impacts teacher pedagogy:

> Teachers are largely affected. They start preparing from September. That means they are modifying how they teach because of this test. I don't think I've ever had a year of EQAO where I haven't had teachers crying in my office. Ever!

Jordan's mother also explained how based on her experiences providing various support services in classrooms, Grade 3 becomes dominated largely by discussions and conversations affiliated with EQAO testing. She expressed:

> For kids specially being in Grade 3, I find it a lot of teachers are pushing the test. Everything is "oh we are going to do this today and it's going to be on your EQAO test," like everything that whole year is pushed on kids about being about and on the EQAO.

Jordan's step-father explained how a lot of the direction comes from the school principal in terms of guidance and investment in different initiatives to prepare children for EQAO tests. Working at a different school than his wife, he explained changes he is experiencing at his school due to having a new principal:

> At my school this year, there is a new principal, and there is a big push for open ended questions and open concept type of thinking where I think that is more geared towards an EQAO type of test where they give you a problem and want to see what you can pull out of it. Depends on the way your school is running and who is running the show.

In further trying to capture the impact of EQAO testing on teacher pedagogy and delivery of the Grade 3 curriculum, I asked children how their teacher prepared them for the EQAO test from September leading up to the when the test was administered in their respective schools. Below are some of their responses:

Deshaun:	She gave us a (pause), like a prep booklet for EQAO and it had similar questions from previous years.
Jordan:	She like makes us practice. She doesn't give us a booklet but she shows us what it's gonna be like practice questions.
Kobe:	We did a lot of tests the months before the EQAO like practice questions.
Chantel:	We did practice questions.
Christopher:	She gave us like some EQAO packages from 2001 and 2008 and other stuff.

Madison: I've been mostly out of the class every day. Umm (pause), we got to go to the library, and get some help with some things like money, coins, shapes, and lots of other things.

A common theme was teachers using previous years EQAO booklets as practice to prepare children for the EQAO test. As well, teachers did practice questions in class to model EQAO format, and in some cases teachers also sent home more questions as homework for extra practice.

Some of the parents further expanded and contextualized how their child's teacher prepared them for the EQAO test:

Madison's mother: To get ready for the test, they did a lot of in-class work and they took Madison out to work with her individually. They work with them one-on-one with an EA [Educational Assistant] and then they spend a lot of time working with her one-on-one getting her ready for the testing.

Kobe's mother: They did a lot of tests the months before the EQAO like practice questions. He had weekly homework; every week, two EQAO questions, throughout the school year from September.

Jordan's mother: They did old EQAO booklets and we just go through it actually with them and the teacher will do a mock test just to show them. They actually do some of the questions with the kids just to show them what it's gonna be like.

Malcolm's step-father: Basically it was laid out. The homework was laid out. They gave suggestions of things you can do with your child and they gave you a calendar where you do these things this day and this day (pretending to point down a list).

Parents' responses corroborated children's explanations outlining heavy reliance by teachers on previous years EQAO booklets and practice questions to get students ready for the EQAO test. In some cases, it can even be inferred that teachers are teaching to the test to improve school EQAO scores.

It was important for me as part of the study to explore, from the children and parental perspective, how the EQAO testing fits in with the routine delivery of the Grade 3 curriculum. Hence, I asked children and parents their opinion on how EQAO tests, in terms of preparing for and writing it, were similar or different to other activities in school. Kobe's father as a parent and a school administrator stated:

> The pedagogy often changes like for a while leading up to the EQAO. Like what we know about good teaching and learning is that, you know, kids need to learn from each other, right, they need to construct knowledge, they need to be doing group work, they need to be active, but all of this stuff kind of goes out the window, because it's like the test is coming so this afternoon we are doing EQAO prep and everybody is at their desk with a pencil and a paper and they don't move. It really shifts, at least in the lead up time to the test. It shifts what is happening and how learning and interaction is taking place in a classroom.

Similarly, Malcolm's step-father as a parent and an elementary school teacher stated:

> A lot of times they're teaching towards the test, not actually teaching, kind of like, they're preparing for this test the entire year and they're neglecting the curriculum and other things that the kids should be learning like behaviour or the learning skills and the work habits. That kind of stuff. So they neglect that just for the test in my opinion. You know it's tough. It's tough. I understand the pressures the teachers are under but also you know the kids are here to learn other things other than the academic piece.

Madison's mother also expressed she feels EQAO testing impacts the school culture negatively the entire year. She explained:

> I think in terms of the focus of the testing, it is right from the beginning of the year, right through, and you know, how it affects the school. Kids are always talking about "oh you're in Grade 3 you have to do your testing this year," "oh you're in Grade 6 you have to do your test this year," and the older kids and the younger kids they talk about it and it's such a big part of (pause) it. That one week affects their curriculum so much because they are so focused on those particular results and how it affects their school.

I asked Madison's mother to expand on what she means specifically with regard to these specific "affects" on the school. She expressed:

> I think it's a negative impact because it affects their curriculum. They stop teaching what they are supposed to teach just so that they can get better

results and teach kids how to answer questions on the test. Like in Grade 3 they are at such different levels and they spend so much time just teaching you how to answer questions. I think they teach to the test.

Both Ontario provincial teacher unions, the Elementary Teachers' Federation of Ontario and the Ontario Secondary School Teachers' Federation, have publicly criticized and opposed the practice of EQAO standardized testing in schools. The main reason being it impacts delivery of the curriculum in a negative way by placing stress on administrators, teachers, and the students as many judgements and inferences are made about the school such as the quality of education offered and the teachers' competencies based on EQAO scores and school rankings.

With EQAO test preparation being perceived by many of the parents interviewed as having a negative influence on delivery of the curriculum, I wondered where EQAO testing fits in the equation of "best practices" in education related to teaching and learning. Describing differences in the pedagogy of preparing for the EQAO test compared to how the curriculum is delivered the remainder of the school year, Chantel's mother stated:

I think EQAO testing is more based on looking at thought processes and how she [Chantel] does things whereas in school the math that has been coming home is more numbers, patterns, and very straight forward. I didn't feel there was a lot of "explain your thinking" in the homework as they do on the EQAO.

Similarly, Kobe's mother explained how EQAO testing impacts teacher pedagogy in many different ways:

I think, from a parent perspective, she [Kobe's teacher] had created this homework book and she had photocopied questions from EQAO booklets and that was to prepare him, but I am fairly certain if there was no such thing as an EQAO test, she wouldn't have done that which tells you it's not really a best practice. So I think that right now, teachers cater towards the test, where really we shouldn't do anything in terms of preparing them, and that would give you a more authentic reading.

Overall, pressure is placed on all stakeholders working in the education system to improve EQAO scores including principals, teachers, parents, and children because EQAO scores have been normalized and legitimized as a major source of data highly valued in the public sphere. All stakeholders are directly and indirectly impacted in various capacities due to meanings, interpretations, and inferences attached to EQAO test scores and school rankings at the individual and community level.

Implications

Ontario Teachers' Federation (2011) points out, "There is an enormous difference between instruction for improving student learning and instruction for improving student test scores" (p. 7). It is important to distinguish that improvement in test scores does not equate to improvement in student learning and instruction, although sometimes that can be the case. When so much attention is placed on administrators and teachers to improve test scores, both internally within the institution of education and externally in the public sphere through ranking of schools, it pressurizes teachers to work backwards by teaching to the test.

The major event defining Grade 3 has become administration of EQAO standardized tests. Children feel apprehensive and nervous about how they will do on the test, a process that begins in September when they are informed it is an EQAO testing year. Despres et al. (2013) explain, "Pressure within a classroom may interfere with the development of an atmosphere of positive learning and discovery, particularly amongst the youngest children" (p. 10). Leading up to the EQAO testing week, more time is allocated towards EQAO preparation. Kohn (2000), who is critiquing standardized testing in the context of United States, points out,

> Teachers often feel obliged to set aside other subjects for days, weeks, or (particularly in schools serving low-income students) even months at a time in order to devote themselves to boosting students' tests scores. Indeed, both the content and the format of instruction are affected; the test essentially becomes the curriculum. (p. 29)

Private educational companies and organizations have taken advantage of pressure on schools and teachers to improve EQAO test scores by producing resources that can be purchased, in reproducible hand-out format or online via games and activities, geared specifically for EQAO test preparation. These profitable EQAO preparation resources have become part of the hegemonic machinery that normalizes and legitimizes standardized tests as an accountability tool to measure how schools are doing. Yet, as Weiner (2014) argues, "Standardization is an ideological principle that attempts to legitimate the decontextualization of learning and teaching in the service of raising the academic bar" (p. 5). In other words, although as educators we might be assisting children to perform better on standardized tests, does that equate to them gaining the necessary relevant knowledge and skills to be successful in today's society?

In Ontario, within the TDSB, EQAO results are a major source of data used in developing and finalizing School Improvement Plans (SIPs) with input from various grade teachers and administrators. Kobe's mom confirmed this process and shed some light on how EQAO data is used by administrators to allocate resources. Although this can be theoretically well intended, as supported by the dominant narrative expressed by EQAO, it may not always be the most effective way as EQAO numbers do not accurately capture the complex lives of students and issues impacting families and communities, particularly racialized students and parents. In response to what extent EQAO is used as part of designing School Improvement Plans, Kobe's mom expressed:

> EQAO is used so much. It's highly problematic. So we use that data, and some principals solely use that data, to dictate student performance. Now, we are trying to push back at that, meaning we have to use quantitative, qualitative, and perceptual data but for sure I think EQAO is the fail safe which is like ground zero. For example, when we have to assign reading coaches to schools, we base what schools they should go to based on EQAO scores which is a problem, because for all you know they had 3 kids who had some sort of IEPs or identifications and shouldn't have written the test in the first place and that sunk their school scores.

The above response contextualizes how EQAO scores are used as a main indicator to allocate support services and resources to schools such as "reading coaches," yet such scores do not always accurately capture the needs of the student demographics attending the school. As a result, resource distribution is not accurately aligned with needs of specific schools and inequitable learning conditions can be perpetuated or go unnoticed.

EQAO results are used by administrators and teachers as a baseline measure to plan school initiatives and improvement plans. Yet, the reality is that the next cohort of students entering Grade 3 could have drastically different set of needs compared to the cohort of students who wrote the EQAO test the previous year. As Jordan's step-father explains,

The School Improvement Plan is based on last year's results and that becomes problematic. We have a staff meeting, examine the results, and the emphasis is guided by the results from last year's Grade 3 results. There is more pressure on the principal, more pressure on the superintendents and all this comes out the can and ends up on us and ends up on them. We also target students to move them up in grade levels from let's say level two to three.

When so much value and currency is attached to EQAO test scores, it diminishes the capacity to use other "best practices" such as critical pedagogy to facilitate holistic and healthy development in young children. Kohn (2000) emphasizes that "Time spent preparing students to succeed on such tests is time that could have been spent helping them become critical, creative, curious thinkers" (p. 33). Kohn further outlines,

As excitement about learning pulls in one direction, covering the material that will be on the test pulls in the other. Thoughtful discussions about current events are especially likely to be discarded because what's in today's paper won't be on the exam. Furthermore, it is far more difficult for teachers to attend to children's social and moral development—holding class meeting, building a sense of community, allowing time for creative play, developing conflict-resolution skills, and so on—when the only thing that matters is scores on tests, that, of course, measure none of these. (p. 30)

Racialized children and their parents interviewed as part of this study have echoed similar concerns. They have collectively experienced teachers teaching to the test by using previous year's EQAO booklets and constantly doing practice questions with the students. When the test indirectly becomes the curriculum, due to the amount of currency and meaning attached to the value of the scores, even though there might be improvements in achievement level of students on these tests, it does not translate to students gaining the necessary relevant and transferrable life skills required to be successful citizens within the twenty-first-century context such as having critical thinking and conflict-resolution skills, as well as demonstrating effective oral communication and creativity.

Recommendations

I therefore recommend a test trial for EQAO to collect data using *growth portfolios* to compile and track examples of progress, improvement, and high achievement levels throughout the school year with input from students and parents. Near the end of each three-months period in the school year—November, February, and May—teachers should have a "parents-student-teacher" conference meeting to assess and discuss progress of students in different subjects, particularly their strengths and areas needing improvement. The aim of the "parent-student-teacher" conference is to collaboratively decide on student work exemplars to input into the portfolio demonstrating skills and mastery of curriculum content in different subjects. School administrators should self-report and input all student achievement levels into a central database created by Ministry of Education or EQAO officers can collect all portfolios and input the data themselves to mitigate bias or false reporting. This port-folio approach should continue and be built upon every school year as students advance to the next grade.

I therefore recommend a test trial for EQAO to switch to random testing of schools in various geographical neighbourhoods or by school boards to gain baseline data of student achievements instead of census-style testing where every student in every school is tested. This can provide a comparative method to explore alternative assessment models and their pros and cons.

FINDING #7

Parents and children felt the government, EQAO, and schools in general need to expand the definition of success beyond academics and a micro-scopic focus on Reading, Writing, and Mathematics.

In response to what they would change about the EQAO, the children expressed:

Chantel: I would tell the government to add arts to it because it's more fun than math and I want to see the boys draw and see them suffer.
Kobe: More play time.
Malcolm: I would tell them that they should umm (pause) tell teachers to help the students a little more if it's too hard for them because on the test they couldn't help you.

Most of the children interviewed suggested they would like to see other subjects be tested as part of EQAO testing to make it more engaging and fun. Suggested subjects included arts and physical education, which they stated were subjects they enjoyed more.

From a parent's perspective, in response to what advice they would give to the government to improve EQAO testing, Jordan's mother stated:

> I think with EQAO testing, it glorifies language and math therefore, pushing other subjects to the side, and I don't think that's fair, because a lot of kids excel in other subjects like science or gym. I feel like why emphasize it just on these two subjects? Why is those two more important than everything else? We need to teach kids as a whole and teach them everything not "oh, language and math those are the most important things and that's it, if you don't have that, then you don't have anything." You shouldn't shut down kids that actually excel and do well in other subjects. I think we are glorifying these two elements and the kid who struggles in those two elements, we are breaking them down even more. They push it more on the students and you are taking away from them doing things that that they are good at and forcing them to do something they are not good at, and we are devaluing them and our students and it's the whole process.

The current model of EQAO testing privileges numeracy and literacy as superior subjects at the expense of marginalization to other subjects such as "science or gym," particularly at the elementary level. This does not assist in judging children in a holistic manner as it places more importance on subject areas tested at the expense of overlooking other areas that children might excel but appears less important due to the limited amount of time devoted to it. This can have a profound impact on the confidence and engagement level of racialized children and those from lower socioeconomic status who due to inequitable access to resources and services systemically might start school at lower levels in domains of reading and writing.

This leads to another problematic nature of EQAO testing which does not take into account preferred learning styles of children. Explaining the difference between her two daughters who are one year apart and both participated in EQAO testing, Madison's mother states:

> Madison's older sister does not have the same level of anxiety and she doesn't really care about tests so she would just rush through her test so she can go outside. You know she is like that with her school work too. She's just more interested in creating things and more artistic that way. And I know I said earlier it doesn't matter what the test results were, but when they came back and they weren't positive, for a second I was like (puzzled face), but after I was like, you know what, like the way that they do the test and how quick they are, we can't use those as regulators or indicators of where are kids are really at.

Malcolm's step-father also emphasized the importance of not taking EQAO school scores at face value as there is a social aspect to schools which impacts student achievement that standardized tests do not capture. He explained:

> Look at the social aspect of things within the school environment. Look at the teacher efficacy within the school environment. Look at the well-being within the school environment and use the test as well to judge the schools and judge the people in these schools operating these schools. Don't just look at the test and say the score is low so this school is not up to par. You have to look at other aspects as well and by doing that you are gonna improve the school environment and the school system.

The use of differentiated instruction by teachers to meet the needs of students' preferred learning styles and the positive school climate that is welcoming and inclusive are prime examples of other important factors that influence student motivation and engagement. This is particularly important for racialized students in the context of Ontario as systemically they have "lower reading scores, higher grade failures, higher drop-out rates and much poorer employment opportunities" (Curtis et al., 1992, p. 7; Dei, 2008; Block & Galabuzi, 2011; James, 2012; Kearns, 2016). EQAO standardized tests do not capture the complexities associated with racialized identities being disadvantaged by inequality of opportunity across various public sectors systemically. The focus of standardized testing exclusively on outcomes in terms of quantitative achievement scores, with disregard for processes that impact teaching and learning at the community and school level, does not provide rich data to address the needs of specific social groups via an equity approach.

Implications

The emphasis on subjects that are tested by EQAO, predominantly Reading, Writing and Mathematics, leads to hierarchization of subjects with numeracy and literacy prioritized as superior relative to other subjects such as Arts and Health and Physical Education. This contributes to marginalization of a holistic model of education that takes into consideration domains beyond academics as part of overall healthy development of children. A common change that occurs in schools as a means of improving achievement scores of children on standardized tests is programmes and clubs with a focus on numeracy and literacy are prioritized and given more funding and resources. On the other hand, programmes and clubs not affiliated with tested subjects such as Arts and/or Physical Education are limited, and in extreme cases, eliminated and replaced, with their funding given to other programmes that focus on knowledges assessed on standardized tests.

Obsession with quantitative forms of assessment that support efficiency and accountability discourses undervalues higher-level thinking, knowledges, and skills that cannot be quantified. Gunzenhauser (2003) argues that standardized testing promotes a unique positivist philosophy of education. He goes on to state:

> The phenomenon of high-stakes testing, and standards movement from which it springs, emerges from a particular philosophy—a behaviorist, positivist philosophy that places great emphasis on what can be measured quantitatively. This is a philosophy that not only has implications for education but builds from a philosophy of reality and the ability of science to perceive that reality. (p. 53)

The assumption within the "positivist philosophy" is that numbers can measure learning accurately and consistently. This is problematic as it exclusively focuses on "outputs," and hence subjects, skills, and learning experiences that cannot be quantified are excluded from being assessed such as spirituality and emotional intelligence.

Kearns (2016) critiques the current state of standardized testing by pointing out, "Literacy is not multiple when it is reduced to a written test score, and requires a particular cultural capital to pass" (p. 125). The hegemonizing of "worthy" knowledge to domains that can be measured quantitatively is detrimental to students—their passion for learning and their sense of self-esteem and self-confidence—especially for racialized students who do not perform well on performance-based assessments in those specific domains (Masood, 2008). As a result, many students become disengaged from their schooling experience, potentially leading to greater dropout rates or further poor performance in subsequent assessments due to not caring about marks since their school experiences does not reflect their passions, interests, and lived experiences (Dei, 2008; James, 2012; Kempf, 2016).

Portelli and Konecny (2013) make the connection between neoliberal ideologies and the hierarchization of domains of knowledge in education by pointing out,

> The way of life that has emerged from neoliberalism is not consistent with the soul of democracy, for it has put aside the power of the humanities and thoughtful social sciences in favour of privileging standardization and promoting empirical evidence to the exclusion of the domains of the moral, critical, spiritual, artistic, and philosophical. Evidence has been reduced to one kind, empirical, and no other forms of evidence qualify as such. (p. 93)

Within this neoliberal paradigm, "improvement" and "success" are viewed and judged from a limited lens. This is not to say that numeracy and literacy are not important, but rather that "measuring achievement in literacy and numeracy to the exclusion of other domains can result in the diversion of resources from those domains, to the narrowing of school curricula, and to a focus on rote learning and test preparation" (People for Education, 2013, p. 3).

Recommendations

I therefore recommend the Ministry of Education to advise EQAO to implement the use of *growth portfolios* as an authentic assessment tool to track and compile examples of student progress, improvement, and achievement levels for every subject in elementary schools. This includes Language, French, Mathematics, Science and Technology, Social Studies, Health and Physical Education, and the Arts. Non-academic areas should also be identified and tracked as part of implementation of *growth portfolios.*

I therefore recommend the federal, provincial, and local governments in collaboration with Ministry of Education, EQAO, school boards, and external organizations to commit funding and resources to host an annual two-day provincial conference on *Student Success in Elementary Years and Beyond.* One of the major focuses of the conference should be on authentic and alternative assessments of children in the early years. The conference would create collaborative opportunities to bridge theory with practice involving educational stakeholders and practitioners from different fields who directly and indirectly work with young elementary-aged children. This includes, but is not limited to, researchers, teachers, early childhood educators, social workers, psychologists, child and youth care workers, special needs assistants, educational assistants, and community leaders and activists. It is imperative that the cost of attending the conference is kept to a reasonable and affordable price to allow individuals from all walks of life to attend the conference as a means of engaging with multiple voices, perspectives, and lived experiences to explore *Student Success in Elementary Years and Beyond.*

REFERENCES

Block, S., & Galabuzi, G. (2011). Canada's colour coded labour market: The gap for racialized workers. Wellesley Institute and Canadian Centre for Policy Alternatives. Retrieved from http://www.wesleyinstitute.com/wp-content/uploads/2011/03/Colour_Coded_Labour_MarketFINAL.pdf

Bourdieu, P., & Passeron, J. (1977). *Reproduction in education, society, and culture.* Beverley Hills, CA: Sage.

Curtis, B., Livingstone, D. W., & Smaller, H. (1992). *Stacking the deck: The streaming of working-class kids in Ontario schools* (Vol. 24). Toronto: James Lorimer & Company.

Dei, G. J. S. (2008). Schooling as community: Race, schooling, and the education of African youth. *Journal of Black Studies, 38*(3), 346–366.

Despres, S., Kuhn, S., Ngirumpatse, P, & Parent, M. (2013). *Real accountability or an illusion of success? A call to review standardized testing in Ontario.* Action Canada. Retrieved from http://www.actioncanada.ca/wp-content/uploads/2014/04/TF3-Report_Standardized-Testing_EN.pdf

Education Quality and Accountability Office. (2013). *EQAO: Ontario's provincial assessment program- Its history and influence 1996–2012.* Toronto: Queen's Printer for Ontario. Retrieved from http://www.eqao.com/en/about_eqao/about_the_agency/communication-docs/EQAO-history-influence.pdf

Education Quality and Accountability Office. (2017). *Highlights of the provincial results.* Toronto: Queen's Printer for Ontario. Retrieved from http://www.eqao.com/en/assessments/results/communication-docs/provincial-report-highlights-elementary-2017.pdf

Education Quality and Accountability Office. (2018). *Accountability outcomes.* Toronto: Queen's Printer for Ontario. Retrieved from http://www.eqao.com/en/about_eqao/about_the_agency/Pages/accountability-outcomes.aspx

Eizadirad, A. (2016). Is it "bad" kids or "bad" places? Where is all the violence originating from? Youth violence in the City of Toronto. *Review of Education, Pedagogy, and Cultural Studies, 38*(2), 162–188.

FairTest. (2017). Fact sheet for families on testing and young children. The National Center for Fair and Open Testing. Retrieved from http://www.fairtest.org/sites/default/files/YoungChildTestingFactSheet2017.pdf

Fiore, L. (2012). *Assessment of young children: A collaborative approach.* New York: Routledge.

Fraser Institute. (2018). *School performance.* Retrieved from https://www.fraser-institute.org/school-performance

Gunzenhauser, M. G. (2003). High-stakes testing and the default philosophy of education. *Theory into Practice, 42*(1), 51–58.

Hart, D., & Kempf, A. (2015). *Public attitudes toward education in Ontario 2015: The 19th OISE survey of educational issues.* OISE, University of Toronto. Retrieved from https://tspace.library.utoronto.ca/bitstream/1807/76898/2/Final_Report_-_19th_OISE_Survey_on_Educational_Issues_2015.pdf

James, C. E. (2012). *Life at the intersection: Community, class and schooling.* Halifax, NS: Fernwood Publishing.

Kearns, L. (2016). The construction of 'illiterate' and 'literate' youth: The effects of high-stakes standardized literacy testing. *Race Ethnicity and Education, 19*(1), 121–140.

Kempf, A. (2016). *The pedagogy of standardized testing: The radical impacts of educational standardization in the US and Canada.* New York: Springer.

Kohn, A. (2000). *The case against standardized testing: Raising scores, ruining the schools.* Portsmouth, NH: Heinemann.

Masood, O. (2008). *At risk: The racialized student marked for educational failure.* (Unpublished doctoral dissertation). University of Toronto, Toronto, ON.

Miller, J. P. (2000). *Education and the soul: Toward a spiritual curriculum.* New York: SUNY Press.

Ontario Ministry of Education. (2010). *Growing success: Assessment, evaluation, and reporting in Ontario schools.* Toronto: Queen's Printer for Ontario. Retrieved from http://www.edu.gov.on.ca/eng/policyfunding/growSuccess.pdf

Ontario Ministry of Education. (2014). *How does learning happen? Ontario's pedagogy for the early years: A resource about learning through relationships for those who work with young children and their families.* Toronto: Queen's Printer for Ontario. Retrieved from http://www.edu.gov.on.ca/childcare/HowLearningHappens.pdf

Ontario Teachers' Federation. (2011). A new vision for large-scale testing in Ontario. Retrieved from https://www.otffeo.on.ca/en/wp-content/uploads/sites/2/2013/09/new_vision.pdf

People for Education. (2013). *Broader measures of success: Measuring what matters in education.* Toronto, ON: People for Education. Retrieved from https://peopleforeducation.ca/wp-content/uploads/2017/08/Broader-measures-of-success-Measuring-what-matters-in-education.pdf

Portelli, J., & Konecny, P. C. (2013). Neoliberalism, subversion, and democracy in education. *Encounters on Education, 14*, 87–97.

Portelli, J., & Vilbert, A. (2002). Standards, equity, and the curriculum of life. *Analytic Teaching, 22*(1), 4–19.

Russo, L. (2012). "Standardized" play and creativity for young children? The climate of increased standardization and accountability in early childhood classrooms. *Counterpoints, 425*, 140–156.

Sharma, M. (2009). *Inner city students: Stamped, labeled and shipped out! Deficit thinking and democracy in an age of neoliberalism.* (Unpublished master's thesis). University of Toronto, Toronto, ON.

Stiggins, R. (2014). *Revolutionize assessment.* Thousand Oaks, CA: Corwin.

Weiner, E. (2014). *Deschooling the imagination: Critical thought as social practice.* Boulder, CO: Paradigm Publishers.

CHAPTER 9

External Assessment as Stereotyping

Within this chapter I present my theory of *external assessment as stereotyping*. Although the foundation of the theory presented is rooted in the data collected via semi-structured interviews focusing on lived experiences of racialized children, parents, and educators with EQAO standardized testing, the theory is further supported by alarming statistics in different institutions beyond education outlining persistent systemic inequities impacting racialized identities. I argue that standardized tests, as a political accountability tool, are detrimental to student's growth and development given how they are currently administered and the results used. Through external assessment as stereotyping, we can begin to see how EQAO diminishes the student's soul and passion for learning leading to lowering their self-esteem and producing feelings of inadequacy and being incompetent. Side-effects of standardized testing include, but are not limited to, perpetuation of a neoliberal deficit model of education that situates failure exclusively on individualistic factors such as lack of effort and preparation, constructing a narrow definition of success predominantly judged by quantifiable indicators in domains of literacy and numeracy, reduction in passion for learning due to boredom and lack of connections to curriculum content, and an increase in stress and anxiety levels leading to greater absenteeism.

© The Author(s) 2019
A. Eizadirad, *Decolonizing Educational Assessment*,
https://doi.org/10.1007/978-3-030-27462-7_9

CRITICAL RACE THEORY REVISITED

Addressing the achievement gap between racialized identities and white students as well as between those from higher socio-economic status and lower socio-economic status through equitable practices is one of the top priorities of current education systems around the world at all levels. A key question to consider is whether EQAO standardized testing, as an account-ability tool and the way it is currently administered, helps to address iden-tified inequities within the education system or is it further perpetuating and widening the already existing inequities and the achievement gap across various social groups?

Before going into the analysis, Critical Race Theory is revisited as a theoretical framework to help situate the lens through which I make the argument for external assessment as stereotyping. Critical Race Theory (CRT) is used to deconstruct responses of children, parents, and educa-tors interviewed who self-identified as racialized. I use Knoester and Au's (2017) definition of CRT:

> Critical Race Theory is a conceptual framework useful in understanding how racism operates, including within institutions such as schools, by paying careful attention to the differential resources and opportunities available to students of different races, as opposed to the more common form of racial theorizing, focusing on individual acts of hatred or racism. (p. 4)

Knoester and Au (2017) further explain that

> [A] key tenet of Critical Race Theory is that such inequality is regularly obscured under the guise of race-less or race-neutral laws and policies and is instead framed around individual equality as expressed through concepts such as meritocracy—that success is purely the result of individual hard work and not the function of social, historical, or institutional process. (p. 4)

The notion of "meritocracy" contributes to advancing a deficit model of education in today's schools blaming the student for their failure without examining systemic barriers and challenges such as access to resources and social support services available.

All the participants interviewed, except one child and parent, self-identified as racialized. Their lived experiences as a form of valuable embodied knowledge provide significant and insightful counter-narratives to explore the impact of EQAO standardized testing on racialized identities. I want to emphasize that when I use the term racialized, it is beyond the binary of black and white. It focuses on power dynamics at the institutional level. I use Block and Galabuzi's (2011) definition of racialization which is defined as

> The process through which groups come to be designated as different and on that basis subjected to differential and unequal treatment. In the present context, racialized groups include those who may experience differential treatment on the basis of race, ethnicity, language, economics, [and] religion. (p. 19)

At the core of racialization and being a racialized person is navigating inequitable power dynamics at the institutional and societal level in the form of systemic barriers related to accessibility to opportunities and services. Baszile (2009) explains the importance of listening to counter-stories from a CRT lens:

> They are told from the perspective of the marginalized and are intended to challenge the universality and often the efficacy of the majoritarian story, not simply in its context but also in its very structure. The story-counterstory frame not only works to uncover subjugated knowledge but it also allows one to see and examine the relationship between the stories and the role race and other subjectivities play in shaping their differences. (pp. 10–11)

The essence of this book is about providing an avenue for racialized identities to express their counter-stories based on their lived experiences. By taking time to listen to their counter-stories, told by voices of racialized children, parents, and educators about their experience with EQAO standardized testing, we can confirm, challenge, oppose, and look into the nuances, complexities, and contradictions associated with the dominant narrative disseminated by EQAO regarding the benefits of EQAO standardized testing as an accountability tool within schools. Particularly, we can learn more about how specific social groups, in this case racialized identities, are impacted by EQAO testing and whether this is a practice that needs to be phased out or altered to better meet their educational needs, particularly in the early years where often the foundation and passion for learning is established.

FINDING #8

Racialized children and parents expressed that the EQAO test is culturally and racially biased as it promotes a Eurocentric curriculum and way of life. They felt the content of EQAO standardized tests reflects lived experiences of families from higher socio-economic status and lacks relevant connections to the identity and lived experiences of racialized students and families from lower socio-economic status.

Racialized parents interviewed expressed that one of the positive aspects of EQAO testing is its potential to assist schools with identifying certain gaps in the system particularly areas needing further improvement. This is often a point that is also emphasized by EQAO and its dominant narrative about the benefits of EQAO testing in the early years. Yet, this data needs to be supplemented with other sources to capture the complexities and nuances that impact the school-community interface and its teaching and learning conditions. Administrators and teachers can deconstruct their school's EQAO data to allocate certain resources and support services to specific students or classrooms to assist with greater student achievement. Yet, the achievement gap between racialized identities and white students, as well as those from higher socio-economic status and lower socio-economic status has not been drastically reduced systemically within the education system since the inception of EQAO standardized testing in 1996. Therefore, we must ask, who does the current policy of EQAO standardized testing enactment benefit and privilege, and which social groups are disadvantaged and oppressed?

Relative to the issue of accessibility to resources and support services, parents interviewed felt that the current model of education and EQAO administration creates competition amongst schools to compete for limited resources available whether in terms of funding or tangible resources such as district coaches or computers. Jordan's step-father explained from a teacher perspective that

> Hand to hand with EQAO, it pits different areas against each other. Resources kind of fall under the same category where schools right down the street here who might not have a lot of resources or money won't be able to have a nice computer lab, lots of field trips or food programs. Schools that are in more affluent neighbourhoods who have a lot more money and whose parent councils are twenty-five people or more are more involved and

there is all this fundraising happening, you know. The balance needs to come down a bit across all boards, especially if the board wants everybody to move up together. I think personally they are creating a big gap between the upper class versus middle to bottom class. I think resources are one of the key factors. More resources need to be pumped into the schools that need it and there needs to be more emphasis on giving them more opportunities to do well.

Laila's mother who is also a teacher echoed similar concerns. She stated in response to how to improve schools that the focus has to be more on equitable funding and allocation of resources to different schools. She expressed, "Ways to improve school would be with funding. Also to think about the areas schools are in and the different types of funding and funding models they get. This is just not equal amongst schools."

The current model of EQAO administration is based on the assumption and the normalized metanarrative that EQAO standardized tests capture student achievement levels accurately and "objectively" with an over-emphasis on its positive impact. At the institutional level, the Ministry of Education or EQAO does not engage in much discussion about negative or harmful effects of EQAO testing on children. Yet, as Ricci (2004) states, "By not examining the students holistically, but merely statistically, students suffer and society suffers" (pp. 355–356). From an equity lens, it is important to engage in dialogues and discussions about whether writing EQAO tests are beneficial to all students given their unique needs, personalities, and lived experiences? I asked racialized parents for their opinion on this issue, and below is some of their responses:

Kobe's mother: There is a huge disadvantage for young people who might have some form of a disability. For example, we might have kids who struggle with severe anxiety and having them sit and write a test will make them very anxious. So in a regular school, they might chunk it, meaning they give small parts or let them write it in a different context so they are comfortable. But you would think they just shouldn't have to write the test, but if you don't write the test, the child gets an automatic zero which means the average of the school goes down. So you will find this very precarious position of administrators and teachers who don't want to get a lower mark because of the reflection of the school and the political piece. They make children write it who probably shouldn't be writing a test like that. There is all kinds of accommodations meaning you can give someone a quiet space with an assistant in the room, and while I think that is a great accommodation which might make them perform better intellectually, kids being excluded from a classroom to write this test away from their peer group is often enough to trigger anxiety because they feel different.

Deshaun's mother: On one hand, it's good because you want to make the comparison of where everybody's level is at. The only downfall to that is just that some children have different learning abilities, ways that they learn or ways that they apply what they've learned, so it might not be in the same format that standardized testing is given.

Kobe and Deshaun's mother provide great examples of how for certain students such as those with identified exceptionalities, the EQAO test and the way it is administered is counter-productive and harmful as it makes them feel excluded and different, further triggering socio-emotional anxiety and stress associated with test-taking. Yet, due to the currency and importance associated with school rankings, and the process that all students who do not write the EQAO test receive an automatic zero in aggregating overall school scores, the needs of certain students are sacrificed and overlooked for political purposes affiliated with school rankings. This is an issue that needs to be re-examined particularly from an equity lens where the objective is to level the playing field when it comes to accessibility to opportunities and improving learning conditions for social groups that are systemically disadvantaged and marginalized.

Similarly, Malcolm's step-father who is a teacher, expressed he feels the EQAO test is geared towards white students and it privileges them because the test content is predominantly Eurocentric. He goes on to state, "This test [the Grade 3 EQAO test] is not geared towards all students. It's geared towards a specific type of student." I followed up by asking Malcolm's step-father who is the typical student that the EQAO standardized test is "geared for" in his opinion. He responded by stating, "It's the middle class, probably white (pause), yea, it's middle class white students it's basically based for." When asked what he thinks of how EQAO results are used, he stated,

A lot of times the results are used to rate the school, rate the teachers as well, and uhhh (pause) it's for the Ministry. The Ministry uses it for their statistics and numbers and things of that nature. For the academia it's effective, but for the human aspect, I don't think so because the test is geared for a specific type of student and there is so many diverse students here so it's kind of not an equal playing field.

Reflecting on his experiences administrating different sets of EQAO tests over the years, Kobe's father who is currently a vice-principal stated:

> Some of the standardized testing that I've seen done (pause) like it's always Eurocentric. So I remember a reading assessment we used to give to kids in Grade 3 and it was about (pause) one of the questions was about sheep farming and the kids in the community where I was teaching knew nothing about sheep farming so it was very difficult for them to make sense of the question, not because they didn't know how to read or answer a question, but because they didn't have the context to make sense of it.

Kobe's father emphasizes that it is not that children do not "know how to read or answer a question" but rather the test questions sometimes do not reflect the lived experiences of children in the community. Kobe's mother also jumped in and gave her opinion as a parent and principal.

> Anyone who is economically advantaged, I think the testing is more culturally relevant to them. So an example would be there was a question about swimming across the lake at a cottage. So you know only a certain economic group would know and has access to swimming across a lake on a cottage. So anyone who is reading that question and has actually swam across a lake at a cottage is going to feel a little bit more relaxed and have (pause) you know a connection whereas someone who hasn't won't. So I think there is absolutely a cultural bias!

Overall, racialized parents who worked in the education system felt EQAO questions privilege white affluent students and their Eurocentric values and experiences. Jordan's step-father, also as a parent and a teacher expressed,

> It's basically, from my perspective, a standardized test that basically the board and the province want to see what the areas (pause) like how well different areas are doing based on this test that is kind of focused towards one group of people who I would say more so are white.

Jordan's step-father, similar to Malcolm and Kobe's father, expressed concerns about how EQAO questions can marginalize racialized identities due to lack of relevance of the questions to the students' lived experiences and community circumstances. He went on to state,

It's almost as if they want to put everybody inside this box and most people don't fit in that box. The language for the test is a lot different than most kids would know; you know, it's kind of geared towards kids who experience more things, have a little more money, and a little more privileged. For example, how many inner city kids can tell you where Algonquin Park is or where Markham is? Even for math, there are kids who never had more than twenty dollars in their hands and you're asking them complex questions. Culturally it is not reflective of most cultures, especially in a city like Toronto.

Collectively responses from the racialized parents express that EQAO tests function under a one-size-fits-all approach making the assumption that all students have certain experiences when this is not the case. The scenarios which are made reference to as part of EQAO questions often reflect the lifestyles and experiences of those from higher socio-economic status, hence disadvantaging racialized identities and those from lower socio-economic status as the content is less relatable to them.

IMPLICATIONS

Several initiatives have emerged in recent years to try to mitigate the high dropout rates amongst racialized students in TDSB schools. In Toronto, the idea of an Africentric Alternative School was proposed, debated, and implemented. The school began operating in September 2009 with 90 elementary students enrolled into its unique programme. The Africentric Alternative School is not exclusively restricted to black students or teachers, but the teachers are predominantly of African descent and the curriculum is based on an African paradigm and Seven Principles of Nzugo Saba which focuses on nurturing a strong sense of community and African culture. Africentric Alternative School continues to operate today and the Africentric curriculum has been expanded as part of Grades 9 and 10 courses in two high schools in Toronto.

Stiggins (2014) raises a critical question about assessment methods which asks, "Should we assess what is easy to measure or what is important?" (p. 76). Similarly, Ball (1990) warns us that "policy is clearly a matter of authoritative allocation of values," and "values do not float free of their social context" (p. 3). Therefore, we must ask whose interests does standardized testing serve and at what costs? It is significant to continuously question "commonsense" assumptions about standardization and its benefits, and ask furthermore whose values and knowledges are established as the norm and used as a baseline measure for judgement and comparison through standardized testing. Price (2003) questions the neutrality and "objectivity" of standardized tests by pointing out,

> While all tests have biases, standardized tests are biased in standardized ways. Standardized tests list towards specific views and knowledge-sets in both intended and unintended ways—but by their very nature they exclude a diversity of interpretations in support of hegemonic views. (p. 718)

Similarly, Tupper and Cappello (2008) critique standardized testing for its shortcomings by emphasizing, "Mainstream education is an extension of colonization insofar as it has been used to promote a dominant narrative of the past and privilege certain ways of knowing" (p. 563). Through normalization and legitimization of standardized testing as an accountability tool, certain knowledges are normalized and legitimized, and consequentially a hierarchy of knowledges constructed which often marginalizes indigenous, oral, and non-hegemonic epistemologies and languages (Eizadirad, Martinez, & Ruminot, 2016). As part of the current system, literacy and numeracy are prioritized as more important subjects, supported with narratives associated with "Back to Basics" movements.

I refer to earlier studies discussed in detail in Chap. 4 and expand on Nezavdal's (2003) theoretical framework of "assessment as a social construct" (p. 69) and Hori's (2013) definition of "structural violence" (p. 4), to form the argument that externally administered standardized tests such as EQAO based on how they are currently administered and the results used, function as a political tool for stereotyping of racialized students and communities. *External assessment as stereotyping* is structurally violent for racialized children and those from lower socio-economic status as it serves to diminish their self-confidence, create doubt in their competencies, and in the long run leads absenteeism due to boredom and lack of connections to curricular content. Holistically this consequentially leads to lower access to opportunities for upward social mobility through streaming of racialized identities into applied fields and over-representation in special education based on how standardized test results are interpreted and used by educators and school administrators (Curtis, Livingstone, & Smaller, 1992; Dei, 2008; Hori, 2013; James, 2012).

It is important to note and distinguish that not all assessment types are harmful or detrimental to student's development and growth; the key is how the tests are administered and the results used. The argument being made here is that when standardized tests such as EQAO are assessed via an external third-party agency without consideration and knowledge from an ecological place-based perspective about the power dynamics and socio-political conditions that impact the teaching and learning conditions, vis-à-vis the school-community interface, it cannot reproduce rich data that is useful in improving student learning. Therefore, *external assessment as stereotyping* functions at three levels:

a. *Stereotypes and constructs the racialized student as a low achiever from a young age.*

This can occur in two ways: psychologically or socio-emotionally by the student through their self-critique and self-perception about how they did on the EQAO test leading to a self-fulfilling prophecy, or by the teacher or administrators in Grade 4 upon returning EQAO individual student results through their direct and indirect actions in the classroom and in the larger context of the school. The first set of EQAO standardized tests are administered at the end of Grade 3 when children are still developing and experiencing many changes physically, psychologically, and socio-emotionally. The labelling of the child as an "under-achiever" or "at-risk" in the mind of the child and the teacher according to their achievement level on the Grade 3 EQAO test can serve as a starting point and a spark to manifest the stereotype. This feeds into the student being judged through a deficit lens (Portelli & Sharma, 2014), a liability to the school reputation and school rankings, that blames them for their failure without examining holistically their unique identities, life circumstances, and systemic barriers impacting their academic performance such as level of accessibility to resources, opportunities, and social support services (Hulchanski, 2007). As Au (2010) argues, standardized tests advance "an ideology of meritocracy that fundamentally masks structural inequalities related to race and economic class" (p. 7). Similarly, Curtis et al. (1992) in *Stacking the Deck: The Streaming of Working-Class Kids in Ontario Schools* point out how deficit thinking has implications for working-class children as "Explicit streaming in elementary school is carried out through the placement of kids labelled 'behavioural,' 'slow learning,' and 'learning disabled' in classes of special education" (p. 53).

b. *Perpetuates and reconfirms the stereotype of the racialized student being a low achiever with poor intellectual skills, a trend that continues as the student goes on to middle school and high school.*

Curtis et al. (1992) argue that "The evidence points to an educational system that segregates many students from their peers, often for long periods of time, in low expectation 'behavioural' programmes on the basis of subjective reporting and culturally-biased testing. Such students come disproportionately from the families of the working class, and ethnic/racial minorities" (p. 64). Placing children in behavioural and/or special education classes from an early age, with the decision profoundly influenced by standardized test results in elementary settings, can be damaging to healthy development of the child and it can further disengage them from school activities through lack of motivation, boredom, and lack of effort in completing and participating in school initiatives. Furthermore, from a teacher and administrator perspective, "low-achievers are perceived as a liability" and become a threat to bringing down the overall school scores which indirectly can lead to "devaluing of less successful students" (Froese-Germain, 2001, p. 118). The powerful impact of the stereotype, as a label and an ideology loaded with assumptions, is planted in the early years derived from results on EQAO standardized tests and perpetuated through subsequent years that leads to "Students who did not meet the provincial standard early in their schooling most likely to continue not meeting the standard in later grades," and in contrast "Students who met the provincial standard early in their schooling were most likely to also meet the standard in secondary school" (Shulman, Hinton, Zhang, & Kozlow, 2014, p. 3).

   c. *Challenges the stereotype of the racialized student being a low achiever by producing positive achievement results. Although positive at the surface, the constant effort of defending one's intellectual abilities while navigating predominantly white elite spaces embedded with hierarchical power relations saturated with stereotypical assumptions about one's race, culture, ethnicity, and/or socio-economic status is exhausting and socio-emotionally draining contributing to subsequent poor performance, feelings of exclusion and not belonging, and/or triggering identity issues and crisis that can lead to absenteeism and dropping out of school.*

In the long term, this leads to dropout, or as Dei, Holmes, Mazzuca, McIsaac, and Campbell (1995) call it "push-out," disengagement, and not wanting to be within a learning environment that does not make one feel good about themselves, even though they are intellectually competent compared to their peers (hooks, 2003; Kearns, 2016; Ladson-Billings, 1994; Razack, 2002). This is supported by the trend that many racialized students and even professors of colour as full-time faculty feel out of place attending predominantly white affluent schools, experiencing micro aggressions in classrooms and on campus and having to constantly explain their identity and culture such as their hair and food and other cultural and racial factors about themselves to their peers with respect to stereotypes made about them (Rodriguez, 2018). This trend and harmful impact of the stereotype manifests itself systemically via statistics where in Ontario in 2015, there was a 69 per cent high school graduation rate for black students and 50 per cent for Indigenous students, versus 84 per cent for white students (Colour of Poverty and Colour of Change, 2019, p. 1).

Ahmed (2007) explains in *A Phenomenology of Whiteness* how social spaces are engrained with whiteness:

> So yes they walk into the room, and I notice that they were not there before, as a retrospective reoccupation of a space that I already inhabited. I look around, and re-encounter the sea of whiteness. As many have argued, whiteness is invisible and unmarked, as the absent centre against which others appear only as deviants, or points of deviation. Whiteness is only invisible for those who inhabit it, or those who get so used to its inhabitance that they learn not to see it, even when they are not it. Spaces are orientated "around" whiteness, insofar as whiteness is not seen. We do not face whiteness; it "trails behind" bodies, as what is assumed to be given. The effect of this "around whiteness" is the institutionalization of a certain "likeness," which makes non-white bodies feel uncomfortable, exposed, visible, different, when they take up this space. (p. 157)

As Ahmed explains, whiteness as an "invisible and unmarked" force is sprinkled and embedded within all social settings and used as a framework to judge behaviour and actions of others. As a result, actions, behaviours, and embodied identities and existences of racialized identities and persons of colour are judged relative to a white frame of reference that has historically been normalized and legitimized, labelling those different as deviant. Rodriguez (2018) in her book *Decolonizing Academia: Poverty, Oppression, and Pain* discusses how as a person of colour seeking a tenure-track professor position, she often experienced constant micro aggressions by other colleagues, particularly white male professors, when she opposed the status quo. She goes on to explain how her identity and actions were labelled different in a negative light by stating, "Not all of us have the luxury to speak freely without getting penalized by being called too radical, too emotional, too angry, or even not scholarly enough" (p. 12).

Overall, *external assessment as stereotyping* as a theoretical concept argues that externally mandated standardized tests administered via third-party agencies cause great damage to racialized students' identities; particularly minoritized non-white students and those from lower socio-economic backgrounds as it contributes to impeding their healthy and holistic development. As Curtis et al. (1992) point out,

> The educational potential of vast members of people continues to be wasted through streaming. It is a form of institutionalized violence that convinces many working-class people that they belong in dead-end programmes with stunted curricula, to be followed by insecure, low-paid employment. The disgust with learning, hatred of teachers, distrust of intellectual work, and generalized resistance to authority which many drop-outs acquire are not a result of their biological or cultural "deficiencies." Rather, the main cause lies in socially discriminatory forms of schooling, and in the false promises of competition in a system which demands that many fail. (p. 99)

Bhabha (1983) states, "The objective of colonial discourse is to construe the colonised as a population of degenerate types on the basis of racial origin, in order to justify conquest and to establish systems of administration and instruction" (p. 22). Labelling children as "low achievers" or "behavioural" allows those in positions of authority in the school system to justify specific types of administration, instruction, and surveillance upon students often holding them back from their full potential. Bhabha (1983) further explains,

> The stereotype is not a simplification because it is a false representation of a given reality. It is a simplification because it is an arrested, fixated form of representation that, in denying the play of difference (that the negation through the Other permits), constitutes a problem for the representation of the subject in significations of psychic and social relations. (p. 26)

External assessment as stereotyping, produced via the political currency and importance given to EQAO test scores and school rankings, perpetuates deficit thinking by inscribing a negative label in the form of a "fixated form of representation" on racialized, minoritized, non-white students, and those from lower socio-economic backgrounds within the "psychic and social relations" in schools. Current examples of normalized negative labels used in schools that perpetuate stereotypes include the student being referred to as "at-risk," "illiterate," "behavioural," or being an "applied" student (Kearns, 2011; Masood, 2008). Consequentially, the negative ideologies affiliated with such negative labels impacts how racialized students view themselves and interact and build relations with others in schools including peers, teachers, and administrators. The big picture consequences and implications are greater absenteeism and limited access to opportunities and in the long term diminished pathways for upward social mobility.

Currently, we are focusing too much attention on equality of outcome symbolized by standardized test scores as a signifier of overall student achievement. As long as we continue to abandon examining the processes that lead to the outcome, vis-à-vis the opportunity gap, the achievement gap will not be minimized sustainably and instead further intensify. As Curtis et al. (1992) argue, "the school system convinces many working-class kids that they are stupid, incapable, incompetent, and that their aim in life should be to show up at work on time while being polite to their bosses. This is part of the violence that streaming does to working-class kids" (p. 3). This aligns with what Anyon (1980) found as part of her ethnographic comparative study where she spent time in working-class and affluent schools and concluded that students in affluent schools receive more challenging and interdisciplinary curriculum that promotes higher-level thinking, whereas students in working-class schools receive lower-level thinking curriculum that focuses on rote memorization and learning appropriate behaviours and mannerism.

Another consequence of having limited access to opportunities for upward social mobility is living in poverty or not being able to climb into a higher socio-economic class. Polanyi, Wilson, Mustachi, Ekra, and Kerr (2017) in their report titled, *Unequal City: The Hidden Divide among Toronto's Children and Youth: 2017 Toronto Child and Family Poverty Report Card*, use 2016 census data to outline how specific racialized social groups and those from lower socio-economic status are disadvantaged systemically compared to their white and affluent counterparts. They provide the following statistics to make their case:

- Indigenous families with children in the City of Toronto experience an extremely high poverty rate of 84%.
- Children in racialized families are more than twice as likely to be living in poverty compared to children in non-racialized families (25.3% compared to 11.4%) in the Toronto region.

- Almost one in two children who are of West Asian (46.8%) or Arab (46.7%) background live in poverty in the Toronto region. This is more than four times the rate of poverty of children in non-racialized families.
- Child poverty rates for children who are second- and third-generation Canadian remain particularly high for Black and Latin American families in the Toronto region.
- 37.8% of children in lone-parent families in the Toronto region live in poverty, while the rate for children in female lone-parent households is 40%, more than twice the poverty rate of two-parent families.
- The gap in child poverty rates across Toronto neighbourhoods remains stark, ranging from 4.1% in Kingsway South to 60.1% in Thorncliffe Park.
- Thirteen city wards have areas of child poverty where rates are 50% or more. (p. 1)

These statistics contextualize how unequitable distribution of resources and social services across spatial geographies makes it unrealistic to expect all children to achieve at the same level, as they do not all have access to the same privileges when starting school in the early years given their unique identities and the neighbourhood conditions they live in.

Closing the Achievement Gap via Rebalancing the Opportunity Gap

We need to shift our focus to realigning the opportunity gap in a more equitable manner as a long-term sustainable approach and strategy towards closing the achievement gap between racialized and non-racialized students and those from higher and lower SES. This approach goes beyond a microscopic focus on outcome-based standardized test scores to considering synergic collaborative efforts between schools and outside organizations in the community offering holistic services to address barriers that currently exist at a systemic level for specific social groups. We must continue to engage in dialogue about whether standardized testing is contributing to closing the achievement gap or further perpetuating and intensifying the disparity between the haves and the have-nots. As Nezavdal (2003) states, "Educating students is about maximizing learning by meeting needs, by propelling passions, and by nurturing human curiosity, not closing doors forever because of one test" (p. 72), and that "we must strive towards a reconciliation of the split between teaching, teacher education, and policy making" (p. 76).

TDSB's *Enhancing Equity Task Force Report and Recommendations* released in December 2017 is a good starting point to acknowledge some of the current systemic barriers that exist within the educational system and work towards identifying specific areas needing change to create more equitable policies and practices. But we must go beyond simply acknowledging barriers and systemic challenges to acting upon them and trying new alternative approaches and changes to address unmet needs of students. The *Enhancing Equity Task Force Report and Recommendations* states,

> The Enhancing Equity Task Force's mandate is to support the TDSB as it seeks to ensure that the framework of "equity for all" infuses every aspect of the Board's work, for students and staff alike. Equity is a question of fundamental human rights; it is also the foundation for excellence for all students, and for student achievement, well-being, and belonging. (p. 4)

Under the subheading "Recommendations," as a means of aligning TDSB's practices with the mandate and vision of "equity for all," the Task Force "made recommendations in the following six areas, so as to":

1. Ensure equitable educational access, experiences, and opportunities for all students in all schools;
2. Make students whole: effectively addressing school incidents and complaints;
3. Ensure equitable access to funding and resources among schools;
4. Meaningfully engage students, families, and communities in building a culture of equity at school;
5. Ensure equity in staff employment, transfer, and promotion; and,
6. Provide professional learning on equity, anti-racism, and anti-oppression for all. (p. 5)

These identified six areas can serve as starting reference points where new changes can be discussed and implemented to make education policies and practices more equitable for racialized and minoritized students. Yet, interestingly the practice of EQAO preparation, administration, and use of data by schools was not questioned as part of the report. This is an area that needs to be further examined, knowing that the current practice is further perpetuating inequities in the achievement gap. There needs to be a Task Force Committee which exclusively examines through community consultations with students, parents, teachers, administrators, scholars, researchers, and community members the larger impact of EQAO testing on educational stakeholders, with the core question being whether EQAO preparation and administration should be altered or completely eliminated.

When asked for suggestions on how to improve schools from the perspective of a parent and an administrator, Kobe's father stated:

> I think we need two things. One, we need schools and teachers and administrators who are not racist or classist or sexist because those things are systems that play out in schooling that dramatically impact the outcomes of kids and not necessarily intentionally, as people who support these systems, but without a critical consciousness we feed into a system that continues to maintain those inequities. So we need educators who are able to challenge those things, so we need to, you know, do professional learning around that training and some people need to go and other people need to come in to shift those kind of structures. The other thing that needs to happen is we need to think of a more equity based as opposed to an equality based model for education so that we can do things, like in a school with high needs, like some of the communities we know of, that are high needs, there needs to be a different model. We need to be able to pull the best teachers in the city to work in those communities, because the needs are so much greater and there are structures that are currently in place that don't allow us to get rid of people that are detrimental to particular communities. In some communities, really, it's a life or death situation, because if some of these young people do not have access to quality education, we know where they will end up. So we have to do much more radical moves to impact change in those communities. We can't play within the same rules and norms. We need to be able to step outside of that to think critically about how we are going to ensure all those young people have access to education that is critical to their livelihood really in the long run.

Kobe's father reiterates that investing in closing the opportunity gap as a means of addressing the current disparity in the achievement gap has its challenges within an education system that operates within hierarchical power relations resisting dramatic change and often imposing uniformity across spatial geographies.

One effective approach that some schools are using to close the opportunity gap is synergic collaboration with external organizations including grassroots non-profit organizations at the local community level involving practitioners from other sectors to provide socio-culturally relevant and responsive services relative to the holistic needs of the student population and community demographics. Two effective programmes that function as synergic collaborations offering holistic services which can serve as models for "best practices" in contributing to closing the achievement gap are TDSB's *Model Schools for Inner Cities (MSIC)* and *Youth Association for Academics, Athletics, and Character Education (YAAACE) Summer Institute*. Before describing these programmes in detail in terms of how they operate and their impact, it is important to note that when an initiative is labelled as "best practices," it should not be taken at face value in the sense that it should be copied and pasted into another community or spatial location. "Best practices" should be interpreted as containing a framework and guidelines that can be beneficial if replicated, but in order for it to be effective, the structure of the programmes and its contents offered must be tailored relative to the needs and demographics of the participants and the power dynamics embedded within the community where the programme is offered.

TDSB's *Model Schools for Inner Cities* (MSIC) "is a board wide initiative that addresses the impacts of poverty on students' achievement and well-being" (TDSB, 2017b, p. 64). The programme began in 2006 with selection of 3 schools based on the Learning Opportunity Index (LOI) and over time has grown to be implemented within 150 schools serving over 56,000 students. According to the TDSB (2017a), "The LOI ranks each school based on measures of external challenges affecting student success. The school with the greatest level of external challenges is ranked number one and is described as highest on the index" (p. 2). There are separate lists created for elementary and secondary schools. MSIC allocates a budget ranging from $10,000 to $14,000 for selected schools ranked near the top of the LOI (TDSB, 2018). Schools have flexibility to plan, outline, and document how the money is used in specific identified areas to increase opportunities for student success. The five identified areas which the money can be used towards are:

1. Innovative teaching and learning practices
2. Providing support services to meet social, emotional and physical well-being of students
3. Establishing schools as the heart of the community
4. Researching, reviewing and evaluating students and programs
5. An ongoing commitment to share successful practice. (TDSB, 2018, para. 2)

Examples of services offered as part of *MSIC* initiatives include hearing and vision screenings for students, parent workshops, after school recreation programmes in partnerships with other agencies, nutrition, snack, and lunch programmes, and addition of specialized staff such as teaching and learning coaches or community support workers assigned to work with cluster of schools. Administrators receiving the money as part of *MSIC* have the flexibility to decide where the money is best spent given the needs of the student demographics as well as the larger needs of the community in which the school is situated within. This allows for ecological place-based policy enactment and funding implementation which is what is needed to close the achievement gap in a sustainable manner.

Another programme that models "best practices" is *Youth Association for Academics, Athletics, and Character Education (YAAACE) Summer Institute*. In 2007, being fed up with the violence plaguing the community and the constant negative media exposure affiliating Jane and Finch with guns, gangs, and crime, Devon Jones an elementary school teacher within the Jane and Finch neighbourhood decided to create a non-profit organization to mitigate the inequality of opportunity that was consuming many of his students towards a life of crime leading them to being incarcerated or dying at a young age. Jordan Manners and Kwasi Peters were his students who were killed at a young age due to gun violence amongst many others where he attended their funerals and was heart-broken by them dying at such a young age (Williams, Jones, & Bailey, 2013).

Being an elementary school teacher in the Jane and Finch community, Jones recognized that children are largely influenced by their surrounding environments in terms of their identity development and decision-making. When he was planning the design of a logo for his organization which would be called Youth Association for Academics, Athletics, and Character Education (YAAACE), the colour of the logo was chosen as purple with intentionality (see Image 9.1) as a means to mitigate the turf war that was making children choose sides from an early age in the Jane and Finch community; with the Crips dominating the housing projects in Finch's south side and the Bloods dominating the housing projects on the Finch's north side (Friesen, 2018, Para. 5). Friesen (2018) further expands, "It's a segregation expressed mainly through clothing, blue for Crips and red for Bloods, and it has existed for a decade. Nor is it limited to serious criminals, but extends all the way to 13-year-old wannabes" (Para. 6). Jones selected the colour purple both for its neutrality and for its symbolism for togetherness as when red and blue are mixed you get purple. It was

Image 9.1   YAAACE
logo (YAAACE, 2018)

intended to bring youth from both sides of the community into a neutral space where they could learn and grow together without worrying about turf confrontations or having to belong to a gang for safety purposes. Hiring respected leaders from the community as staff to lead its programmes, YAAACE intended to break the ideological concept that one had to choose between either the Bloods or the Crips to survive and be sheltered from violence; the children and youth needed hope and faith that a better alternative exists.

In terms of programming and services offered, Devon Jones merged school and community to one socio-culturally relevant and responsive enterprise that offers holistic services focusing on increasing accessibility to opportunities for members of the Jane and Finch community. What makes YAAACE stand out and be unique from other programmes available within the neighbourhood or across the City of Toronto is its synergic collaboration with external organizations and agencies at the local community level involving practitioners from other sectors that work with children, youth, and young adults to provide socio-culturally relevant and holistic services relative to the needs of the community members and the demographics of the participants enrolled in their programmes. The objective of YAAACE is to help marginalized, racialized, and poor children and youth from under-resourced communities through "year round comprehensive programming and activities" (YAAACE, 2018, para. 1). YAAACE strives to close the achievement gap by focusing on minimizing the opportunity gap through its Social Inclusion Strategy. According to YAAACE (2018),

YAAACE's social inclusion strategy is a socio-mechanism co-constructed by frontline workers, educators, researchers, academics, law enforcement personnel and stakeholders with a vested interest in children, youth and community. The objective of the social inclusion strategy is to nurture and incubate the vast potential of children and youth becoming twenty first century learners and global citizens. The program design pivots on the provision of comprehensive year round programming (academics, athletics, recreation, technology and the arts). The operational framework is as follows: outreach and wraparound; arts, athletics and expanded opportunities; academic intervention and support (the Weekend Academy and Summer Institute); research and curriculum development (specifically, the creation of a curriculum that targets reflective education and seeks to mitigate negative environmental factors that compromise academic engagement for students in racialized communities). (Para. 3)

Through "comprehensive year round programming," YAAACE via its "social inclusion strategy" seeks to neutralize the negative social conditions and circumstances plaguing the Jane and Finch neighbourhood impacting the majority racialized population of the community manifested through inequitable access to resources and social support services.

Whereas YAAACE began as an organization predominantly offering recreation and sport programmes for youth, over the years it changed its mandate to centre education as a key component of all its programmes. YAAACE also recognized the importance of the early years as foundational for development of children's character and good habits, so it began to offer programmes to young children as early as four- and five-year olds starting kindergarten. YAAACE recognized that the negative pull factors in the community such as guns and gangs try to consume the children at a young age. Hence, the Social Inclusion strategy intends to surround the children and youth from the community with as much intentional quality programming as possible within any given week and throughout the year as a means to offset exposure to negative pull factors. The earlier this process begins, the more likely that the children will not be consumed by negative community pressures. By creating accessibility to quality programmes and services, YAAACE seeks to support community members to be resilient and develop the character traits and life skills required to overcome the systemic challenges plaguing the neighbourhood.

One of the most popular programmes offered by YAAACE is its Summer Institute programme which operates during the July and August summer months. It operates based on a school within a camp model.

Whereas children from higher socio-economic backgrounds remain or improve in their reading and writing scores over the summer months due to exposure to quality programmes and experiential learning opportunities, children from lower socio-economic backgrounds often decrease in their academic competencies due to lack of accessibility or affordability for quality programmes. In single-parent households or dual households living in poverty where both parents are constantly working multiple jobs to support their families, watching television or playing outside become common activities for the children during the summer months to occupy themselves. As Lalani (2016) reports, "The [YAAACE] summer program was created in part to address educational attrition during the summer months which many students experience, while also providing a fun and safe environment. It takes in around 300 students from Kindergarten to Grade 8 each summer for a relatively affordable price of $150" (YAAACE, 2018, para. 9). Children's reading, writing, and mathematics levels are assessed for diagnostic purposes at the beginning of the YAAACE Summer Institute and once again at the end of the summer in order to track their academic progress over the weeks as well as provide extra support for the children and their parents during the school year from September to June. The assessment data has been collected for participants in the YAAACE Summer Institute over the last five years and the results have indicated that it has made a drastic difference in some of the children's academic competencies and achievement throughout the summer and subsequent school years. The data is currently being compiled as part of a larger academic study to be published in the near future.

YAAACE's collaborative partnerships are synergic in nature as each partnership builds on another and contributes to enhancing the overall quality of programmes and services offered in a manner that is socio-culturally relevant to the members of the Jane and Finch community and their short- and long-term needs. At the heart of all programmes offered through YAAACE is the philosophy of accessibility and affordability. There have been many cases where children have been taken in free of cost or on subsidized payment plans to accommodate the needs of the family. Currently, after 12 years as a non-profit organization, YAAACE has long-term partnerships with the following organizations and agencies which offer it funding, goods, or services in various capacities; Toronto District School Board, Toronto Police Services, Solaro, Canada Elite sponsored by Under Armour, Canadian Tire Jumpstart, Canadian Youth Basketball League, Leslois Shaw Foundation, Telus, Laidlaw Foundation, Second

Harvest Food Rescue, City of Toronto, Province of Ontario, Service Canada, Black Creek Community Health Centre, Department of Justice Canada, and Michael "Pinball" Clemons Foundation. It is this extensive network of partnerships that makes YAAACE unique in what it offers as a means of addressing the systemic inequities plaguing the community.

Some of these aforementioned partnerships and collaborations play an essential role in creating quality comprehensive programmes and services offered as part of the YAAACE Summer Institute where the participants are members of the Jane and Finch community and are predominantly racialized, minoritized, and from lower socio-economic backgrounds (Eizadirad, 2017; Williams et al., 2013). The TDSB supports educational programmes offered by YAAACE by providing Ontario Certified Teachers to work at the summer camp which is known as the Summer Institute. Students are grouped by age, grade, and maturity level and led by a TDSB teacher and multiple counsellors who are high school students for seven weeks. Many of the teachers who work at the YAAACE Summer Institute teach in the local schools situated in the Jane and Finch community, and therefore, are able to keep in communication with the students and their parents throughout the year. The Summer Institute follows a school within a camp model where students receive educational instruction within a classroom for part of the day in a fun, hands-on, inquiry-based, experiential manner and the remaining time participate in recreational and cooperative learning activities such as swimming, basketball, music, and arts and crafts. One day a week is devoted to outdoor experiential learning through field trips. Funding from Service Canada and TDSB's Focus on Youth programme allows high school youth from the neighbourhood to be hired as Summer Institute camp counsellors to support the teachers in the classrooms. This gives an opportunity for the older youth to earn an income and to develop their leadership skills by giving back to the community in which they live and to mitigate them resorting to selling drugs or committing crime due to lack of income. Second Harvest Food Rescue donates healthy snacks and sandwiches on a daily basis to the Summer Institute programme which are given to children who cannot afford snacks or lunches regularly to facilitate a healthy child development. Funding secured from various other partnerships goes into buying equipment and supplies to offer quality educational and sport programmes such as the robotics programme offered to the children as part of the Summer Institute where they learn to code and programme robots to complete various tasks. More recently, within the last few years, a partnership with

University of Waterloo has created the opportunity for the children attending the Summer Institute programme to have their eyes checked and if needed provided with glasses free of charge.

As of 2011, 65 per cent of the Jane and Finch population are visible minorities (City of Toronto, 2018). YAAACE seeks to shatter the stereotypes associated with the neighbourhood and its residents as being dangerous and violent (Eizadirad, 2017; Williams et al., 2013). By engaging members of the Jane and Finch community, particularly the racialized, minoritized, and lower SES demographic in various educational and sport programmes offered year round, YAAACE creates sustainable change within the community by providing access to quality programmes at an affordable cost. This type of holistic and interdisciplinary programming and synergic collaborative partnership is what is required to minimize the achievement gap via focusing on aligning the opportunity gap between those from lower and higher SES.

Recommendations

I therefore recommend the TDSB to set yearly timelines to review their findings and update the public on new changes proposed and implemented in the six specific identified areas as part of their *Enhancing Equity Task Force Report and Recommendations* to ensure "equity for all." It is recommended for the TDSB to work closely with the provincial Anti-Racism Directorate Office which has outlined a three-year strategic plan that "targets systemic racism by building an anti-racism approach into the way government develops policies, makes decisions, evaluates programs, and monitors outcomes. It calls for a proactive, collaborative effort from all government ministries and community partners to work toward racial equity" (Ontario Anti-Racism Directorate, 2016, para. 34). The Ontario Anti-Racism Strategic Plan outlines various approaches and strategies that can be utilized by school boards to ensure better equity for specific social groups including racialized students. The plan groups its proposed initiatives under four categories: Policy, Research, and Evaluation; Sustainability and Accountability; Public Education and Awareness; and Community Collaboration (Ontario Anti-Racism Directorate, 2016). Some of the relevant action-oriented suggestions listed under these four categories that can be implemented as part of school board policies and practices are disaggregated race-based data collection, passing on anti-racism legislation, publicly reporting on progress of goals, public education and awareness about various social issues, an anti-racism conference, and most importantly implementation of population-specific anti-racism initiatives. The three areas that the strategic plan identifies as a priority to focus on are anti-black racism, Indigenous-focused anti-racism, and Ontario public service anti-racism. As part of implementing Indigenous-focused anti-racism, school boards and schools should look for opportunities to enact new changes that align with the Truth and Reconciliation 94 Calls to Action (Truth and Reconciliation Commission of Canada, 2015).

I therefore recommend the Ministry of Education, school boards, and schools to invest in creating and maintaining more sustainable long-term synergic collaborations with external organizations involving practitioners from other sectors that work with children, youth, and young adults to provide socio-culturally relevant holistic services relative to the needs of the students and the local community in which schools are situated within. Two effective programmes that can serve as "best practices" having shown promising results in closing the achievement gap through rebalancing and minimizing the opportunity gap are TDSB's *Model Schools for Inner Cities* and *Youth Association for Academics, Athletics, and Character Education's Summer Institute*. It is encouraged for family of schools, which are schools located in close proximity to each other in a given neighbourhood, to share their best practices and strategies that are effective by hosting two meetings throughout the school year. This can be done as a conference call or as part of professional development for teachers and administrators.

REFERENCES

Ahmed, S. (2007). A phenomenology of whiteness. *Feminist Theory, 8*(2), 149–168.
Anyon, J. (1980). Social class and the hidden curriculum of work. *Journal of Education, 162*(1), 67–92.
Au, W. (2010). *Unequal by design: High-stakes testing and the standardization of inequality*. London: Routledge.
Ball, S. (1990). *Politics and policy making in education: Explorations in policy sociology*. London: Routledge.
Baszile, D. T. (2009). Deal with it we must: Education, social justice, and the curriculum of hip hop culture. *Equity & Excellence in Education, 42*(1), 6–19.
Bhabha, H. (1983). The Other question. *Screen, 24*, 18–36. Retrieved from https://pdfs.semanticscholar.org/0c8e/a96f2957d6b0d64e902d-c25e07ea7e714880.pdf
Block, S., & Galabuzi, G. (2011). Canada's colour coded labour market: The gap for racialized workers. Wellesley Institute and Canadian Centre for Policy Alternatives. Retrieved from http://www.wellesleyinstitute.com/wp-content/uploads/2011/03/Colour_Coded_Labour_MarketFINAL.pdf

City of Toronto. (2018). Neighbourhood improvement area profiles. Retrieved from https://www.toronto.ca/city-government/data-research-maps/neighbourhoods-communities/nia-profiles/

Colour of Poverty and Colour of Change. (2019). Fact sheets. Retrieved from https://colourofpoverty.ca/fact-sheets/

Curtis, B., Livingstone, D. W., & Smaller, H. (1992). *Stacking the deck: The streaming of working-class kids in Ontario schools* (Vol. 24). Toronto: James Lorimer & Company.

Dei, G. J. S. (2008). Schooling as community: Race, schooling, and the education of African youth. *Journal of Black Studies, 38*(3), 346–366.

Dei, G. J. S., Holmes, L., Mazzuca, J., McIsaac, E., & Campbell, R. (1995). *Drop out or push out. The dynamics of Black students' disengagement from school.* Toronto, Canada: Ontario Institute for Studies in Education.

Eizadirad, A. (2017). The university as a neoliberal and colonizing institute; A spatial case study analysis of the invisible fence between York University and the Jane and Finch neighbourhood in the City of Toronto. *Journal of Critical Race Inquiry, 4*(1), 25–53.

Eizadirad, A., Martinez, X., & Ruminot, C. (2016). Comparative analysis of educational systems of accountability and quality of education in Ontario, Canada and Chile: Standardized testing and its role in perpetuation of educational inequity. *Interfaces Brasil/Canadá, 16*(2), 54–88.

Friesen, J. (2018, April 25). Canada's toughest neighbourhood. *The Globe and Mail.* Retrieved from https://www.theglobeandmail.com/news/national/canadas-toughest-neighbourhood/article1086849/

Froese-Germain, B. (2001). Standardized testing + High-stakes decisions = Educational inequality. *Interchange, 32*(2), 111–130.

hooks, b. (2003). *Teaching community: A pedagogy of hope.* New York: Routledge.

Hori, M. M. (2013). *The Toronto District School Board & Structural Violence.* Mahad. M. Hori.

Hulchanski, J. D. (2007). *The three cities within Toronto: Income polarization among Toronto's neighbourhoods 1970–2005.* Toronto, ON: Cities Centre Press, University of Toronto. Retrieved from http://www.urbancentre.utoronto.ca/pdfs/curp/tnrn/Three-Cities-Within-Toronto-2010-Final.pdf

James, C. E. (2012). *Life at the intersection: Community, class and schooling.* Halifax, NS: Fernwood Publishing.

Kearns, L. (2011). High-stakes standardized testing and marginalized youth: An examination of the impact on those who fail. *Canadian Journal of Education, 34*(2), 112–130.

Kearns, L. (2016). The construction of 'illiterate' and 'literate' youth: The effects of high-stakes standardized literacy testing. *Race Ethnicity and Education, 19*(1), 121–140.

Knoester, M., & Au, W. (2017). Standardized testing and school segregation: Like tinder for fire? *Race Ethnicity and Education, 20*(1), 1–14.

Ladson-Billings, G. (1994). *The dreamkeepers: Successful teachers for African-American children.* San Francisco: Jossey-Bass.

Lalani, A. (2016, October 5). Devon Jones wins praise for changing lives for the better. *Toronto Star.* Retrieved from https://www.thestar.com/yourtoronto/education/2016/10/05/devon-jones-wins-praise-for-changing-lives-for-the-better.html

Masood, O. (2008). *At risk: The racialized student marked for educational failure.* (Unpublished doctoral dissertation). University of Toronto, Toronto, ON.

Nezavdal, F. (2003). The standardized testing movement: Equitable or excessive? *McGill Journal of Education, 38*(1), 65–78.

Ontario Anti-Racism Directorate. (2016). *A better way forward: Ontario's 3-year anti-racism strategic plan.* Retrieved from https://www.ontario.ca/page/better-way-forward-ontarios-3-year-anti-racism-strategic-plan#section-2

Polanyi, M., Wilson, B., Mustachi, J., Ekra, M., & Kerr, M. (2017). *Unequal city: The hidden divide among Toronto's children and youth. 2017 Toronto child and family poverty report card.* Retrieved from http://torontocas.ca/sites/torontocas/files/CAST%20Child%20Poverty%20Report%20Nov%202017.pdf

Portelli, J., & Sharma, M. (2014). Uprooting and settling in: The invisible strength of deficit thinking. *LEARNing Landscapes, 8*(1), 251–267.

Price, D. (2003). Outcome-based tyranny: Teaching compliance while testing like a state. *Anthropological Quarterly, 76*(4), 715–730.

Razack, S. (2002). When place becomes race. In S. Razack (Ed.), *Race, Space and the law: Unmapping a White Settler Society.* Toronto: Between the Lines.

Ricci, C. (2004). The case against standardized testing and the call for a revitalization of democracy. *Review of Education, Pedagogy, and Cultural Studies, 26*(4), 339–361.

Rodriguez, C. (2018). *Decolonizing academia: Poverty, oppression, and pain.* Winnipeg, MB: Fernwood Publishing.

Shulman, R., Hinton, A., Zhang, S., & Kozlow, M. (2014). Longitudinal results of province-wide assessments in English- language schools: Trends in student achievement and implications for improvement planning in Mathematics and Literacy. Education Quality and Accountability Office. Retrieved from http://www.eqao.com/en/research_data/Research_Reports/DMA-docs/cohort-tracking-2012.pdf

Stiggins, R. (2014). *Revolutionize assessment.* Thousand Oaks, CA: Corwin.

Toronto District School Board. (2017a). *2017 Learning opportunities index: Questions and answers.* Retrieved from http://www.tdsb.on.ca/Portals/research/docs/reports/LOI2017.pdf

Toronto District School Board. (2017b). *Enhancing equity task force: Report and recommendations.* Toronto. Retrieved from http://www.tdsb.on.ca/Portals/0/community/docs/EETFReportPdfVersion.pdf

Toronto District School Board. (2018). *Model schools for inner cities.* Toronto. Retrieved from http://www.tdsb.on.ca/Community/Model-Schools-for-Inner-Cities

Truth and Reconciliation Commission of Canada. (2015). *Truth and Reconciliation Commission of Canada: Calls to Action.* Retrieved from http://www.trc.ca/websites/trcinstitution/File/2015/Findings/Calls_to_Action_English2.pdf

Tupper, J., & Cappello, M. (2008). Teaching the treaties as (un)usual narratives: Disrupting the curricular commonsense. *Curriculum Inquiry, 35*(1), 559–578.

Williams, C., Jones, D., & Bailey, R. (2013). From the margins: Building curriculum for youth in transition. Ministry of Justice & Youth Association for Academics, Athletics and Character Education. Retrieved from http://yaaace.com/wp-content/uploads/2013/06/From-the-Margins-Building-Curriculum-for-Youth-in-Transitions.pdf

Youth Association for Academics, Athletics, and Character Education. (2018). *About us.* Retrieved from http://yaaace.com/about-us/

CHAPTER 10

Decolonizing Educational Assessment Models

This chapter focuses on defining new possibilities for what decolonization and decolonizing pedagogy can be theoretically and in praxis in our current context within education and beyond, specifically focusing towards decolonizing educational assessment. The process of decolonization begins by decolonizing our minds, spirits, and imaginative souls to envision alternative methods, policies, techniques, strategies, approaches, and practices that differ from what currently exists and has been historically and socio-economically constructed, normalized, and legitimized, such as the practice of using standardized testing to demonstrate accountability. In other words, we must first dream and think differently ideologically, even if it seems abstract or against the grain, before we can act upon our ideas and seek to implement alternative visions for the future.

We must also shift our thinking away from settling for a single magical solution for our current educational problems such as the achievement gap amongst different social groups. Schools are situated within communities and cities, and impacted by surrounding social, political, and socio-economic factors. Therefore, in acknowledging that there cannot be a single solution to challenging systemic barriers, we must also recognize that we cannot settle for a single definition of decolonization. Decolonization as a process and pedagogy will be different and unique to each setting and spatial location in relation to the unique power relations embedded within each space. Key features of decolonization and decolonizing pedagogy are characteristics of interconnectivity, reciprocity, radical love, and unlearning (Lather, 1986;

© The Author(s) 2019
A. Eizadirad, *Decolonizing Educational Assessment*,
https://doi.org/10.1007/978-3-030-27462-7_10

Rodriguez, 2018; Smith, 1999) with a big picture focus on addressing the unmet needs of learners and communities. These characteristics have their roots originating from Indigenous ways of life, teaching, and learning focused on relationship building with nature, the land, and people of all ages from children to elders. Decolonization and decolonizing pedagogy has to be rooted and implemented using an ecological place-based approach where community members have a platform and a medium to voice their concerns and experiences and be given the tools, resources, and the accessibility to relevant social support systems to address inequities and systemic barriers that are co-constructed by institutional policies and practices whether intentionally or unintentionally. Discussions around decolonization from a place-based vantage point can provide the opportunity and the platform to connect social issues and their root causes to larger historical, political, and socio-economic forces such as racism, colonialism, imperialism, and knowledge production processes. This can assist in identifying and implementing new ideas and multi-modalities to reduce systemic barriers and minimize its impact on vulnerable populations in society who are oppressed and marginalized by it.

As it relates to the use of standardized testing in schools, it is important to note, as mentioned in the previous chapter, that not all assessment types are harmful or detrimental to student's development and growth; the key is whom the tests are administered by, how the tests are administered, and how the results are used. The current way EQAO standardized tests are administered—whether intentional or as an unintended consequence—is not helping address the needs of the racialized student population in the early years in a manner that facilitates closing the achievement gap or fosters holistic healthy development. This is evident by the voices of the children, parents, and educators expressing their racialized experience with schooling and EQAO standardized testing in the early years, supplemented and supported with statistical trends outlining that racialized identities and communities face systemic barriers within Ontario which places them at a great disadvantage when it comes to equality of opportunity.

Overall, findings expressed throughout the book indicate that the Grade 3 EQAO standardized test is more harmful than beneficial for healthy holistic development of children. The harmful impacts of standardized testing are identified under the umbrella term the *invisible scars and traumatizing effects of standardized testing* which include examples such as perpetuation of fear of failure, lowering of self-confidence and self-worth, development of test-taking anxiety, increase in stress and anxiety, troubled sleeping, and creation of self-doubt. Furthermore, identifying *external assessment as stereotyping*, it is argued EQAO tests are culturally and racially biased as it promotes a Eurocentric curriculum and way of life privileging white students and those from higher socio-economic status while simultaneously lacking relevant connections to the identity and lived experiences of racialized students and families from lower socio-economic backgrounds. We need to invest in equitable practices that close the opportunity gap as a means of achieving the outcome-oriented goal of closing the achievement gap. This requires a policy and praxis shift from equality to an equity lens.

The remaining of this chapter will discuss and explore what decolonization can look like in various forms and how it can be implemented as a process-oriented pedagogy. As well, various suggestions are provided on where we can go from here to better serve the needs of racialized, minoritized, and students from lower socio-economic backgrounds at the elementary level as it relates to the use of standardized testing and decolonizing educational assessment. Investing in decolonizing educational assessments is an important step in the right direction if we want to make the institution of education more equitable and socially just. A decolonized education model begins with assessing the needs of students and the local communities; how students socio-emotionally and culturally enter the learning environment and the power dynamics embedded in the community and the learning space. This involves practices such as validating the histories and lived experiences of students as a form of valuable knowledge; recognizing their interests, passions, and their preferred learning styles; and recognizing what resources are available and what new resources can be secured through cooperation and synergic collaborations with external organizations. Above all, a decolonized education focuses on providing support to teachers in numerous ways in order for them to assess in multiple ways and in different contexts the potential and competencies of students in relation to their unique needs, learning styles, and personalities.

The objective of a decolonized education model would be to internally motivate students to care about themselves and their communities through relationship building, empowerment, reflexivity, and a sense of shared responsibility while acknowledging inequality of opportunity as a systemic barrier to achieving success. This translates into cultivating unique student potentials and cultural capitals in relation to their identities and strengths and further empowering them to be agents of social change. Learning within such model is not linear and at times messy and loud. We must deviate away from always wanting students to sit at their desks in silence and completing worksheets. Decolonizing pedagogy as a process-oriented practice involves allowing students to express themselves and make mistakes—including their anger, frustration, and happiness—invite them to think, and most importantly challenge them to solve problems both in the classroom and in the larger context of their communities and the world. This is accomplished through horizontal sharing of power and control where all community members including the students recognize that they have a role to play in their own success and success of others. Within this paradigm, success manifests itself in many forms and it is context-specific accompanied with themes of love, cooperation, reciprocity, and sacrifice; components which cannot be measured quantitatively but rather qualitatively over time through students' thoughts, words, actions, and deeds. Each student is guided to be the best they can be, to compete with himself or herself, and to contribute to the betterment of their community and the nation instead of competing with other students locally, nationally, and internationally for the sake of rankings, rewards, and marks.

The emphasis on community and shared responsibility is significantly different from the standardized testing accountability paradigm; whereas "there is a threat implicit in accountability model" (Ungerleider, 2003, p. 283) in the form of shame, punishment, or fear of failure, the shared responsibility model encourages all educational stakeholders including parents, teachers, administrators, and community members to play an active role in developing students holistically, recognizing that meaningful teaching and learning takes place beyond the walls of the classroom within and through many spaces within the community. As Kobe's mother states,

> I think the government [and all institutions including schools] has to be prepared to identify and challenge systemic barriers. It's not an easy thing to do but I think unless they are prepared to do that I don't think we can get education to where it needs to go.

As Kobe's mother expresses, the process of making education more equitable begins with a willingness of the government, and I would add other institutions, to acknowledge there are systemic barriers within their policies and practices and that something needs to be done about it through a collective approach. It requires commitment, effort, and energy from various stakeholders to collectively and collaboratively as a community of learners work towards creating sustainable change with equity and social justice at the heart of the decisions and new actions being implemented to close the achievement gap. Minimizing the opportunity gap through investing in a decolonized education model is a great place to start the change.

Exploring Alternative Approaches and Pathways

Overall, eight findings were identified that emerged from the voices of the racialized children, parents, and educators interviewed with respect to preparation and administration of EQAO standardized tests in the early years. These findings are summarized here and following the listing of each finding, further areas to explore are discussed as a means of exploring alternative future pathways to decolonizing assessment methods. Keep in mind, there is no ideal solution that can be copied and pasted into all communities. These strategies and approaches have to be tailored to reflect the needs of the school based on their student demographics and the needs of the community in which the schools are situated within.

1. Most children experienced high-intensity socio-emotionally induced stress and anxiety subjectively attributing it to fear of failure and poor performance. The level of stress and anxiety was so severe in some cases that the child could not sleep the night before the test or refused entering the classroom on test day to participate in writing the EQAO test.

Since this qualitative study is exploratory in nature due to its small sample size, school boards and schools should invest in more avenues in different formats such as surveys, interviews, and focus groups to listen to the voices of children and youth with respect to how they are impacted by preparing and writing EQAO standardized tests. We need to give importance to subjective experiences of racialized students as expressed through their voices. Consultations with racialized students, parents, and educators should be done regionally within neighbourhoods and communities which historically have done poorly on EQAO standardized tests based on their school results as well as within neighbourhoods which have consistently done well. This provides a comparative method to explore and contrast relevant experiential and community factors that impact student learning and performance on EQAO standardized tests beyond examining individualistic factors such as student effort. Data collected can be used to explore and analyse other important relevant factors such as school culture and climate, opportunities available such as sport teams, clubs and leadership initiatives, and accessibility to support services and extra help amongst other factors that can assist in engaging children and facilitating their healthy development.

Longitudinal studies administered by approved third-party external organizations can be another approach to invest in better understanding the long-term impact of standardized testing on young children in a context-specific manner relative to geography, race, gender, and socio-economic status. Tracking the same cohort of children must go beyond simply examining how they do in Grade 3 compared to the other years EQAO standardized tests are administered. To gain a more complex and holistic understanding of the impact of EQAO standardized testing on children, longitudinal studies should track specific cohort of students based on contextual factors relative to their lived experiences with a focus on specific factors such as race, geography, gender, socio-economic status, teacher pedagogy, access to support services, and so on. Data collected using this approach will allow educational researchers to make connections between in-school factors and the larger community factors that interact and intersect dynamically to influence the child holistically in terms of motivation and engagement in school.

2. Most parents expressed, based on changes they observed in emotions and behaviours of their child preparing and writing the Grade 3 EQAO test that the test is more harmful than beneficial. All parents tried to counter and mitigate the test-induced anxiety, stress, and fear of failure in their child. Strategies used included encouraging their child to try their best, having informal conversations with them about the non-impact of test results on their marks and advancement to Grade 4, and doing practice questions to familiarize them with types of questions on the test and to reduce their test-taking anxiety.

3. Parents from higher socio-economic status had a better understanding of EQAO standardized testing and its purpose as a political accountability tool including how the test is administered and how the results are used. Whereas most parents preferred the Grade 3 EQAO test to be eliminated entirely, some parents including those

who work within the educational system, were in favour of maintaining the test, but strongly felt it requires changes in its content and format to be effective and socio-culturally relevant to the identities, knowledge, skills, and lived experiences of twenty-first-century learners.

To align educational assessment practices in schools with primary purpose of improving student learning by investing more in "assessment of learning" and "assessment as learning," (Ministry of Education, 2010) government officials, educational administrators, researchers, and teachers need to hold consultation meetings with children, parents, and educators in various communities to receive feedback regarding:

a. Whether they support or oppose the current practice of administering EQAO standardized tests in Grade 3 given its current monetary and social costs? If the majority consensus is that it is not worth it to be maintained, supported with evidence, consider eliminating and phasing out the EQAO test and explore reallocating the funds to other social support services to create a more equitable educational system. If the majority consensus is to maintain administration of EQAO tests, supported with evidence, go to step b;

b. Explore ways the current model of administrating the Grade 3 EQAO test can be altered and improved to be more effective pedagogically and practically. This includes constructively examining the EQAO test from multiple perspectives: how the test is designed in terms of format (e.g. paper and pencil), type of questions asked (e.g. predominantly multiple choice, true and false, and short answer questions), when the test is administered, when the results are returned, what type of feedback is provided as part of individual results (descriptive feedback versus overall achievement level scores) and school results, and how the data is used by schools, school boards, and the general public.

These are not simple endeavours but areas we need to explore to further make our schools and education system more equitable by addressing needs of all students across a spectrum of different identities and communities, particularly racialized children who face systemic barriers embedded within educational policies and practice. This process will take time, energy, effort, and collaboration involving professionals across multiple sectors working with children including teachers, administrators, social workers, child and youth care practitioners, early childhood educators, educational assistants, and others. This can become a more tangible task to accomplish if there is a signed commitment from the Ministry of Education in the form of a proposed yearly plan along with specific goals to work towards. This proposed yearly plan should be accompanied with committed funding from various relevant local organizations and the provincial and the federal government.

4. Most children did not understand why they write the Grade 3 EQAO test and how the results are used.

Schools should explore alternative avenues of communicating with children and parents about how EQAO results are used at the individual and school level and systemically on a larger scale by school boards and Ministry of Education. More importantly, schools should explore how teachers can have a conference meeting with the child and their parents, in person or via alternative methods such as by phone or email, to deconstruct and discuss individual EQAO results with the objective of helping students improve and mitigate the *invisible scars and traumatizing effects of standardized testing* associated with children's self-critique of themselves and parent's critique of their child based on EQAO scores.

5. According to the parents, EQAO standardized testing relative to its structure, format, and administration does not align with "best practices" in education associated with meaningful teaching and learning in schools.
6. Teacher pedagogy and delivery of curriculum is negatively impacted by Grade 3 EQAO test preparation leading to teaching to the test. This is attributed to the pressure placed on teachers and administrators to increase their school scores, as schools are judged and ranked by external organizations such as the Fraser Institute based on overall performance of students on EQAO tests.

Teachers and administrators are under extensive stress and pressure to improve their EQAO school test scores as overall school rankings by the Fraser Institute are used to judge the identity of the school and label the surrounding community as "good" or "bad." This creates a domino effect on teachers indirectly placing stress on children to be prepared to do well on EQAO tests. This is exemplified with large amount of time devoted to preparing for EQAO tests which makes it a big spectacle for the children and their peers. Similar to an athlete practicing and getting ready for competition day, children prepare all year for the EQAO test with the goal of performing to the best of their abilities during testing week.

One of the primary objectives of EQAO is to provide students, parents, schools, and school boards with data about achievement level of students and what can be done to improve their competencies in the domains assessed. This is the stance that the EQAO takes and the dominant narrative it promotes to justify the maintenance of EQAO testing at various levels. Currently schools use EQAO results to co-construct improvement strategies as part of the School Improvement Plan (SIP). This includes strategies such as identifying marker students to work with individually, identifying students who might need an IEP with accommodations and/or modifications to their learning expectations, where to allocate resources and support services, and establishing new clubs or initiatives to improve student learning and achievement. A question which needs to be explored and considered is whether a similar set of data can be collected locally at the school level without needing externally administered standardized tests?

Ontario Teachers' Federation (2011) emphasizes, "Classroom-based formative assessment is a more reliable indicator of individual achievement and more closely aligned with the best strategies for individual student improvement. It is also the best predictor of student achievement" (p. 5). Schools need to explore how teachers can use "assessment as learning" and "assessment for learning" throughout the school year to collect data that demonstrates "assessment of learning." This might sound complex, but if implemented consistently across school boards, it will yield more practical data and reduce the *invisible scars and traumatizing effects of standardized testing*. A more local place-based ecological approach to collecting data in partnership with classroom teachers will save the Ministry of Education millions of dollars associated with administrating external EQAO tests in various grades. The money saved can be funnelled into providing more relevant and appropriate support services to schools and students. As well, it will alleviate teachers feeling the pressure to teach to the test allowing for more organic and authentic interdisciplinary and holistic learning to take place which benefits the students in the long run and focuses on the needs of specific social groups who are systemically disadvantaged by current educational policies and practices.

As part of a proposed place-based ecological model to collect data about student learning, teachers should use *growth portfolios* to assess student achievement levels in various subjects including Reading, Writing, and Mathematics. *Growth portfolio's* objective is to track and compile examples of progress, improvement, and high achievement levels throughout the school year with input from the students and their parent(s). The portfolio can be subdivided by specific subjects. Teachers should begin the school year with a diagnostic assessment of children to identify what level they are starting the school year at. This is already being done in schools as a natural process of learning more about the students and how to tailor teaching content to reflect their needs and preferred learning styles, hence, no new funding is required to implement this initiative. Near the end of each three-month period in the school year—November, February, and May—teachers should have a "parents-student-teacher" conference meeting to assess and discuss the progress of students in different subjects particularly their strengths and identified areas needing improvement. The aim of the "parent-student-teacher" conference is to collaboratively decide on student work exemplars to input into the *growth portfolio* demonstrating skills and mastery of curriculum content in various subjects. This approach opens the lines of communication by giving a voice to students and parents to be involved in the assessment process collaboratively, and as a process establishing a connection between learning conditions at home and at school. Also, it provides more holistic and richer data about the student's strengths and areas needing improvement spanning from September to June instead of a snapshot in a week which is what EQAO tests capture. This *growth portfolio* approach should continue and be built upon every school year as students advance to the next grade.

School administrators such as principals can use data from student *growth portfolios* at the end of Grade 3 to identify each student's final achievement level and self-report the data into a central database created by Ministry of Education. If ethical issues with self-reporting is a concern, in early implementation stages of this new approach, EQAO can send educational officers or trainers to schools to examine the content of the *growth portfolios* collaboratively with the respective Grade 3 teachers in the school and input the data through their EQAO staff. At later stages, once the programme is more established, schools can self-report the data themselves with random schools being selected for auditing to ensure proper reporting techniques are followed consistently.

Another option to consider and explore, if the decision is to maintain the current way EQAO standardized tests are administered, is switching to random testing of schools in various geographical neighbourhoods or by school boards to gain baseline data of student achievements and make inferences from the data instead of census-style testing where every student in every school is tested. It is important to keep in mind that although random testing of schools will save money in terms of administration costs, this approach is also problematic as it perpetuates similar inadequacies that currently exist with the way EQAO tests are administered. Once again, the question to keep in mind is which approach yields the most accurate and useful data given the costs and resources it requires?

7. Parents and children felt the government, EQAO, and schools in general need to expand the definition of success beyond academics and a microscopic focus on Reading, Writing, and Mathematics.

The Ministry of Education in partnership with EQAO should explore how they can work in collaboration with schools, non-profits, and external organizations across different communities and neighbourhoods to advance a more holistic model of education that assesses various subjects and contextual factors that impact student learning and healthy child development. This process begins by expanding the definition of success and redefining it in broader terms (Dei, 2008; Miller, 2000; People for Education, 2018). Rebranding success in the public sphere and within education institutions requires transition to a more holistic model of education that encompasses academic and non-academic components. As Dei (2008) suggests in *Schooling as Community*,

> We must define success broadly to include the academic, moral, social, spiritual, and cultural development of the learner. Similarly, failure cannot be the flip side of success. The success of some students cannot be justifiably served for consumption in terms of explaining the failure of others. (p. 360)

Rebranding success to include Howard Gardner's Theory of Multiple Intelligences (Gardner, 1983) would be a great starting point to empower children in their early years to find their strengths, build their self-confidence, and provide them with constructive descriptive feedback on areas to improve. Lowe (2016) states, "Gardner's theory argues that every individual possesses all eight intelligences—linguistic, logical-mathematical, spatial, bodily-kinesthetic, musical, interpersonal, intrapersonal and naturalist—but the strength of these intelligences in each person varies" (p. 17). Gardner (1983) strongly opposed the use of Intelligence Quotient (IQ) tests and other standardized tests arguing they are limited tools in capturing authentically and effectively the complex competencies students have across multiple domains.

Portelli and Vilbert (2002) similarly suggest a shift away from standardized testing towards a more place-based, relational, and socio-culturally relevant pedagogy identified as "curriculum of life." Curriculum of life is defined as "a curriculum that is grounded in the immediate daily world of students as well as in the larger social political context of their lives" (p. 4). They further expand:

> The curriculum of life is rooted in the school and community world to which the students belong, addressing questions of who we are and how we live well together; it extends into the larger world of possibilities beyond school and community bounds; and it addresses questions about the larger social and political contexts in which these worlds are embedded. (p. 15)

Organizations such as People for Education (https://peopleforeducation. ca/) and FairTest (https://www.fairtest.org/) can work collaboratively with EQAO to construct and implement more authentic and organic local assessment techniques to measure indicators of school success and student achievement. People for Education is "an independent, non-partisan, charitable organization working to support and advance public education through research policy, and public engagement" (People for Education, 2018, para. 1). They have begun a multi-year project looking at identifying "key domains that are essential for student success" (para. 3). They have narrowed their search to five specific domains, which are Health, Citizenship, Creativity, Social-Emotional Learning, and Quality Learning Environments (People for Education, 2018). Collaboration, dialogue, and cooperation with external organizations such as People for Education can begin the process of designing more effective assessment tools which recognizes children as complex beings who need much more than foundational skills in literacy and numeracy for long-term success in the twenty-first century.

8. Racialized children and parents expressed that the EQAO test is culturally and racially biased as it promotes a Eurocentric curriculum and way of life. They felt the content of EQAO standardized tests

reflects lived experiences of families from higher socio-economic status and lacks relevant connections to the identity and lived experiences of racialized students and families from lower socio-economic status.

Freire (1998) in *Pedagogy of Freedom: Ethics, Democracy, and Civic Courage* points out, "education is ideological," (p. xiii) and "what empirical studies often neglect to point out is how easily statistics can be manipulated to take away the human face of the subjects of study through a process that not only dehumanizes but also distorts and falsifies reality" (p. xxv). The fear of remaining competitive in a globalized world pressurizes communities, governments, and nations to conform to spending more funding and resources on "worthy" knowledges to demonstrate on the international stage the high-quality education offered in their countries. Although these neoliberal ideologies are presented as ideal solutions for improving education for all, what is often silenced and not mentioned is the devastating impact of such policies and practices on certain identities and their local communities, particularly Indigenous and racialized communities and their local, oral, and land-based knowledges and way of life, especially in the context of Canada.

The ideologies of neoliberalism and its promotion for standardization function as a colonizing tool pressurizing and controlling Indigenous populations to conform to evidence-based outcomes or risk being perished through violence. Canada and its treatment of Aboriginals, who were the founders of the land, can serve as a prime example of how Native identities were appropriated through standardization of language; including the forced attendance of Aboriginal students to residential schools to be assimilated into Canadian culture, the exclusion and dismissal of oral culture and spirituality as "worthy" domains within the official curriculum of schools at all levels, and the horrendous disciplining of Aboriginal students to speak "proper" English as a means of demonstrating their progress towards being "civilized" and adapting to "modern" conditions of Canadian society (Smith, 1999). In essence, the curriculum is directly driven by standardization which dictates and inscribes on to others what type of learning and knowledges need to be taught and learned, including within Indigenous communities, which historically have lived life and learned in different ways relative to their own spiritual and traditional values, morals, and ethics. As Ricci (2004) emphasizes, "the curriculum ignores student needs by implementing a standard curriculum that is expected to fit all students" (p. 359). This results in the promotion of a one-size-fits-all curriculum.

The curriculum also ignores the unique needs of communities and their local place-based ecological contexts. Instead, standardization promotes competition which directly opposes the indigenous notion of cooperation and collective and shared responsibility. Standardization also promotes rewards and punishment; those who conform are rewarded with access to economical avenues leading to a higher income whereas those who fail to conform and get poor results in academic domains risk their survival by not finishing high school and consequentially having limited access to a sustainable well-paid income due to lack of education and relevant job experience.

RECOMMENDATIONS

The following recommendations are listed within one subsection to address and mitigate the overall concerns raised about the negative impact of EQAO standardized testing and to promote discussions and dialogue towards a decolonized educational assessment model that is more equitable:

1. School boards and schools should immediately invest in mitigating the short- and long-term *invisible scars and traumatizing effects of standardized testing* by investing in offering more mental health and mindfulness initiatives for racialized children and parents.

2. School boards and schools should immediately invest in creating more avenues and mediums, such as focus groups and online surveys, to engage racialized children participating in writing EQAO standardized tests to express how they are socio-emotionally, spiritually, and psychologically impacted by the process before, during, and after writing the tests. The post-impact examination should have a special one-year time frame, particularly exploring the direct impact on children's identities when they receive their EQAO results in Grade 4.

3. School boards and schools should track cohort of students through longitudinal and intersectional studies administered by neutral external organizations to further examine the impacts of standardized testing on young children based on contextual factors with a focus on specific factors including geography, race, gender, socio-economic status, teacher pedagogy, and access to support services.

4. To address concerns associated with ineffective timing of when EQAO results are returned to children, a test trial for a year should be conducted where EQAO administers Grade 3 EQAO tests in late September at the start of Grade 4. If the objective is to assess students organically of their knowledge acquisition and mastery of content in the primary grades until end of Grade 3, it is reasonable to select start of Grade 4 to administer the EQAO test. This diminishes the opportunity for teachers to spend time prepping children and teach to the test as a means of getting children to perform better and to increase overall school scores. Upon administrating EQAO tests in late September, individual student results are to be scored and returned to the children by end of January of the same school year.

5. To address concerns about how individual EQAO student results contain only raw achievement scores with limited descriptive feedback about children's strengths, weaknesses, and where errors are made, EQAO should digitalize all marked EQAO booklets by scanning them and making them available to students and parents online through a secure website that allows them to log in with a personalized username and password. Once logged in securely, students and parents can download their individualized marked booklets and read more specific comments and suggestions as a form of feedback about how they did. This allows children and parents to visually see what questions they did well on, where they made errors, and how they can improve in various areas.

6. Schools should host "parent-student-teacher" meetings, in person or via alternative methods such as by phone or email, to explain to children and parents how to effectively interpret EQAO results in a constructive manner to improve student learning and mitigate the *invisible scars and traumatizing effects of standardized testing* associated with children's self-critique of themselves and parent's critique of their children based on EQAO scores. It is recommended "parent-student-teacher" meetings are conducted as soon as EQAO results are returned to children in late September or early October. As part of this conference meeting, the child, the parent(s), and the teacher should collaboratively co-construct an individualized personal action plan for the school year outlining short- and long-term goals for areas of improvement along with plans on how to achieve those goals. This individualized personal

plan produced based on Grade 3 EQAO results should be supplemented with other teacher assessments. The goals outlined as part of the action plan should be monitored relative to its progress at various intervals throughout the school year, particularly leading up to when report card marks are finalized to facilitate students receiving descriptive feedback about their strengths and identified areas needing improvement to increase their marks. These "check-in" meetings on the progress of the goals should be revisited with the parent(s) and the child every three months.

7. EQAO should collect data using *growth portfolios* to compile and track examples of progress, areas needing improvement, and achievement levels throughout the school year with input from students and parents. Near the end of each three-month period in the school year—November, February, and May—teachers should have a "parents-student-teacher" conference meeting to assess and discuss progress of students in different subjects. The aim of the "parent-student-teacher" conference is to collaboratively decide on student work exemplars to input into the portfolio demonstrating skills and mastery of curriculum content in different subjects. School administrators should self-report and input all student achievement levels into a central database created by Ministry of Education, or EQAO officers can collect portfolios and input the data themselves to mitigate bias or false reporting. This portfolio approach should continue and be built upon every school year as students advance to the next grade.

8. EQAO should consider conducting a test trial to switch to random testing of schools in various geographical neighbourhoods or by school boards to gain baseline data of student achievements instead of census-style testing where every student in every school is tested.

9. The federal, provincial, and local governments in collaboration with Ministry of Education, EQAO, school boards, and external organizations should commit funding and resources to host an annual two-day provincial conference on *Student Success in Elementary Years and Beyond.* One of the major focuses of the conference will be on authentic assessments of racialized children in the early years. The conference would create collaborative opportunities to bridge theory with practice involving educational stakeholders and practitioners from different fields who directly and indirectly work with young elementary-aged children. This includes, but is not limited

to, researchers, teachers, early childhood educators, social workers, psychologists, child and youth care workers, special needs assistants, educational assistants, and community leaders and activists.

10. The TDSB should set yearly timelines to review their findings and update the public on new changes proposed and implemented in the six identified areas as part of their *Enhancing Equity Task Force Report and Recommendations* to ensure "equity for all" (TDSB, 2017, p. 4). It is recommended that the TDSB works closely with the provincial Anti-Racism Directorate Office which has outlined a three-year strategic plan that targets systemic racism. Some of the relevant action-oriented suggestions made by Anti-Racism Directorate Office which can be implemented by schools include disaggregated race-based data collection, passing on anti-racism legislation, publicly reporting on progress of goals, public education and awareness about various social issues, an anti-racism conference, and most importantly implementation of population-specific anti-racism initiatives.

11. The Ministry of Education, school boards, and schools should invest in creating and maintaining sustainable long-term synergic collaborations with external organizations at the local community level involving practitioners from other sectors that work with children, youth, and young adults to provide socio-culturally relevant holistic services relative to the needs of students and the local community. Two effective programmes that can serve as "best practices" to be replicated having shown promising results in closing the achievement gap through minimizing the opportunity gap are TDSB's *Model Schools for Inner Cities* and *Youth Association for Academics, Athletics, and Character Education's Summer Institute.*

MODERNIZATION OF EQAO: A RESPONSE TO CONCERNS RAISED FROM PUBLIC CONSULTATIONS

In December 2018, EQAO produced a document in response to the concerns raised from the report *Ontario: A Learning Province: Finding and Recommendations from the Independent Review of Assessment and Reporting* and the government's public consultation on educational issues. The EQAO responded with a document titled *Supporting Student Learning Through Assessment and Accountability* where it outlines how

EQAO plans to modernize its policies and practices in various ways to improve its current practices. As the document states, EQAO "seeks to support the government's consultation by outlining a proposal for what modernized large-scale assessments could look like—and how they could better support students, parents, guardians, educators and the rest of Ontario" (EQAO, 2018, p. 3). The document further states that EQAO continues to strongly advocate that census-style standardized testing is more effective than random sampling and concludes with listing some ideas that EQAO is considering to implement to improve its current practices:

- Assessments currently administered in Grades 3 and 6 could be administered at the beginning of Grades 4 and 7 respectively (e.g., September to October). When assessments are administered digitally at the beginning of the school year, results can be generated and disseminated quickly (e.g., digitally through a secure portal) to parents, guardians, and educators within the same school year. This change would increase the assessments' formative value, and results could be more easily leveraged to benefit students. The assessments would continue to evaluate the reading, writing, and math skills students are expected to have learned by the end of Grades 3 and 6, and, so long as the assessments are census-based, provide the same degree of accountability.
- Assessments could provide clearer results through more descriptive feedback.
- The Ontario Secondary School Literacy Test (OSSLT) could be shortened and have multiple administration dates during the Grade 10 school year. This would allow students to write when they're ready and enable them to rewrite the test as needed starting in Grade 10. It would also enable students who are struggling with their literacy skills to continue to access the specialized course (the Ontario Secondary School Literacy Course) to improve their literacy skills prior to graduation.
- Administration periods for the primary- and junior-division assessments could be expanded to four- to six-week windows. (pp. 5–6)

Although some of these suggestions will facilitate more effective administration of EQAO standardized testing at various levels, it still does not question the premise of using EQAO standardized testing as an accountability tool, and how these changes will address the needs of specific social groups such as racialized and Indigenous students who face systemic barriers in the education system.

Conclusion

The significant findings identified as part of this book contribute to research in the field associated with standardized testing of racialized children in elementary schools. The findings holistically reveal that racialized children experience high-intensity socio-emotionally induced stress and anxiety attributing it to fear of failure and poor performance, and delivery of the curriculum impacted by pressures placed on teachers and administrators to increase their EQAO school scores. Students who do poorly on EQAO tests are labelled as "illiterate," "at-risk," or "low achievers." This process is "structurally violent" because "it denies students upward social mobility and therefore socioeconomically marginalized and racially excluded students get streamed towards less desired labour jobs" (Hori, 2013, p. 37).

The current normalized and legitimized neoliberal market-driven model of education, with its reliance on standardized testing as an accountability tool, homogenizes the needs of all students and communities by disregarding them as holistic beings and dynamic communities and instead judges them predominantly by results and performance on standardized tests (Miller, 2016; Portelli & Vilbert, 2002). As a whole, standardization penetrates all spheres of education, managing education from a neoliberal business model while paradoxically proclaiming efficiency and accountability. It is significant that we, as educators and caring adults, continuously question hegemonic assumptions about how learning should be assessed, in a way that is empowering to students rather than harmful. Particular attention needs to be given to engaging in dialogue about standardization in education from every facet ranging from the curriculum content to assessment of learning. The discussion needs to shift from an equality paradigm to an equity lens that asks, "Whose values and knowledges are established as the 'norm' and consequentially utilized as a baseline measure for judgement and comparison?" and "Whose interests does this approach serve and in what ways and at what costs?"

Currently the symbiotic fusion of the Ontario curriculum, the Tyler Rationale, and EQAO standardized testing in Ontario constructs a narrow definition of success that is based on a market-driven ideology of education supplemented by efficiency and accountability discourses. This model is counter-productive as it has harmful effects on marginalized students including racialized, Indigenous, ESL learners, and students from lower socio-economic status. It has led to intensifying and widening of the achievement gap in education rather than closing the achievement gap. Questioning and critiquing this market-driven model of education from an equity and social justice lens is at the core of the power struggle to revolutionize and decolonize our minds, imaginations, and educational systems in order to open it up to new alternatives and possibilities.

If we want to close the achievement gap between different social groups in the education system and to specifically address the systemic barriers that are present and persistent in schools for racialized identities and communities, we need to invest in programmes and policies that view education as symbiotic with the larger community and other institutions outside of schools (Dei, 2008; Miller, 2016; Williams, Jones, & Bailey, 2013). We cannot address the achievement gap without first addressing the inequality of opportunity that plagues our educational system and further marginalizes our most vulnerable student populations. As long as schools continue to operate under a one-size-fits-all mandate and schools located in higher socio-economic status communities continue to get better access to funding, opportunities, resources, and social support services, the achievement gap will continue to exist and further intensify, particularly as it impacts racialized children. As Rodriguez (2018) points out, "The lethal silence and complicity not only sustains existing destructive structures but keeps blizzard-like conditions intact so persons of colour cannot even move" (p. 112). By investing in creating equality of opportunity for racialized, Indigenous, gendered, ESL learners, and students from lower socio-economic backgrounds through collaborative alternative programmes such as Model Schools for Inner Cities and Youth Association of Academic, Athletic, and Character Education, we can work towards building confidence in students and empower them to make a difference in their own lives and in their communities. This kind of difference and alternative approach to improving student achievement goes beyond a test score and has real-life implications for all living within the school-community space.

Education alone, and quality of education, cannot be judged exclusively through standardized tests and their quantifiable indicators. Accountability needs to be measured using multi-models, with some focusing on qualitative factors such as the strength of relationships amongst students, teachers, and administrators within schools. Students have to be seen as holistic beings with different social, emotional, academic, and psychological needs

(Miller, 2016). More alternative programmes that offer holistic services such as TDSB's *Model Schools for Inner Cities* and The Summer Institute offered by *Youth Association for Academics, Athletics, and Character Education* need to be introduced, implemented, and supported with funding and resources as exemplars of modern programmes that are effective in meeting needs of students and communities through a social inclusion strategy focusing on factors such as student motivation, health, emotional well-being, and systemic challenges in the local community. As Ricci (2004) states,

> A test-driven curriculum that imposes a monoculture of training will limit the biodiversity of ideas, knowledge, culture, and history. By limiting the biodiversity of ideas in schools, the less chance we have of critically challenging the status quo and thinking of creative alternatives to the injustices that need to be challenged within our society. We must fight for the biodiversity of learning and eliminate a test-driven, monocultural training environment. (p. 359)

Equity and social justice need to be at the centre of introducing and implementing new decolonized alternative programmes to address closing the achievement gap. We need to deviate away from standardization and instead work towards promoting "biodiversity of ideas, knowledge, culture, and history." This will assist in shattering the one-size-fits-all approach to teaching and learning and instead work towards creating alternative programmes designed to address specific needs of racialized children and communities.

The work of decolonization extends beyond schools and applies to communities as well, particularly racialized communities. In order for decolonization of communities to be effective and lead to empowerment and breaking free of spiritual enslavement, we must be able to create decolonized spaces, alter the dynamics of existing spaces, and make these spaces accessible to allow for the cultivation of racialized and minoritized social and cultural capital. As a result, decolonization as a process and a pedagogy becomes personal and political, blossoming in different ways in each unique setting relative to power relations embedded within that spatial setting. Important settings to consider are homes, schools, businesses, the media, and government agencies. The objective at the core of creating decolonized spaces is empowerment of one's sense of identity and the instilling of the belief that one has the potential to succeed and be an agent of social change in numerous capacities. This is inspired by acts of resistance, subversion, and expressions of radical love in the face of unjust policies and practices. Simply put, one has to gain the feeling that he or she matters! As Freire (1970) phrases it, "the oppressed must reach this conviction as Subjects, not as objects" (67).

Exposure to critical pedagogy and anti-racism within decolonized spaces can provide students with the racial literacy that gives them the language to meaningfully express their concerns, navigate social spaces, and use critical thinking skills to tackle complex issues in their communities. As Dei and Doyle-Wood (2009) point out, the struggle for racialized and minoritized individuals "is the struggle—as living embodiments of knowledge—to be heard, recognized, acknowledged as human, and the struggle to maintain a sense of agency in the face of normalizing systems of power" (157). Anti-racism recognizes that many racialized bodies have internalized negative ideas about who they are as a result of their lived experiences within a system that historically marginalizes them, racially excludes them through inequality of opportunity, and delegitimizes their way of being and knowing simply due to their race, culture, and place of residence. Therefore, we must collectively as a community of learners and social activists continue to care and work towards resignifying what it means to be racialized and a member of a racialized community. We must through education and service-oriented collaboration help each other heal and continue to give each other hope for a new day.

Implementing a decolonizing pedagogy also involves exploring how we can draw upon the Land and Earthly teachings and decolonial curriculum to subvert colonial, racist, and imperial consciousness. Accessibility to decolonized spaces and mobilization within these spaces will allow for discussion and convergence towards questioning the hierarchy in place and working in solidarity to resist, interrupt, and subvert the hegemonic and normalizing systems of power that perpetuate a racial hierarchy. Yet to reach that stage a sense of hope has to be renewed. In order for a sense of hope to be renewed, especially for racialized and minoritized individuals who doubt themselves and their competencies, we must not be afraid to take risks and engage with pain and struggle as a form of pedagogy. We must be willing to expose our own vulnerabilities and to enter an uncomfortable state by asking questions that take us out of our comfort zones. As hooks (2003) states, "Dominator culture has tried to keep us all afraid, to make us choose safety instead of risk, sameness instead of diversity. Moving through that fear, finding out what connects us, revelling in our differences; this is the process that brings us closer, that gives us a world of shared values, of meaningful community" (197).

In conclusion, we have to keep in mind that at the core of our struggle for systemic change is a hierarchy and its colonizing and inequitable power relations and institutional practices perpetuated through a dominator culture and its meta-narratives. Therefore, we cannot fight systems of oppression alone as individuals. We must fight the systems collectively as communities and in solidarity with one another, keeping in mind commonalities in our goals, values, objectives, and philosophies to end oppression in its various forms. As Rodriguez (2018) points out, "If we are truly committed to the work of decolonizing, we must listen to the silences, that which is not written, and pay attention to the internal dynamics of communities and how we label their experiences" (p. 33). We must continue to question hegemonic narratives and their symbolic and ideological implications for various social groups. We must continue to imagine counter-hegemonic possibilities and narratives that oppose, resist, and seek to interrupt the essentialist and determinist deficit discourse perpetuated by market-driven neoliberal ideologies. We must work collaboratively with the power of ideas, individuals, and institutions and their interconnectedness. Change is inevitable. But what is significant and what we continuously want to insert into the discussion through a decolonial and an anti-racist perspective is change for whose benefits and at what costs? At the grassroots level, this translates into striving to create equality of opportunity by working collectively and in solidarity to challenge injustice and inequity in various spheres of everyday life, with the hope of creating sustainable systemic change where institutions can play a pivotal role in eradicating oppression rather than perpetuating it through their market-driven, colourblind politics.

Overall, we must strive as individuals and communities to heal, listen, and engage with our pain and other's oppression, work collectively and on a daily basis to constructively process our emotions and experiences, be open-minded, and engage in dialogues and conversations from multiple vantage points and positionalities. Lastly, never give up hope and continue to imagine alternatives and new possibilities, even in the face of inequitable practices. One day a more equitable system will exist. History has taught us systems eventually change; either by collapsing, self-destructing, or by altering from within. What role will you play in changing the system and trying to create a more equitable and social justice-oriented society? Seeking an answer to this question will take you on a life-long journey demonstrated through your thoughts, words, and actions including when you decide to be silent and complicit and when you decide to speak up, resist, and advocate.

I will conclude with a poem titled *Waiting for Wings* reflecting my life journey so far and where I am heading. Concluding with a poem serves two purposes: to disrupt the hegemonic practice of how a book is typically expected to conclude and to deviate from and resist dominant notions around literacy affiliated with "proper" grammar, punctuation, and syntax.

WAITING FOR WINGS

Words alone cannot explain the metamorphosis of my life
simply because the emotions, feelings, and struggles are too real, traumatizing, and complex.
Trying to take it one step at a time, but people constantly asking me, "what's next?"

Didn't want be the average one in school, so I constantly soak up my thoughts with intellect attempting to overcome ideological battles and mental slavery.
Allowing education to set me free, or is it simply the process of obtaining a degree?
Realized change in inevitable.
It's part of the humanly experience.
Not allowing the pleasures of life to interrupt what's dear to my heart
cuz believe it or not, as individuals at one point or another we got to reflect ourselves and the way we behave.
What do we want to let go and what do we want to save?
One life, one love, one struggle, one blood.
Who to blame? Finding ways vs. finding excuses, not as simple as black-and-white.
So many options, but do I have the energy, strength, and the resiliency to keep up the fight?

But it's the struggle from within that makes one want to change.
It's the troubled times that makes you realize who is an acquaintance and who is a true friend.
Too many times I forget to be all appreciative and instead get all rude,
so I brush off my shoulder, not allowing the weight of my responsibilities to bring me down.
But I can't brush off the scars and broken heart
so I wear them on me proudly, showing my imperfection!
Cuz the beauty of one's being is the sum of its parts,
so I arrange my priorities, gonna lead the way!

Goal after goal I'm going to strive to achieve with Plan B, C, D., E. F, G, and H
cuz I am going to be free, from fear of failure.
Creative self-expression, find the purpose to your life, balance out the equation, filter yourself. Cleanse your thoughts and motives, and keep on searching within yourself until you come to understand, self-realize, until you become fulfilled, gain perspective, and believe, you have what it takes, regardless of your past experiences and mistakes.
Because at the end of the day, success can only be measured based on your own values, beliefs, and standards, so as long as you're happy with who you are and the effort you put into things, you'll be fine. Away from dwelling and regrets.
Life is nothing but a journey filled with learning experiences, positive and some negative.
Explore your environment. Incite your mind, heart, body, and soul, find the vision to see through the illusional world we co-exist within, and realize the beauty of growth.
Because true change comes within, and spreads outward, not the other way around.
Which makes me wonder, does a butterfly know how beautiful it has become when it has successfully hatched out of a cocoon?

References

Dei, G., & Doyle-Wood, S. (2009). Is we who Haffi Ride Di Staam: Critical knowledge/multiple knowings-possibilities, challenges, and resistance in curriculum/cultural contexts. In Y. Kanu (Ed.), *Curriculum as cultural practice: Postcolonial imaginations* (pp. 151–180). Toronto, ON: University of Toronto Press.

Dei, G. J. S. (2008). Schooling as community: Race, schooling, and the education of African youth. *Journal of Black Studies, 38*(3), 346–366.

Education Quality and Accountability Office. (2018). *Supporting student learning through assessment and accountability.* Toronto: Queen's Printer for Ontario. Retrieved from http://www.eqao.com/en/about_eqao/modernization/Communication%20Documents/supporting-student-learning-through-assessment-accountability.pdf

Freire, P. (1970). *Pedagogy of the oppressed.* New York: The Continuum International Publishing Group Inc.

Freire, P. (1998). *Pedagogy of freedom: Ethics, democracy, and civic courage.* Lanham, MD: Rowman & Littlefield.

Gardner, H. (1983). *Frames of mind: The theory of multiple intelligences.* New York: Basic Books.

hooks, b. (2003). *Teaching community: A pedagogy of hope.* New York: Routledge.

Hori, M. M. (2013). *The Toronto District School Board & Structural Violence.* Mahad. M. Hori.

Lather, P. (1986). Research as praxis. *Harvard Educational Review, 56*(3), 257–278.

Lowe, S. (2016). *A social constructivist view of neoliberalism as it pertains to the Education Quality and Accountability Office testing and Howard Gardner's Theory of Multiple Intelligences.* Master of Teaching research paper, Department Curriculum, Teaching and Learning, University of Toronto, Toronto, ON.

Miller, J. P. (2000). *Education and the soul: Toward a spiritual curriculum.* New York: SUNY Press.

Miller, J. P. (2016). Equinox: Portrait of a holistic school. *International Journal of Children's Spirituality, 21*(3–4), 283–301. https://doi.org/10.1080/1364436X.2016.1232243

Ontario Ministry of Education. (2010). *Growing success: Assessment, evaluation, and reporting in Ontario schools.* Toronto: Queen's Printer for Ontario. Retrieved from http://www.edu.gov.on.ca/eng/policyfunding/growSuccess.pdf

Ontario Teachers' Federation. (2011). A new vision for large-scale testing in Ontario. Retrieved from https://www.otffeo.on.ca/en/wp-content/uploads/sites/2/2013/09/new_vision.pdf

People for Education. (2018). *Beyond the 3R's: Competencies that matter.* Retrieved from https://peopleforeducation.ca/mwm-sharing-the-thinking/competencies-insight/

Portelli, J., & Vilbert, A. (2002). Standards, equity, and the curriculum of life. *Analytic Teaching, 22*(1), 4–19.

Ricci, C. (2004). The case against standardized testing and the call for a revitalization of democracy. *Review of Education, Pedagogy, and Cultural Studies, 26*(4), 339–361.

Rodriguez, C. (2018). *Decolonizing academia: Poverty, oppression, and pain.* Winnipeg, MB: Fernwood Publishing.

Smith, L. (1999). *Decolonizing methodologies: Research and indigenous peoples.* London: Zed Books Ltd.

Toronto District School Board. (2017). *Enhancing equity task force: Report and recommendations.* Toronto. Retrieved from http://www.tdsb.on.ca/Portals/0/community/docs/EETFReportPdfVersion.pdf

Ungerleider, C. (2003). *Failing our kids: How we are ruining our public schools.* Toronto: National Library of Canada Cataloguing in Publication.

Williams, C., Jones, D., & Bailey, R. (2013). From the margins: Building curriculum for youth in transition. Ministry of Justice & Youth Association for Academics, Athletics and Character Education. Retrieved from http://yaaace.com/wp-content/uploads/2013/06/From-the-Margins-Building-Curriculum-for-Youth-in-Transitions.pdf

Appendices: Key Terms

Critical Theory: Critical Theory includes "theories that view knowledge in social constructionist terms as rooted in subjective experiences and power relations" (Brown & Strega, 2005, p. 68). Furthermore, "Critical research rejects the ideas of value-free science that underpin both qualitative and quantitative approaches to research. Instead, it positions itself as about critiquing and transforming social relations. Critical researchers view reality as both objective and subjective: objective in terms of the real forces that impinge on the lives of groups and individuals, and subjective in terms of the various individual and group interpretations of these forces and the experiences they engender" (Brown & Strega, 2005, p. 9).

Critical Race Theory (CRT): CRT is "[A] conceptual framework useful in understanding how racism operates, including within institutions such as schools, by paying careful attention to the differential resources and opportunities available to students of different races, as opposed to the more common form of racial theorizing, focusing on individual acts of hatred or racism" (Knoester & Au, 2017, p. 4).

Equality: "The achievement of equal status in society in terms of access to opportunities, support, rewards and economic and social power for all without regard to race, colour, creed, culture, ethnicity, linguistic origin, disability, socio-economic class, age, ancestry, nationality, place of origin, religion, sex, gender identity, gender expression, sexual orientation, family status, and marital status" (TDSB, 2017, p. 72).

© The Author(s) 2019   229
A. Eizadirad, *Decolonizing Educational Assessment*,
https://doi.org/10.1007/978-3-030-27462-7

Equity: "The provision of opportunities for equality for all by responding to the needs of individuals. Equity of treatment is not the same as equal treatment because it includes acknowledging historical and present systemic discrimination against identified groups and removing barriers, eliminating discrimination and remedying the impact of past discrimination" (TDSB, 2017, p. 72).

Hegemony: Derived from the works of Antonio Gramsci; "The term hegemony applies to the process whereby ideas, structures, and actions come to be seen by the majority of people as wholly natural, preordained, and working for their own good when in fact these ideas, structures, and actions are constructed and transmitted by powerful minority interests to protect the status quo that serves these interests so well. The subtle cruelty of hegemony is that over time it becomes deeply embedded, part of the natural air we breathe. One cannot peel back the layers of oppression and identify a group or groups of people as the instigators of a conscious conspiracy to keep people silent and disenfranchised. Instead, the ideas and practices of hegemony become part and parcel of everyday life—the stock opinions, conventional wisdom, or commonsense ways of seeing and ordering the world that people take for granted" (Weiner, 2014, p. 40).

Minoritized: Whereas the term "minority" refers to "a group of less than half of the total, a group that is sufficiently smaller in number," the term minoritized has a focus on describing power relations referring to "groups that are different in race, religious creed, nation of origin, sexuality, and gender and as a result of social constructs have less power or representation compared to other members or groups in society" (Smith, 2016, para. 11).

Praxis: Derived from the works of Paulo Freire; "Reflection and action upon the world in order to transform it" (Freire, 1970, p. 51). Freire (1970) argues it is through "conscientization" (p. 67), a process of developing critical awareness about one's social reality through reflection and action, that objects come to see themselves as subjects beholding agency and having capacity to make liberatory change at the micro and macro level.

Neoliberalism: "Neoliberalism is the dominant political and ideological paradigm of our time, embodied by policies and processes that place political control in a handful of private interests. Its defining characteristics include a shift of shared concern for the common good between the state and citizens to a relationship based on economics whereby citizen roles are limited to "taxpayers" in the social order, and a predominant consensual discourse whereby contestation and dissent are compromised. Resulting social policies reflect managerialism, privatisation and a preponderance of punitive accountability mechanisms" (Pinto, 2015, p. 142).

Paradigm: "This is the philosophical stance taken by the researcher that provides a basic set of beliefs that guides action. It defines, for its holder the nature of the world, the individual's place in it, and the range of possible relationships to that world" (Creswell, 2007, p. 248). Denzin and Lincoln (2000) further call this the "net that contains the researcher's epistemological, ontological, and methodological premises" (p. 13).

Racialized/Racialization: "Race is a socially constructed way of judging, categorizing and creating difference among people based on physical characteristics such as skin colour, eye, lips and nose shape, hair texture and body shape. The process of social construction of race is termed "racialization." This is the "process by which societies construct races as real, different and unequal in ways that matter to economic, political and social life. Despite the fact that there are no biological "races," the social construction of race is a powerful force with real consequences for individuals. Someone's "race" can also extend to specific traits which are deemed to be "abnormal" and of less worth. Individuals may have prejudices related to various racialized characteristics. In addition to physical features, these characteristics could include accent, dialect or manner of speech, name, clothing and grooming, diet, beliefs and practices, leisure preferences, and places of origin" (TDSB, 2017, p. 75).

Socio-Culturally Relevant Pedagogy: A form of meaningful teaching and learning that takes into consideration "both micro- and macro-analyses, including: teacher-student interpersonal contexts, teacher and student expectations, institutional contexts, and the societal context. This work is important for its break with the cultural deficit or cultural disadvantage explanations which led to compensatory educational interventions. Next step for positing effective pedagogical practice is a theoretical model that not only addresses student achievement but also helps students to accept and affirm their cultural identity while developing critical perspectives that challenge inequities that schools (and other institutions) perpetuate" (Ladson-Billings, 1995, p. 469).

Socio-Economic Status: "The economic, social and political relationships in which people operate in a given social order. These relationships reflect the areas of income level, education, access to goods and services, type of occupation, sense of ownership or entitlement and other indicators of social rank or class" (TDSB, 2017, p. 75).

Subaltern: Derived from the works of Antonio Gramsci; referring to oppressed subjects or social groups or more generally those of inferior rank (Spivak, 1988).

Systemic Discrimination: "A pattern of discrimination that arises out of apparently neutral institutional policies or practices, that is reinforced by institutional structures and power dynamics, and that results in the differential and unequal treatment of members of certain groups" (TDSB, 2017, p. 76).

REFERENCES

Brown, L., & Strega, S. (2005). *Research as resistance: Critical, indigenous, and anti-oppressive approaches.* Toronto, Canada: Canadian Scholars' Press.

Creswell, J. W. (2007). *Qualitative inquiry and research design: Choosing among five approaches* (2nd ed.). Thousand Oaks, CA: Sage.

Denzin, N., & Lincoln, Y. (2000). Introduction: The discipline and practice of qualitative research. In *Handbook of qualitative research.* London: Sage Publications.

Freire, P. (1970). *Pedagogy of the oppressed.* New York: The Continuum International Publishing Group Inc.

Knoester, M., & Au, W. (2017). Standardized testing and school segregation: Like tinder for fire? *Race Ethnicity and Education, 20*(1), 1–14.

Ladson-Billings, G. (1995). Toward a theory of culturally relevant pedagogy. *American Educational Research Journal, 32*(3), 465–491.

Pinto, L. E. (2015). Fear and loathing in neoliberalism; School leader responses to policy layers. *Journal of Educational Administration and History, 47*(2), 140–154.

Toronto District School Board. (2017). *Enhancing equity task force: Report and recommendations.* Toronto. Retrieved from http://www.tdsb.on.ca/Portals/0/community/docs/EETFReportPdfVersion.pdf

Spivak, G. C. (1988). Can the subaltern speak? Reflections on the history of an idea. In C. Nelson & L. Grossberg (Eds.), *Marxism and the interpretation of culture* (pp. 21–78). London: Macmillan.

Weiner, E. (2014). *Deschooling the imagination: Critical thought as social practice.* Boulder, CO: Paradigm Publishers.

Interview Guide for Parents

Before

Can you tell me a little about your child's school and its surrounding community?

Were you born in Canada? If not, how long have you been in Canada?

Is English your mother tongue language? What other languages can you speak?

What is your opinion of your child's school and school teacher? What do you like? What do you dislike?

What is different in Grade 3 compared to other years of your child being in school?

Have you received any communication from your child's teacher or school regarding EQAO testing? If so, what have you learned about EQAO testing in Grade 3?

Based on your understanding, what is the EQAO test? Why does your child write it in Grade 3?

What have you observed in your child in terms of emotions and behaviours in relation to preparing for the EQAO test?

How do you support your child's learning at school?

How do you support your child to prepare for the EQAO test?

What do you think the results of EQAO are used for?

During

How important is it that your child does well?

How did you feel on the first EQAO test day?

How did your child feel on the first EQAO test day? Any differences before and after he/she got home?

What is the mood of your child? What does he/she do when home after writing the test?

How are you supporting your child this week to do well on the EQAO test?

Is your child stressed? Any changes in behaviour or attitude during testing week?

What is your child's opinion about the test?

In your opinion, how is the EQAO test different or similar to other things your child does in school?

Have standardized tests come up in family talks as a point of concern or anxiety?

Do you think your child likes writing the EQAO test? Why or why not?

After

How do you think your child did on the EQAO test?

How are parents affected by standardized tests?

What is your opinion of the EQAO test? Strengths? Weaknesses?

Would you change anything about the test? What? Why?

How do you think the EQAO test helps your child as a student?

Do you see any positive or negative changes in the school's curriculum or procedures as a result of EQAO standardized testing?

What advice would you give other parents to prepare their children for the EQAO test?

If you could tell the government about ways to improve schools, what would you say?

What would you tell the government about the EQAO test in particular? Why?

INTERVIEW GUIDE FOR GRADE 3 STUDENTS

Before

Can you tell me a little about your school and its surrounding community?

Were you born in Canada? If not, how long have you been in Canada?

Is English your mother tongue language? What other languages can you speak?

What do you like about school? What do you dislike about school?

What is your favourite subject? What is your least favourite subject?

What do you like to do in your spare time?

What is different in Grade 3 compared to your other years in school?

Based on your understanding, what is the EQAO test? Why do you write it?

How does your teacher explain EQAO testing to you?

How do you feel about writing the EQAO test this year?

How do you prepare for the EQAO?

How does your teacher prepare you for the EQAO test?

How do your parents prepare you for the EQAO test?

During

How did you feel on the first EQAO test day? When you got the first booklet?

What was the typical day and routine during test week?

How was this test different or similar to other things you do in school?

What is the mood in the school during EQAO testing days?

What are you doing to prepare to do well on the EQAO test?

What do you do when you get home after writing the EQAO test?

What are your teacher and parents doing to support you to do well on the EQAO test during test week?

Do you like writing the EQAO test? Why or why not?

After

How do you think you did on the EQAO test?

What is your opinion of the EQAO test? Strengths? Weaknesses?

Would you change anything about the test? What? Why?

How do you think the EQAO test helps you as a student?

Next time, for example when you have to write the EQAO test again in Grade 6, how would you prepare differently for the EQAO test?

What do you think the EQAO results are used for?

What advice would you give to Grade 2 students to prepare for the EQAO test next year?

If you could tell the government about ways to improve schools, what would you say?

What would you tell the government about the EQAO test in particular? Why?

ABBREVIATIONS

BIPSA	Board Improvement Plan for Student Achievement and Well Being
CRT	Critical Race Theory
EA	Educational Assistant
EQAO	Education Quality and Accountability Office
ERF	Educational Resource Facilitator
ESL	English as a Second Language

ETFO	Elementary Teachers' Federation of Ontario
FairTest	The National Center for Fair and Open Testing
IEP	Individual Education Plan
IQ	Intelligence Quotient
ISR	Individual Student Report
LOI	Learning Opportunity Index
MSIC	Model Schools for Inner Cities
NDP	New Democratic Party
OSSD	Ontario Secondary School Diploma
OSSLT	Ontario Secondary School Literacy Test
OSSTF	Ontario Secondary School Teachers' Federation
RCOL	Royal Commission on Learning
SES	Socio-Economic Status
SIP	School Improvement Plan
TA	Thematic Analysis
TDSB	Toronto District School Board
YAAACE	Youth Association for Academics, Athletics, and Character Education

References

Ahmed, S. (2007). A phenomenology of whiteness. *Feminist Theory, 8*(2), 149–168.

Anyon, J. (1980). Social class and the hidden curriculum of work. *Journal of Education, 162*(1), 67–92.

Anyon, J. (1981). Social class and school knowledge. *Curriculum Inquiry, 11*(1), 3–42.

Apple, M. (1978). Ideology, reproduction, and educational reform. *Comparative Education Review, 22*(3), 367–387.

Apple, M. W. (2004). *Ideology and curriculum.* New York: Routledge.

Au, W. (2010). *Unequal by design: High-stakes testing and the standardization of inequality.* London: Routledge.

Ball, S. (1990). *Politics and policy making in education: Explorations in policy sociology.* London: Routledge.

Basu, R. (2004). The rationalization of neoliberalism in Ontario's public education system, 1995–2000. *Geoforum, 35*(5), 621–634.

Baszile, D. T. (2009). Deal with it we must: Education, social justice, and the curriculum of hip hop culture. *Equity & Excellence in Education, 42*(1), 6–19.

Bhabha, H. (1983). The Other question. *Screen, 24*, 18–36. Retrieved from https://pdfs.semanticscholar.org/0c8e/a96f2957d6b0d64e902d-c25e07ea7e714880.pdf

Block, S., & Galabuzi, G. (2011). Canada's colour coded labour market: The gap for racialized workers. Wellesley Institute and Canadian Centre for Policy Alternatives. Retrieved from http://www.wellesleyinstitute.com/wp-content/uploads/2011/03/Colour_Coded_Labour_MarketFINAL.pdf

Bourdieu, P., & Passeron, J. (1977). *Reproduction in education, society, and culture.* Beverley Hills, CA: Sage.

© The Author(s) 2019

A. Eizadirad, *Decolonizing Educational Assessment,*
https://doi.org/10.1007/978-3-030-27462-7

Bourdieu, P., & Wacquant, L. J. (1992). *An invitation to reflexive sociology.* Chicago: University of Chicago press.

Bower, J., & Thomas, L. (2013). *De-testing + de-grading schools; Authentic alternatives to accountability and standardization.* New York, NY: Peter Lang Publishing.

Brown, L., & Strega, S. (2005). *Research as resistance: Critical, indigenous, and anti-oppressive approaches.* Toronto, Canada: Canadian Scholars' Press.

Brown, R. (2009). *Making the grade: The grade 9 cohort of fall 2002: Overview.* Research Report, Toronto: Retrieved from http://www.tdsb.on.ca/Portals/research/docs/reports/MakingTheGrade2002-07Overview.pdf

Campbell, C., Clinton, J., Fullan, M., Hargreaves, A., James, C., & Longboat, K. (2018). *Ontario: A learning province. Findings and recommendations from the independent review of assessment and reporting. Ontario Ministry of Education.* Toronto: Queen's Printer for Ontario. Retrieved from http://www.edu.gov.on.ca/CurriculumRefresh/learning-province-en.pdf

City of Toronto. (2018). Neighbourhood improvement area profiles. Retrieved from https://www.toronto.ca/city-government/data-research-maps/neighbourhoods-communities/nia-profiles/

Clarke, V., & Braun, V. (2017). Thematic analysis. *The Journal of Psychology, 12*(3), 297–298. https://doi.org/10.1080/17439760.2016.1262613

Colour of Justice Network. (2007). Colour of poverty. Retrieved from http://www.learningandviolence.net/lrnteach/material/PovertyFactSheets-aug07.pdf

Colour of Poverty and Colour of Change. (2019). Fact sheets. Retrieved from https://colourofpoverty.ca/fact-sheets/

Creswell, J. W. (2007). *Qualitative inquiry and research design: Choosing among five approaches* (2nd ed.). Thousand Oaks, CA: Sage.

Curtis, B., Livingstone, D. W., & Smaller, H. (1992). *Stacking the deck: The streaming of working-class kids in Ontario schools* (Vol. 24). Toronto: James Lorimer & Company.

Dei, G., & Doyle-Wood, S. (2009). Is we who Haffi Ride Di Staam: Critical knowledge/multiple knowings-possibilities, challenges, and resistance in curriculum/cultural contexts. In Y. Kanu (Ed.), *Curriculum as cultural practice: Postcolonial imaginations* (pp. 151–180). Toronto, ON: University of Toronto Press.

Dei, G. J. S. (2000). Towards an anti-racism discursive framework. In G. Dei & A. Calliste (Eds.), *Power, knowledge and anti-racism education: A critical reader.* Toronto, ON: Fernwood Publishing Co.

Dei, G. J. S. (2008). Schooling as community: Race, schooling, and the education of African youth. *Journal of Black Studies, 38*(3), 346–366.

Dei, G. J. S., Holmes, L., Mazzuca, J., McIsaac, E., & Campbell, R. (1995). *Drop out or push out. The dynamics of Black students' disengagement from school.* Toronto, Canada: Ontario Institute for Studies in Education.

Delgado, R., & Stefancic, J. (2000). *Critical race theory: The cutting edge.* Philadelphia: Temple University Press.

Denzin, N., & Lincoln, Y. (2000). Introduction: The discipline and practice of qualitative research. In *Handbook of qualitative research*. London: Sage Publications.

Despres, S., Kuhn, S., Ngirumpatse, P, & Parent, M. (2013). *Real accountability or an illusion of success? A call to review standardized testing in Ontario*. Action Canada. Retrieved from http://www.actioncanada.ca/wp-content/uploads/2014/04/TF3-Report_Standardized-Testing_EN.pdf

Du Bois, W. E. B. (2008). *The souls of black folk*. Rockville, MD: Arc Manor.

Education Quality and Accountability Office. (1997). *Education quality and accountability office/Office de la qualite et de la responsibilite en education by-law no. 1*. Toronto: Queen's Printer for Ontario. Retrieved from http://www.eqao.com/en/about_eqao/about_the_agency/communication-docs/EQAO-By-Law-No1.pdf#search=eqao%20by%20law%20

Education Quality and Accountability Office. (2011). *EQAO tests in elementary school: A guide for parents*. Toronto: Queen's Printer for Ontario. Retrieved from https://www.rainbowschools.ca/wp-content/uploads/2016/04/EQAO_ParentGuide_PrimaryJunior2011.pdf

Education Quality and Accountability Office. (2012). *The power of Ontario's provincial testing program*. Toronto: Queen's Printer for Ontario. Retrieved from http://www.eqao.com/en/assessments/communication-docs/power-provincial-testing-program.PDF

Education Quality and Accountability Office. (2013). *EQAO: Ontario's provincial assessment program- Its history and influence 1996–2012*. Toronto: Queen's Printer for Ontario. Retrieved from http://www.eqao.com/en/about_eqao/about_the_agency/communication-docs/EQAO-history-influence.pdf

Education Quality and Accountability Office. (2015). *Top reasons you can't compare standardized testing in Ontario and the United States*. Toronto: Queen's Printer for Ontario. Retrieved from http://www.eqao.com/en/about_eqao/media_room/communication-docs/EQAO-US-comparison.pdf

Education Quality and Accountability Office. (2017a). *Highlights of the provincial results*. Toronto: Queen's Printer for Ontario. Retrieved from http://www.eqao.com/en/assessments/results/communication-docs/provincial-report-highlights-elementary-2017.pdf

Education Quality and Accountability Office. (2017b). *Achievement results; Primary division*. Toronto: Queen's Printer for Ontario. Retrieved from http://www.eqao.com/en/assessments/results/assessment-docs-elementary/provincial-report-primary-achievement-results-2017.pdf

Education Quality and Accountability Office. (2018a). *About the agency*. Toronto: Queen's Printer for Ontario. Retrieved from http://www.eqao.com/en/about-eqao/about-the-agency

Education Quality and Accountability Office. (2018b). *Accountability outcomes*. Toronto: Queen's Printer for Ontario. Retrieved from http://www.eqao.com/en/about_eqao/about_the_agency/Pages/accountability-outcomes.aspx

Education Quality and Accountability Office. (2018c). *Board of Directors.* Toronto: Queen's Printer for Ontario. Retrieved from http://www.eqao.com/en/about-eqao/about-the-agency/board-of-directors

Education Quality and Accountability Office. (2018d). *EQAO agrees that further discussion is required regarding the recommendations of the premier's education advisors.* Toronto: Queen's Printer for Ontario. Retrieved from http://www.eqao.com/en/about_eqao/media_room/Pages/further-discussion-required-recommendations-04-24-2018.aspx

Education Quality and Accountability Office. (2018e). *Supporting student learning through assessment and accountability.* Toronto: Queen's Printer for Ontario. Retrieved fromhttp://www.eqao.com/en/about_eqao/modernization/Communication%20Documents/supporting-student-learning-through-assessment-accountability.pdf

Education Quality and Accountability Office. (2019a). *Highlights of the provincial results. Literacy.* Toronto: Queen's Printer for Ontario. Retrieved from http://www.eqao.com/en/assessments/results/communication-docs/provincial-report-highlights-literacy-2018.pdf

Education Quality and Accountability Office. (2019b). *Highlights of the provincial results. Mathematics.* Toronto: Queen's Printer for Ontario. Retrieved from http://www.eqao.com/en/assessments/results/communication-docs/provincial-report-highlights-mathematics-2018.pdf

Education Quality and Accountability Office Act. (1996). *Education Quality and Accountability Office Act. SO 1996, c, 11.*

Egan, K. (1978). What is curriculum? *Curriculum Inquiry, 8*(1), 65–72.

Eizadirad, A. (2016). Is it "bad" kids or "bad" places? Where is all the violence originating from? Youth violence in the City of Toronto. *Review of Education, Pedagogy, and Cultural Studies, 38*(2), 162–188.

Eizadirad, A. (2017). The university as a neoliberal and colonizing institute; A spatial case study analysis of the invisible fence between York University and the Jane and Finch neighbourhood in the City of Toronto. *Journal of Critical Race Inquiry, 4*(1), 25–53.

Eizadirad, A. (2018). Legitimization and normalization of EQAO standardized testing as an accountability tool in Ontario: Rise of quantifiable outcome-based education and inequitable educational practices. *OISE Graduate Student Research Conference Journal, 1*(1), 6–18.

Eizadirad, A., Martinez, X., & Ruminot, C. (2016). Comparative analysis of educational systems of accountability and quality of education in Ontario, Canada and Chile: Standardized testing and its role in perpetuation of educational inequity. *Interfaces Brasil/Canadá, 16*(2), 54–88.

Eizadirad, A., & Portelli, J. (2018). Subversion in education: Common misunderstandings and myths. *International Journal of Critical Pedagogy, 9*(1), 53–72.

Elementary Teachers' Federation of Ontario. (2010). EQAO testing. Retrieved from   http://www.etfo.ca/defendingworkingconditions/issuesineducation/pages/eqao%20testing%20-%20advice%20to%20members.aspx

Elementary Teachers' Federation of Ontario. (2015). ETFO bargaining bulletin: Central collective bargaining updates published by ETFO.

Elementary Teachers' Federation of Ontario. (2018). ETFO. Retrieved from http://www.etfo.ca/Pages/Home.aspx

FairTest. (2017). Fact sheet for families on testing and young children. The National Center for Fair and Open Testing. Retrieved from http://www.fairtest.org/sites/default/files/YoungChildTestingFactSheet2017.pdf

FairTest. (2018). About FairTest: The National Center for Fair and Open Testing. Retrieved from https://www.fairtest.org/about

Fiore, L. (2012). *Assessment of young children: A collaborative approach.* New York: Routledge.

Fraser Institute. (2018). *School performance.* Retrieved from https://www.fraser-institute.org/school-performance

Freire, P. (1970). *Pedagogy of the oppressed.* New York: The Continuum International Publishing Group Inc.

Freire, P. (1998). *Pedagogy of freedom: Ethics, democracy, and civic courage.* Lanham, MD: Rowman & Littlefield.

Friesen, J. (2018, April 25). Canada's toughest neighbourhood. *The Globe and Mail.* Retrieved from https://www.theglobeandmail.com/news/national/canadas-toughest-neighbourhood/article1086849/

Froese-Germain, B. (2001). Standardized testing + High-stakes decisions = Educational inequality. *Interchange, 32*(2), 111–130.

Galletta, A. (2013). *Mastering the semi-structured interview and beyond: From research design to analysis and publication.* New York: NYU Press.

Gardener, D. A. K. (2017). *EQAO Preparation and the Effects on In-Classroom Instruction.* Master of Teaching research paper, Department of Curriculum, Teaching and Learning, University of Toronto, Toronto, ON.

Gardner, H. (1983). *Frames of mind: The theory of multiple intelligences.* New York: Basic Books.

Garrison, M. (2009). *A measure of failure: The political origins of standardized testing.* Albany, NY: State University of New York Press.

Gidney, R. (1999). *From hope to Harris: The reshaping of Ontario's schools.* Toronto: University of Toronto Press.

Giroux, H. (2003). Spectacles of race and pedagogies of denial: Anti-Black racist pedagogy under the reign of neoliberalism. *Communication Education, 52*(3-4), 191–211.

Giroux, H. (2007). Where are we now? In P. McLaren & J. Kincheloe (Eds.), *Critical Pedagogy: Where Are We Now?* New York: Peter Lang Publishing Inc..

Glesne, C. (2015). *Becoming qualitative researchers: An introduction.* Boston, MA: Pearson.

Gordon, A. (2017, September 6). Ontario to launch review of how students are tested. *Toronto Star.* Retrieved from https://www.thestar.com/news/gta/2017/09/06/ontario-to-launch-review-of-how-students-are-tested.html

Gorlewski, J., Porfilio, B., & Gorlewski, D. (2012). *Using standards and high-stakes testing for students: Exploiting power with critical pedagogy.* New York, NY: Peter Lang Publishing, Inc.

Gramsci, A. (1995). *Further selections from the prison notebooks.* Minneapolis: University of Minnesota Press.

Gramsci, A. (2000). *The Gramsci reader: Selected writings, 1916–1935.* New York: NYU press.

Green, J., Willis, K., Hughes, E., Small, R., Welch, N., Gibbs, L., et al. (2007). Generating best evidence from qualitative research: The role of data analysis. *Australian and New Zealand Journal of Public Health, 31*(6), 545–550.

Grenfell, M. J. (Ed.). (2014). *Pierre Bourdieu: Key concepts.* New York: Routledge.

Grey, M. K. (2017). *Perpetuating inequities in Ontario schools: A large-scale practice of assessment.* Master of Teaching research paper, Department Curriculum, Teaching and Learning, University of Toronto, Toronto, ON.

Gunzenhauser, M. G. (2003). High-stakes testing and the default philosophy of education. *Theory into Practice, 42*(1), 51–58.

Hamilton, L., Stecher, B., & Klein, S. (2002). *Making sense of test-based accountability in education.* Santa Monica, CA: RAND.

Hart, D., & Kempf, A. (2015). *Public attitudes toward education in Ontario 2015: The 19th OISE survey of educational issues.* OISE, University of Toronto. Retrieved from https://tspace.library.utoronto.ca/bitstream/1807/76898/2/Final_Report_-_19th_OISE_Survey_on_Educational_Issues_2015.pdf

Hart, D., & Kempf, A. (2018). *Public attitudes toward education in Ontario 2018: The 20th OISE survey of educational issues.* OISE, University of Toronto. Retrieved from https://www.oise.utoronto.ca/oise/UserFiles/Media/Media_Relations/OISE-Public-Attitudes-Report-2018_final.pdf

hooks, b. (2003). *Teaching community: A pedagogy of hope.* New York: Routledge.

Hori, M. M. (2013). *The Toronto District School Board & Structural Violence.* Mahad. M. Hori.

Hulchanski, J. D. (2007). *The three cities within Toronto: Income polarization among Toronto's neighbourhoods 1970–2005.* Toronto, ON: Cities Centre Press, University of Toronto. Retrieved from http://www.urbancentre.utoronto.ca/pdfs/curp/tnrn/Three-Cities-Within-Toronto-2010-Final.pdf

Hunkins, F. P., & Hammill, P. A. (1994). Beyond Tyler and Taba: Reconceptualizing the curriculum process. *Peabody Journal of Education, 69*(3), 4–18.

James, C. E. (2012). *Life at the intersection: Community, class and schooling.* Halifax, NS: Fernwood Publishing.

Kearns, L. (2008). *Equity, literacy testing and marginalized youth: The social construction of 'illiterate' identities.* (Unpublished doctoral dissertation). University of Toronto, Toronto, ON.

Kearns, L. (2011). High-stakes standardized testing and marginalized youth: An examination of the impact on those who fail. *Canadian Journal of Education, 34*(2), 112–130.

Kearns, L. (2016). The construction of 'illiterate' and 'literate' youth: The effects of high-stakes standardized literacy testing. *Race Ethnicity and Education*, *19*(1), 121–140.

Kempf, A. (2013, June 21). Standardized school tests stress students and system. *Toronto Star*. Retrieved from https://www.thestar.com/opinion/commentary/2013/06/21/standardized_school_tests_stress_students_and_system.html

Kempf, A. (2016). *The pedagogy of standardized testing: The radical impacts of educational standardization in the US and Canada*. New York: Springer.

Kincheloe, J. L., & McLaren, P. (2002). Rethinking critical theory and qualitative research. In Y. Zou & H. Trueba (Eds.), *Ethnography and schools: Qualitative approaches to the study of education* (pp. 87–138). Lanham, MD: Rowman & Littlefield.

Kliebard, H. M. (1970). The Tyler rationale. *The School Review*, *78*(2), 259–272.

Klinger, D., Rogers, W., Anderson, J., Poth, C., & Calman, R. (2006). Contextual and school factors associated with achievement on a high-stakes examination. *Canadian Journal of Education*, *29*(3), 771–797.

Knoester, M., & Au, W. (2017). Standardized testing and school segregation: Like tinder for fire? *Race Ethnicity and Education*, *20*(1), 1–14.

Kohn, A. (2000). *The case against standardized testing: Raising scores, ruining the schools*. Portsmouth, NH: Heinemann.

Kohn, A. (2001). Fighting the tests: A practical guide to rescuing our schools. *Phi Delta Kappan*, *82*(5), 349–357.

Kumashiro, K. (2000). Toward a theory of anti-oppressive education. *Review of Educational Research*, *70*(1), 25–53.

Kumashiro, K. (2004). *Against common sense: Teaching and learning toward social justice*. New York: Routledge.

Ladson-Billings, G. (1994). *The dreamkeepers: Successful teachers for African-American children*. San Francisco: Jossey-Bass.

Ladson-Billings, G. (1995). Toward a theory of culturally relevant pedagogy. *American Educational Research Journal*, *32*(3), 465–491.

Lalani, A. (2016, October 5). Devon Jones wins praise for changing lives for the better. *Toronto Star*. Retrieved from https://www.thestar.com/yourtoronto/education/2016/10/05/devon-jones-wins-praise-for-changing-lives-for-the-better.html

Langlois, H. (2017). *Behind the snapshot: Teachers' experiences of preparing students in lower socioeconomic status schools for the Ontario Secondary School Literacy Test*. Master of Teaching research paper, Department Curriculum, Teaching and Learning, University of Toronto, Toronto, ON.

Lather, P. (1986). Research as praxis. *Harvard Educational Review*, *56*(3), 257–278.

Lewis, S. (1992). Report of the advisor on race relations to the Premier of Ontario, Bob Rae. Retrieved from https://archive.org/details/stephenlewisrepo00lewi

Lock, C. (2001). *The influence of a large scale assessment program on classroom practices*. (Unpublished doctoral dissertation). Queen's University, Kingston, ON.

Lopez, R. G. (2003). The (racially neutral) politics of education: A critical race theory perspective. *Educational Administration Quarterly, 39*(1), 68–94.

Lowe, S. (2016). *A social constructivist view of neoliberalism as it pertains to the Education Quality and Accountability Office testing and Howard Gardner's Theory of Multiple Intelligences.* Master of Teaching research paper, Department Curriculum, Teaching and Learning, University of Toronto, Toronto, ON.

Madison, D. (2012). *Critical ethnography: Methods, ethics, and performance.* Thousand Oaks, CA: SAGE Publications.

Masood, O. (2008). *At risk: The racialized student marked for educational failure.* (Unpublished doctoral dissertation). University of Toronto, Toronto, ON.

McIntosh, P. (1988). White Privilege: Unpacking the Invisible Knapsack. Retrieved from http://hd.ingham.org/Portals/HD/White%20Priviledge%20 Unpacking%20the%20Invisible%20Knapsack.pdf

McLaren, P. (2015). *Life in schools: An introduction to critical pedagogy in the foundations of education.* New York, NY: Routledge.

McMurtry, R., & Curling, A. (2008). *The review of the roots of youth violence.* Toronto, ON: Ministry of Children, Community and Social Services. Retrieved from   http://www.children.gov.on.ca/htdocs/English/professionals/oyap/ roots/index.aspx

McNeil, L. (2000). *Contradictions of school reform; Educational costs of standardized testing.* New York, NY: Routledge.

Miller, J. P. (2000). *Education and the soul: Toward a spiritual curriculum.* New York: SUNY Press.

Miller, J. P. (2016). Equinox: Portrait of a holistic school. *International Journal of Children's Spirituality, 21*(3–4), 283–301. https://doi.org/10.1080/13644 36X.2016.1232243

Morgan, C. (2006). A retrospective look at educational reforms in Ontario. *Our Schools, Our Selves, 15*(2), 127–141.

Nagy, P. (2000). The three roles of assessment: Gatekeeping, accountability, and instructional diagnosis. *Canadian Journal of Education/Revue canadienne de l'éducation*, 262–279.

Nezavdal, F. (2003). The standardized testing movement: Equitable or excessive? *McGill Journal of Education, 38*(1), 65–78.

Noguera, P. A. (2003). Schools, prisons, and social implications of punishment: Rethinking disciplinary practices. *Theory into Practice, 42*(4), 341–350.

O'Grady, W., Parnaby, P. F., & Schikschneit, J. (2010). Guns, gangs, and the underclass: A constructionist analysis of gun violence in a Toronto high school. *Canadian Journal of Criminology and Criminal Justice, 52*(1), 55–77.

Ontario Anti-Racism Directorate. (2016). *A better way forward: Ontario's 3-year anti-racism strategic plan.* Retrieved from https://www.ontario.ca/page/ better-way-forward-ontarios-3-year-anti-racism-strategic-plan#section-2

Ontario Ministry of Education. (1997). *The Ontario curriculum grades 1–8, 1997.* Toronto: Queen's Printer for Ontario. Retrieved from http://www.edu.gov. on.ca/eng/curriculum/elementary/subjects.html

Ontario Ministry of Education. (2010). *Growing success: Assessment, evaluation, and reporting in Ontario schools.* Toronto: Queen's Printer for Ontario. Retrieved from http://www.edu.gov.on.ca/eng/policyfunding/growSuccess.pdf

Ontario Ministry of Education. (2014). *How does learning happen? Ontario's pedagogy for the early years: A resource about learning through relationships for those who work with young children and their families.* Toronto: Queen's Printer for Ontario. Retrieved from http://www.edu.gov.on.ca/childcare/HowLearningHappens.pdf

Ontario Ministry of Education. (2017a). *High school graduation rate climbs to all-time high.* Toronto: Queen's Printer for Ontario. Retrieved from https://news. ontario.ca/edu/en/2017/05/high-school-graduation-rate-climbs-to-all-time-high.html

Ontario Ministry of Education. (2017b). *Ontario appoints new advisors to guide transformation in education system.* Toronto: Queen's Printer for Ontario. Retrieved from https://news.ontario.ca/edu/en/2017/08/ontario-appoints-new-advisors-to-guide-transformation-in-education-system. html?_ga=2.71555795.1779644130.1528468099-1009438681.1520260943

Ontario Ministry of Education. (2018a). *Independent review of assessment and reporting.* Toronto: Queen's Printer for Ontario. Retrieved from http://www. edu.gov.on.ca/CurriculumRefresh/student-assessment.html

Ontario Ministry of Education. (2018b). *Ontario's graduation rate.* Toronto: Queen's Printer for Ontario. Retrieved from http://www.edu.gov.on.ca/eng/

Ontario Ministry of Education. (2018c). *The Ontario curriculum: Elementary.* Toronto: Queen's Printer for Ontario. Retrieved from http://www.edu.gov. on.ca/eng/curriculum/elementary/common.html#display

Ontario Secondary School Teachers' Federation. (2018). *About us.* Retrieved from https://www.osstf.on.ca/about-us.aspx

Ontario Teachers' Federation. (2011). A new vision for large-scale testing in Ontario. Retrieved from https://www.otffeo.on.ca/en/wp-content/uploads/sites/2/2013/09/new_vision.pdf

Paradkar, S. (2017, May 5). The Yonge St. riot of 1992… or was it an uprising?: Paradkar. *Toronto Star.* Retrieved from https://www.thestar.com/news/gta/2017/05/05/the-yonge-street-riot-of-1992-or-was-it-an-uprising-paradkar.html

People for Education. (2013). *Broader measures of success: Measuring what matters in education.* Toronto, ON: People for Education. Retrieved from https://peopleforeducation.ca/wp-content/uploads/2017/08/Broader-measures-of-success-Measuring-what-matters-in-education.pdf

People for Education. (2018). *Beyond the 3R's: Competencies that matter.* Retrieved from https://peopleforeducation.ca/mwm-sharing-the-thinking/competencies-insight/

Pinar, W., Reynolds, W., Slattery, P., & Taubman, P. (1995). *Understanding curriculum: An introduction to the study of historical and contemporary curriculum discourses.* New York: Peter Lang Publishing, Incorporated.

Pinto, L. E. (2015). Fear and loathing in neoliberalism; School leader responses to policy layers. *Journal of Educational Administration and History, 47*(2), 140–154.

Pinto, L. E. (2016). Tensions and fissures: The politics of standardised testing and accountability in Ontario, 1995–2015. *The Curriculum Journal, 27*(1), 95–112.

Polanyi, M., Wilson, B., Maddox, R., Ekra, M., Kerr, M., & Khan, A. (2018). *2018 Toronto child & family poverty report: Municipal election edition.* Retrieved from http://www.torontocas.ca/sites/torontocas/files/2018_Child_Family_Poverty_Report_Municipal_Election_Edition.pdf

Polanyi, M., Wilson, B., Mustachi, J., Ekra, M., & Kerr, M. (2017). *Unequal city: The hidden divide among Toronto's children and youth. 2017 Toronto child and family poverty report card.* Retrieved from http://torontocas.ca/sites/torontocas/files/CAST%20Child%20Poverty%20Report%20Nov%202017.pdf

Pole, C., & Morrison, M. (2003). *Ethnography for education.* Maidenhead: Open University Press.

Portelli, J., & Konecny, P. C. (2013). Neoliberalism, subversion, and democracy in education. *Encounters on Education, 14,* 87–97.

Portelli, J., & Sharma, M. (2014). Uprooting and settling in: The invisible strength of deficit thinking. *LEARNing Landscapes, 8*(1), 251–267.

Portelli, J., & Vilbert, A. (2002). Standards, equity, and the curriculum of life. *Analytic Teaching, 22*(1), 4–19.

Price, D. (2003). Outcome-based tyranny: Teaching compliance while testing like a state. *Anthropological Quarterly, 76*(4), 715–730.

Racial Justice Report Card for Ontario. (2014). Retrieved from http://yourlegalrights.on.ca/sites/all/files/COPC%20Provincial%20Racial%20Justice%20Report%20Card%20_2014_.pdf

Razack, S. (2002). When place becomes race. In S. Razack (Ed.), *Race, Space and the law: Unmapping a White Settler Society.* Toronto: Between the Lines.

Ricci, C. (2004). The case against standardized testing and the call for a revitalization of democracy. *Review of Education, Pedagogy, and Cultural Studies, 26*(4), 339–361.

Rodriguez, C. (2018). *Decolonizing academia: Poverty, oppression, and pain.* Winnipeg, MB: Fernwood Publishing.

Rogers, W. T. (2014). Improving the utility of large-scale assessments in Canada. *Canadian Journal of Education/Revue canadienne de l'éducation, 37*(3), 1–22.

Royal Commission on Learning. (1994). *For the love of learning: Report of the royal commission on learning [Short Version].* Toronto: Queen's Printer for Ontario.

Rushowy, K. (2015, May 14). EQAO standardized testing cancelled over teacher job action. *Toronto Star*. Retrieved from https://www.thestar.com/yourtoronto/education/2015/05/14/teacher-strike-standardized-tests-cancelled-because-of-job-action.html

Russo, L. (2012). "Standardized" play and creativity for young children? The climate of increased standardization and accountability in early childhood classrooms. *Counterpoints, 425*, 140–156.

Sattler, P. (2012). Education governance reform in Ontario: Neoliberalism in context. *Canadian Journal of Educational Administration and Policy, 128*, 1–28.

Sharma, M. (2009). *Inner city students: Stamped, labeled and shipped out! Deficit thinking and democracy in an age of neoliberalism*. (Unpublished master's thesis). University of Toronto, Toronto, ON.

Shulman, R., Hinton, A., Zhang, S., & Kozlow, M. (2014). Longitudinal results of province-wide assessments in English- language schools: Trends in student achievement and implications for improvement planning in Mathematics and Literacy. Education Quality and Accountability Office. Retrieved from http://www.eqao.com/en/research_data/Research_Reports/DMA-docs/cohort-tracking-2012.pdf

Shum, D., & Miller, A. (2016, October 20). EQAO cancels high school online literacy tests due to 'technical issues'. *Global News*. Retrieved from https://globalnews.ca/news/3015060/ontario-high-school-online-literacy-tests-run-into-technical-issues/

Singh, S. (2016). *Critical discourse analysis: The impact the Ontario Secondary School Literacy Test has on ESL teachers' teaching practices and work environments*. Doctor of Education thesis, Faculty of Graduate Studies, University of Calgary, Calgary, Alberta.

Smith, I. (2016). Minority vs. Minoritized: Why the noun just doesn't cut it. Retrieved from https://www.theodysseyonline.com/minority-vs-minoritize

Smith, L. (1999). *Decolonizing methodologies: Research and indigenous peoples*. London: Zed Books Ltd.

Spencer, B. (2006). *The will to accountability: Reforming education through standardized literacy testing*. (Unpublished doctoral dissertation). University of Toronto, Toronto, ON.

Spivak, G. C. (1988). Can the subaltern speak? Reflections on the history of an idea. In C. Nelson & L. Grossberg (Eds.), *Marxism and the interpretation of culture* (pp. 21–78). London: Macmillan.

Stiggins, R. (2014). *Revolutionize assessment*. Thousand Oaks, CA: Corwin.

Tollefson, K. (2008). *Volatile knowing: Parents, teachers, and the censored story of accountability in America's public schools*. Lanham, MD: Lexington Books.

Toplak, M., & Wiener, J. (2000). A critical analysis of Grade 3 testing in Ontario. *Canadian Journal of School Psychology, 16*(1), 65–85.

Toronto District School Board. (2015). *2015–2017 school improvement plan for student achievement& well-being (k-grade 12+)*. Toronto. Retrieved from http://schoolweb.tdsb.on.ca/Portals/humbervalley/docs/SchoolImprovementPlan.pdf

Toronto District School Board. (2017a). *2017 Learning opportunities index: Questions and answers.* Retrieved from http://www.tdsb.on.ca/Portals/research/docs/reports/LOI2017.pdf

Toronto District School Board. (2017b). *Enhancing equity task force: Report and recommendations.* Toronto. Retrieved from http://www.tdsb.on.ca/Portals/0/community/docs/EETFReportPdfVersion.pdf

Toronto District School Board. (2017c). *Special education in Ontario.* Toronto. Retrieved from http://www.edu.gov.on.ca/eng/document/policy/os/onschools_2017e.pdf

Toronto District School Board. (2018). *Model schools for inner cities.* Toronto. Retrieved from http://www.tdsb.on.ca/Community/Model-Schools-for-Inner-Cities

Trevino, J., Harris, M., & Wallace, W. (2008). What's so critical about critical race theory? *Contemporary Justice Review, 11*(1), 7–10.

Truth and Reconciliation Commission of Canada. (2015). *Truth and Reconciliation Commission of Canada: Calls to Action.* Retrieved from http://www.trc.ca/websites/trcinstitution/File/2015/Findings/Calls_to_Action_English2.pdf

Tupper, J., & Cappello, M. (2008). Teaching the treaties as (un)usual narratives: Disrupting the curricular commonsense. *Curriculum Inquiry, 35*(1), 559–578.

Tyler, R. W. (1949). *Basic principles of curriculum and instruction* [Twenty-ninth impression, 1969]. Chicago, IL: The University of Chicago Press.

Tyler, R. W. (1969). *Basic principles of curriculum and instruction.* Chicago: University of Chicago Press.

Ungerleider, C. (2003). *Failing our kids: How we are ruining our public schools.* Toronto: National Library of Canada Cataloguing in Publication.

United Nations Statistics Division. (2018). *Country profile: Canada.* World Statistics Pocketbook. Retrieved from http://data.un.org/en/iso/ca.html

United Way. (2019). *Rebalancing the Opportunity Equation.* Retrieved from https://www.unitedwaygt.org/file/2019_OE_fullreport_FINAL.pdf

Volante, L. (2006). An alternative vision for large-scale assessment in Canada. *Journal of Teaching and Learning, 4*(1), 1–14.

Volante, L. (2007). Educational quality and accountability in Ontario: Past, present, and future. *Canadian Journal of Educational Administration and Policy, 58*, 1–21.

Weale, S. (2017, May 1). More primary school children suffering stress from SATs, survey finds. *The Guardian.* Retrieved from https://www.theguardian.com/education/2017/may/01/sats-primary-school-children-suffering-stress-exam-time#img-3

Weiner, E. (2014). *Deschooling the imagination: Critical thought as social practice.* Boulder, CO: Paradigm Publishers.

Williams, C., Jones, D., & Bailey, R. (2013). From the margins: Building curriculum for youth in transition. Ministry of Justice & Youth Association for Academics, Athletics and Character Education. Retrieved from http://yaaace.com/wp-content/uploads/2013/06/From-the-Margins-Building-Curriculum-for-Youth-in-Transitions.pdf

Wolfer, L. (2007). *Real research: Conducting and evaluating research in the social sciences.* Boston, MA: Pearson Education Inc.

Ydesen, C. (2014). High-stakes educational testing and democracy—Antagonistic or symbiotic relationship? *Education, Citizenship and Social Justice, 9*(2), 97–113.

Youth Association for Academics, Athletics, and Character Education. (2018). *About us.* Retrieved from http://yaaace.com/about-us/

Index

© The Author(s) 2019
A. Eizadirad, *Decolonizing Educational Assessment*,
https://doi.org/10.1007/978-3-030-27462-7

CPSIA information can be obtained
at www.ICGtesting.com
Printed in the USA
LVHW082116301119
639026LV00021B/1064/P